TEACHING
ENVIRONMENTAL
LITERACY

Scholarship of Teaching and Learning
Jennifer Meta Robinson
Whitney M. Schlegel
Mary Taylor Huber
Pat Hutchings
editors

TEACHING ENVIRONMENTAL LITERACY

ACROSS CAMPUS AND ACROSS THE CURRICULUM

Edited by

Heather L. Reynolds, Eduardo S. Brondizio, and

Jennifer Meta Robinson *with*

Doug Karpa and Briana L. Gross

Indiana University Press
Bloomington · Indianapolis

This book is a publication of

Indiana University Press
601 North Morton Street
Bloomington, IN 47404-3797 USA

www.iupress.indiana.edu

Telephone orders   800-842-6796
Fax orders   812-855-7931
Orders by e-mail   iuporder@indiana.edu

Manufactured in the United States of America

Library of Congress Cataloging-in-Publication Data
Teaching environmental literacy : across campus and across the curriculum / edited by Heather L. Reynolds . . . [et al.].
p. cm. — (Indiana series in the scholarship of teaching and learning)
Includes bibliographical references and index.
ISBN 978-0-253-35409-9 (cloth : alk. paper) —
ISBN 978-0-253-22150-6 (pbk. : alk. paper)
1. Environmental education. I. Reynolds, Heather L.
GE70.T38 2009
333.72071—DC22   2009022302
1 2 3 4 5 15 14 13 12 11 10

To my parents, John and Ann, who taught love
and respect for, and citizenship with, nature.
And to Dave, for his constant love and support.

—H. L. R.

To my daughters, Maíra and Júlia, and to their
cousins and friends, who always remind me to
appreciate and enjoy the world around us, and
to respect the rights of their kids to also do so.

—E. S. B.

To my parents, Sam and Catherine,
for Adirondack summers, and
to Jeff for the flowers.

—J. M. R.

We are not likely anytime soon to dispense with disciplinary knowledge, nor do I propose to do so. What I do propose is that we seek out ways to situate disciplinary knowledge within a more profound experience of the natural world while making it more relevant to the great quandaries of our age.

—DAVID W. ORR, *Earth in Mind*

The ecological crisis is upon us because we never imagined that there were limits to the Earth's bounty and resilience. We now know that such limits exist, and we are faced with a grand challenge: How do we live sustainably? Universities could provide the model by serving as loci of hope and transformation—"do tanks" for thinkers. If ever there was an interdisciplinary problem, this is it. It will require not just our scientists and engineers, but also sociologists, geographers, anthropologists, philosophers, economists, artists, and word-smiths, working across disciplines with students in an ennobling endeavor."

—CHRISTOPHER UHL, AMY ANDERSON, AND GARRETT FITZGERALD, "Higher Education: Good for the Planet?"

CONTENTS

ACKNOWLEDGMENTS

This book would not have been possible without the steadfast support of sponsoring editor Rebecca Tolen and Indiana University Press. We also thank Zsuzsa Gille and the two anonymous reviewers for their very helpful feedback on an early version of the manuscript.

We are grateful to the Council for Environmental Stewardship's Environmental Literacy Working Group, including Hans Andersen, Lucille Bertuccio, Jim Capshew, Briana Gross, Katherine Metzo, Heather Reynolds, and Paul Schneller, who originally recognized the need for a campus conversation about environmental literacy, laid the organizational framework, and worked to obtain the initial funding for the seminar series that led to this volume.

Funding for this project was provided by a variety of Indiana University Bloomington sources, including competitive grants programs, matching funds, and in-kind support. We gratefully acknowledge competitive grant awards from the Office of Academic Affairs and Dean of Faculties Multidisciplinary Ventures and Seminars Fund and from the College of Arts and Sciences Arts and Humanities Institute. We thank Jeff White and Linda Smith, who, as Associate Deans for, respectively, the School for Public and Environmental Affairs (SPEA) and the College of Arts and Sciences, provided matching funds to support a SPEA graduate assistant on the project. Many thanks to the Scholarship of Teaching and Learning Program, which provided funds for external speakers and in-kind support in the form of an instructional consultant to facilitate breakout groups. We are also thankful for a grant from the Council of Environmental Stewardship.

Our deep thanks go to SPEA graduate assistant Theryn Henkel for diligent logistical support.

Special thanks go to Briana Gross (then a graduate student) and Doug Karpa (then an instructional consultant) who were instrumental to the project in many ways, both organizationally and intellectually, and as early members of the editorial team.

We thank the many faculty, staff, and students who participated in the original seminar series and the subsequent semesters of meetings. The passion and creativity of all these individuals, who collectively came to be known as the Environmental Literacy and Sustainability Initiative (ELSI), made for a stimulating, meaningful, and productive two years. Finally, we thank our contributing authors, most of whom were also ELSI members, for their patience through the long process of reviews and revisions and for the fine ideas and writing they contributed to this volume.

INTRODUCTION

The Rationale for Teaching Environmental
Literacy in Higher Education

Heather L. Reynolds, Eduardo S. Brondizio,
Jennifer Meta Robinson, Doug Karpa,
and Briana L. Gross

A view of earth from space makes it abundantly clear that the human presence is a subset of the larger earth environment. Humans depend crucially on natural ecosystem processes for basic life support services such as air purification, climate regulation, and waste decomposition, for the flow of goods such as food, pharmaceuticals, and fresh water, and for recreational enjoyment and aesthetic fulfillment (Daily et al. 1997, Millennium Ecosystem Assessment 2003). Indeed, the twenty-first century has been dubbed the Century of the Environment in recognition of the importance of the world's diverse ecosystems for human health, economic vitality, social justice, and national security (Lubchenco 1998). Yet our society perpetuates the myth of an environment that is largely separate from our social and economic concerns (Daly 1996). This myth mattered little when human population size was small and our technology limited, but at nearly seven billion strong and equipped with the power of the agricultural, industrial, and information revolutions, the extent of human domination over earth's ecosystems is making the intimate interconnections between environment and society increasingly clear.

Human activities are causing unprecedented rates and types of environmental changes, from local to global scales. Humans have transformed or degraded one-third to one-half of the earth's land surface, altered atmospheric chemistry, and accelerated rates of both species extinctions and their invasions into previously unoccupied habitat (Vitousek et al. 1997). We see the results in environmental, social, and economic challenges that have increasingly become part of everyone's daily lives: climate change, pervasive pollution of air, water, and soil with industrial and agricultural toxins, soil erosion, and declining reserves of fresh water, oil, and metals (Millennium Ecosystem Assessment 2005). Even as total resource use may already be at a point of exceeding the earth's environmental capacity (Wackernagel et al. 2002), a persistent gap exists in how these resources are distributed, leading to extreme social and economic inequities that are expected to intensify with climate change (United Nations Human Development Report 2007/2008).

A central challenge of twenty-first-century society is thus to bring the nature and scope of the human endeavor into a sustainable relationship with the biosphere. Indeed, sustainability—meeting present needs without compromising the ability of future generations to meet their needs—is widely advocated as a shared organizing principle of society (United Nations Agenda 21 1993, Merkel 1998, Sitarz 1998). However, even as interconnected environmental, social, and economic problems have become increasingly prominent in public discourse, the training people receive to understand and address such concerns has lagged behind. Thirty-odd years after the first Earth Day, for example, only one-third of Americans can pass basic tests of environmental knowledge with grades of C or better, and only about a tenth possesses basic knowledge of energy issues and problems (Coyle 2005). In essence, the American educational system has been turning out "environmental illiterates," ill-equipped to understand emerging information about the environmental, social and economic dimensions of human–environment interactions and make informed choices on the suite of issues, from lifestyles to politics, that will decide whether and how society moves towards a more sustainable economy (Orr 2004).

The learning environment itself is a powerful form of pedagogy—a "hidden curriculum" (Orr 1990, Orr 2004). As students move about campus buildings and grounds every day, they receive important messages about human–environment interactions. Typically, these messages reinforce the paradigm that the earth's resources and capacity to assimilate wastes are infinite and that each individual's energy and resource use is disconnected from the welfare of other humans, other organisms, and the local to global ecosystems in which they are embedded. Alternatively, the campus environment, including buildings, grounds, energy and resource use, waste production, and academic focus, can foster an understanding that humans are embedded in and dependent upon the web of life, that our personal and collective lifestyle choices have both local and far-reaching impacts on other humans, other organisms, and ecosystems, and that sustainable societies must live within the regenerative and assimilative capacity of earth's biosphere (Orr 1997, Uhl et al. 2000, 2001).

In response to global climate change and other increasingly urgent environmental, social, and economic challenges of our day and spurred by the joint efforts of students, staff, and faculty, colleges and universities around the country are developing campus sustainability initiatives that seek to green campus operations (McIntosh et al. 2008). Inspiring examples include the University of California campuses, which are undertaking efforts to offset 100 percent of carbon dioxide emissions, increase renewable energy generation, and offer a 65 percent vegetarian meal option (Hartog and Fox 2008); the University of Pennsylvania, which purchases renewable energy credits, has vegetated roofs and a green building development plan that will see many new buildings achieve LEED Silver certification, and offers locally farmed food (Sustainable Endowments Institute 2008); and the University of Washington, which is 100 percent powered by renewable energy, has installed energy-efficient lighting in dormitories, and offers local food in campus cafeterias (Newsweek Current 2007).

Architecture is indeed a form of pedagogy, but greening operations without "greening the curriculum" misses a large opportunity to reconcile the hidden (or "shadow") curriculum with the traditional academic curriculum, thereby engaging students in the practice and theory of sustainability (Orr 1990, Association of University Leaders for a Sustainable Future 1996, Uhl et al. 2001). Yet, even as "sustainability" becomes a buzzword on campuses, with growing investment in sustainability staff and greener operations, a recent national survey of college and university leadership in sustainability academics and operations finds that academic programs in environment or sustainability lag behind and have even declined over the past decade, as has support and professional development in environmental and sustainability studies for faculty (McIntosh et al. 2008). There are notable exceptions, such as Arizona State University's landmark degree-granting School of Sustainability, established in 2007 (http://schoolofsustain ability.asu.edu/). And many colleges and universities do offer majors or minors in environmental or sustainability studies, but percentages are down (53 percent offering majors or minors in 2008 versus 67 percent in 2001, McIntosh et al. 2008). Furthermore, while new degree and course offerings are important, most institutions still lack mechanisms for systematically advancing environmental literacy as a basic competency for *all* students—and for faculty. Few published models exist to guide interested faculty toward ways of tapping their own expertise and other ready resources to advance broad-based environmental literacy.

This volume offers one such model, and its outcomes. It shares the experiences from a grassroots faculty conversation about teaching environmental literacy and sustainability at Indiana University that coalesced into a multiyear conversation that in turn informed a later, campus-wide sustainability initiative established by the offices of the provost and vice president. The knowledge-sharing practices developed in that context provide an integrative, inquiry-based model that is transferable to other college and university contexts.

The faculty conversation began with these questions: "What should an environmentally literate person actually know?" and "What teaching and learning strategies are most effective in promoting environmental literacy campuswide?" The approximately thirty faculty, staff, and students who convened once a month to discuss these questions approached them as genuine challenges requiring significant and diverse expertise. Consequently, the group that convened included people from a broad range of research fields relating to human–environment interactions, including public and environmental affairs, anthropology, physics, law, geography, economics, philosophy, chemistry, political science, English, religious studies, and biology. It invited the voices of those with teaching specializations—including in service learning, assessment, and scholarship of teaching and learning—and those with influence over significant campus environment and sustainability resources—including the university research and teaching preserve, the arts and sciences dean's office, and the physical plant and purchasing office. Graduate and undergraduate students and their organizations also participated in the discussions.

Over two years of regular conversations, what came to be known as the Environmental Literacy and Sustainability Initiative developed the scope of content for a campus-wide environmental literacy curriculum and recommendations for pedagogies that support it. The conversation considered both in-class and extracurricular learning. In part 1 of this book, we describe the model for our campus conversation. We report the results of that conversation in the following three sections.

In part 2, Core Learning Goals for Campus-wide Environmental Literacy, we identify three themes around which to organize student learning: human dependence on ecosystems (ecosystem services), human domination of ecosystems (ecological footprint), and human stewardship of ecosystems (sustainability). Rather than exhaustively catalogue content areas for student to learn, a futile undertaking given rapidly emerging information about human–environment interactions, these themes function as an organizing framework for the kinds of information, skills, and affective qualities that are essential to environmental literacy. The chapters presented in this section provide some important content and also may serve as examples for the kinds of content faculty members may offer students through the lens of their own disciplinary expertise. In part 3, Strategies for Teaching Environmental Literacy: Beyond the Traditional Classroom, we give an overview of strategies for teaching this new literacy, with an emphasis on reaching the broadest possible audience, promoting learning across disciplinary boundaries, and producing graduates who have gained experience in applying key facts and theory to everyday practices as citizens. In part 4, Beyond Courses: Teaching Environmental Literacy across Campus and across the Curriculum, we discuss models and implications for campus administration, faculty leadership, and student partnership in support of environmental literacy. The book concludes by proposing environmental literacy as a potent access point engaging students in interconnected dimensions—economic, ecological, and social—of our changing world.

The complex web of dependencies and influences between environment and society presents educators with a substantial challenge. Taking lessons from traditional environmental science that keep rigorous science, the complexity of application, and ethical responsibility in focus, we hope to broaden the fields and constituencies implicated in educating college graduates so that they can contribute as responsible citizens and informed architects of a more sustainable future. This distillation of our local conversation, along with our transferable model for faculty engagement, student learning, and administrative leadership offers an example of the synergy possible when an interdisciplinary group comes together around a common theme. It decribes one way to position key stakeholders in higher education to reflect critically on our roles as educators and share strategies for making environmental literacy a core learning goal for all students.

References

Arizona State University. School of Sustainability. At http://schoolofsustainability.asu .edu/ (accessed 2 December 2008).

Association of University Leaders for a Sustainable Future. 1996. Feature: *Learning from the "Shadow Curriculum"—Message from the Director.* 1: May–August. At http://www .ulsf.org/pub_declaration_othvol12.html (accessed 1 December 2008).

Coyle, K. 2005. *Environmental Literacy in America: What Ten Years of NEETF/Roper Research and Related Studies Say About Environmental Literacy in the U.S.* Washington, D.C.: The National Education and Training Foundation.

Daily, G. C., S. Alexander, P. R. Ehrlich, L. Goulder, J. Lubchenco, P. A. Matson, H. A. Mooney, S. Postel, S. H. Schneider, D. Tilman, and G. M. Woodwell. 1997. *Ecosystem Services: Benefits Supplied to Human Societies by Natural Ecosystems.* Washington, D.C.: Ecological Society of America.

Daly, H. E. 1996. *Beyond Growth: The Economics of Sustainable Development.* Boston: Beacon Press.

Hartog, L., and M. Fox. 2008. "Ten That Get It." *Sierra Magazine* September/October: 29–32.

Lubchenco, J. 1998. "Entering the Century of the Environment: A New Social Contract for Science." *Science* 279: 491–497.

McIntosh, M., K. Gaalswyk, L. Julian Keniry, D. J. Eagan. 2008. *Campus Environment 2008: A National Report Card on Sustainability in Higher Education.* National Wildlife

Federation. At http://www.nwf.org/campusEcology/docs/CampusReportFinal.pdf (accessed 2 December 2008).

Merkel, A. 1998. "The Role of Science in Sustainable Development." *Science* 281: 336–337.

Millennium Ecosystem Assessment. 2003. *Ecosystems and Human Well-being: A Framework for Assessment.* Washington, D.C.: Island Press.

———. 2005. *Ecosystems and Human Well-Being: Synthesis.* Washington, D.C.: Island Press.

Newsweek Current. Thursday, 13 September 2007. *Clean and Green: 16 Schools that Care.* At http://blog.newsweek.com/blogs/current/archive/2007/09/13/clean-green-16-schools-that-care.aspx (accessed 2 December 2008).

Orr, D. W. 1990. "Environmental Education and Ecological Literacy." *The Educational Digest* 55: 49–53.

———. 1997. "Architecture as Pedagogy II." *Conservation Biology* 11: 597–600.

———. 2004. *Earth in Mind.* Washington, D.C.: Island Press.

Sitarz, D. 1998. "Introduction." In D. Sitarz, ed., *Sustainable America: America's Environment, Economy, and Society in the 21st Century,* 3–23. Carbondale: Earthpress.

Sustainable Endowments Institute. 2008. *College Sustainability Report Card.* At http://www.greenreportcard.org/ (accessed 2 December 2008).

Uhl, C., and A. Anderson. 2001. "Green Destiny: Universities Leading the Way to a Sustainable Future." *BioScience* 51: 36–42.

Uhl, C., A. Anderson, and G. Fitzgerald. 2000. "Higher Education: Good for the Planet?" *Bulletin of the Ecological Society of America* April: 152–156.

United Nations. 1993. Agenda 21: *Earth Summit—The United Nations Programme of Action from Rio.* At http://www.un.org/esa/sustdev/documents/agenda21/english/agenda21toc.htm (accessed 1 October 2008).

United Nations Human Development Report 2007/2008. *Fighting Climate Change: Human Solidarity in a Divided World.* New York: Palgrave Macmillan.

Vitousek, P. M., H. A. Mooney, J. Lubchenco, and J. M. Melillo. 1997. "Human Domination of Earth's Ecosystems." *Science* 277: 494–499.

Wackernagel, M., N. B. Schulz, D. Deumling, A. Callejas Linares, M. Jenkins, V. Kapos, C. Monfreda, J. Loh, N. Myers, R. Norgaard, and J. Randers. 2002. *Tracking the Ecological Overshoot of the Human Economy.* Proceedings of the National Academy of Sciences 99: 9266–9271.

**Jennifer Meta Robinson and
Heather L. Reynolds**

Communication and Culture, Biology

While most of this volume is dedicated to describing the disciplinary content essential for educating environmentally literate citizens and to recommending promising pedagogical approaches for teaching that content, we begin with the seminar itself from which this book emerged as a model for grassroots, multi-disciplinary faculty inquiry (table part 1.1). Building on a foundation of existing interest and expertise at Indiana University, a multidisciplinary working group of faculty, staff, and students convened to develop a core strategy for promoting teaching and learning about environmental literacy campus-wide. What came to be known as the Environmental Literacy and Sustainability Initiative (ELSI) reached out to administrators, student groups, and operational units in an effort to develop an institutional framework for advancing environmental literacy and sustainability on campus (ELSI, http://www.indiana.edu/~elsi/elsi.html). Key elements of ELSI's two-year conversation are articulated in this edited volume. In addition, the ideas and cross-disciplinary relationships stemming from it laid important groundwork that a campus-wide sustainability task force appointed by the university vice president later could draw on. Members of ELSI were early

Table Part 1.1. A Model for Cultivating a Campus Conversation about Environmental Literacy and Sustainability

1. Building on foundations	• Who are the relevant content experts on campus and in the community? • What existing initiatives complement work on environmental literacy and sustainability?
2. Locating resources	• What internal grants (e.g., teaching, civic engagement, interdisciplinary) exist that could be applied to promote environmental literacy and sustainability? • What offices could provide support within their existing missions (e.g., teaching center, service-learning center, grant development)?
3. Designing the seminar	• What sorts of resources and areas of expertise should be represented in the discussions? • What does bringing together this particular group of people add to what we know? • What kind of format will both build knowledge among the participants and lead to actionable outcomes? • What does the group already know, and what gaps in knowledge should it seek to fill?
4. Gauging outcomes	• Are there opportunities to extend the discussion beyond the original participants? Are there opportunities that emerge serendipitously that will advance some of the seminar's goals? • Are there ways to share core findings and outcomes with related initiatives so that the key goals are carried forward?

advocates for such comprehensive approaches. And some were later tapped to serve on the vice president's task force, which recommended the institutionalization of several items also identified as desirable by ELSI, including the establishment of student campus greening projects; a position for full-time director of campus sustainability; involvement of operational units such as the residence halls, physical plant, and purchasing; and a sustainability advisory board. We offer here key components and lessons from our experience at fostering a sustained, multidisciplinary conversation with the hope that this model can be adopted and adapted at other educational institutions.

Building on Foundations

A major asset of colleges and universities rests in their highly accomplished faculty and staff, who are dedicated to educating students to be responsible contributors to society and who are often well aware of the interrelated environmental, social, and economic imperatives we face. Moreover, through professional and personal networks, they are often aware of existing institutional and local initiatives that can help build momentum toward a campus-wide environmental literacy effort. On the Bloomington campus of Indiana University, the Council for Environmental Stewardship (CFES) was formed in early 1998 as part of a campus-wide initiative to engage students, faculty, and staff in academic programs and administrative efforts designed to enhance campus environment and contribute to a healthy and sustainable world. In 2001, the CFES Environmental Literacy Working Group established that there was no mechanism for promoting environmental literacy as a basic competency across the entire spectrum of IU students. The CFES Environmental Literacy Working Group's focus thus became the development and promotion of such a vehicle for Indiana University. That group recognized the need for a broad-based conversation that would bring experts together to share what they knew. The working group also generated a broad conceptual outline of environmental literacy as an understanding of the ecological, social, and economic dimensions of human–environment interactions and the application of three broad content areas to everyday life: ecosystem services, ecological footprint, and sustainability. This framework guided the selection of seminar participants, the directives to them, and the format of the seminar conversations.

Recognizing existing expertise meant that, even from the beginning, the seminar discussions drew from a strong multidisciplinary base, including experts on campus in the sciences, humanities, and social sciences who not only shared their expertise regarding the causes, impacts, and solutions relevant to being active participants in the "Century of the Environment" (Lubchenco 1998) but who were also already committed to and active in preparing students to make good decisions in times of great environmental challenges. For example, Professor

Diane Henshel led a master's-level capstone class in environmental science that evaluated the conditions and factors that contribute to the development of mold in buildings on campus. The students in this class interviewed administrators, faculty, staff, and students in order to make informed and sustainable recommendations for university-wide management of mold toxins (Henshel 2005). Developing the co-curriculum, Professor Heather Reynolds (Biology) worked with the University's Council for Environmental Stewardship to lead students to replant several large ornamental planters in a high-traffic region of the campus with native plants. They produced signs and pamphlets for the planter sites that educated readers about the environmental impacts of landscaping practices. This project provided an exemplar of using the physical campus as a pedagogical tool. As a third example of building on existing faculty foundations, Paul Schneller, the Physical Plant Coordinator of Development and an adjunct faculty member in the university's School of Public and Environmental Affairs, developed a new Green Internship program. This program placed student interns with the Physical Plant; the University Architects Office; Purchasing; and the Office of Environmental, Health, and Safety Management to work on semester-long sustainability-related projects for course credit.

Locating Resources

Although not many resources are necessary to invite dedicated people into discussion about issues that they are committed to, a greater degree of coordination means a greater likelihood for impact, and such coordination often does benefit from additional resources. For example, local curricular grants may exist that can be used to support development of environmental literacy and sustainability programs. By 2002, the CFES's Environmental Literacy Working Group discussions had gained enough momentum to successfully apply for internal funding from the Office of Academic Affairs and Dean of Faculties Multidisciplinary Ventures and Seminars Fund for a series of meetings that would produce an edited volume of proceedings (Reynolds and Brondizio 2002).

The original proposal was for a faculty seminar titled "Cultivating Freshman Environmental Literacy—A Faculty Seminar" to last one academic year, fall/spring 2003–2004. Ironically, while the funded proposal described a year-long seminar, the conveners were worried that such an extended time frame would cause the discussions to lose momentum, and so shortened the seminar to one fall semester only. Very quickly, however, it became apparent that the conversations would be sufficiently rich to extend into spring 2004 and again into the following year when participants did concerted outreach to administrators, operations staff, and student groups and developed a proposal for institutionalization.

The original proposal to the internal grant program outlined the rationale and timeliness for the subject of the seminar, situating higher education in a position crucial to the goal of environmental sustainability. It highlighted the position of colleges and universities, as centers of enlightenment and learning, to contribute to the global discussion by producing graduates who possess the information, skills, and civic ethic to help our complex, global society move toward economies that operate within the regenerative and assimilative capacities of the earth system. Through readings, invited lectures, discussion, and synthesis, the seminar was proposed to explore the twin concepts of global environmental change and sustainability, their ecological, sociopolitical, and economic underpinnings, and the most appropriate format by which to draw these elements of environmental literacy into an interdisciplinary learning experience. The immediate outcome was intended to be a plan detailing the content and format of a lecture- or web-based course or other vehicle (e.g., orientation packet, video) capable of reaching a significant portion of the freshman population. The seminar participants would also produce edited proceedings to document their work. This project also proposed to forge interdisciplinary collaborations among faculty and students, create a model for other institutions to follow, and foster an ethic of stewardship and civic responsibility in generations of students to come.

The original proposal made the case for this particular university's participation in the conversation given the reference points of peer institutions. It placed the proposed seminar in the context of related activities in the Big Ten, PAC-10, ACC, Ivy League, and other university and college systems. It also reviewed the findings of a survey of U.S. higher education institutions conducted by the National Wildlife Federation's Campus Ecology Project. Although it acknowledged a wealth of relevant courses at nearly every university, including Indiana University, it identified an important gap: most institutions lack both a mechanism for advancing environmental literacy across a broad spectrum of the student population and a mechanism for launching discussions about an informed and intentional environmental literacy program. Indiana University's Bloomington campus thus had the opportunity to take on its own shortfalls in coordinating efforts toward environmental literacy while developing a model for other institutions.

The proposal resulted in a $5,000 award from the Multidisciplinary Ventures and Seminars Fund, which in turn opened the door for additional successful funding proposals to the University's College Arts and Humanities Institute, the CFES, the Scholarship of Teaching and Learning Program, the School for Public and Environmental Affairs, the College of Arts and Sciences, and the campus teaching center. The supplemental funds they provided covered the costs of honoraria for speakers, travel expenses, office/clerical supplies, salary for a teaching assistant, publication costs, and an educational consultant.

Involving People

The original proposal was itself a collaboration by two professors that built on existing foundations. Heather Reynolds, then Assistant Professor of Biology, was serving at that time as chair of the University's Council for Environmental Stewardship and a member of the CFES's Environmental Literacy Working Group. Eduardo S. Brondizio, then Assistant Professor of Anthropology, was serving as Assistant Director of the Anthropological Center for Training and Research on Global Environmental Change. Another key member of the organizing group was Briana Gross, then a graduate student in biology and the leader of the CFES's Environmental Literacy Working Group. These organizers attained support from approximately thirty faculty and administrators from units on campus as diverse as the Schools of Law, Public and Environmental Affairs, and Journalism, and the Departments of Anthropology, English, Biology, History and Philosophy of Science, Religious Studies, Political Science, and Physics.

While the initial grant proposal had proposed a faculty discussion focused on freshman, the initiative quickly expanded to embrace all students and indeed all campus personnel. As a result, staff and graduate students and undergraduate leaders of student groups were invited into the conversation. The campus teaching center provided space in its Scholarship of Teaching and Learning presentation series for keynote seminar speakers to reach a broader spectrum of the university. Doug Karpa, an instructional consultant from that office, joined the core seminar team as a pedagogy expert. The teaching center co-funded two keynote speakers, David Orr (Oberlin) and Christopher Uhl (Penn State), who visited to address the seminar and the campus.

The project funded a half-time (twenty hours per week) graduate student with joint interests in education and human–environment interactions to facilitate key activities and outcomes. The responsibilities of the graduate student included the following:

- Developing web pages on the Council for Environmental Stewardship's website to serve as a locus of information, including the seminar's mission, schedule of events, questions from the month's presenter(s), session minutes (including breakout summaries), and related links;
- Attending each seminar session to participate in discussion and to take notes from which to prepare minutes summarizing the session's main ideas;
- Posting readings, presenter questions, and monthly minutes on the

website, and emailing reminders of upcoming meetings to seminar participants; and

· Assisting with room reservations and refreshment orders.

The seminar series was successful in terms of both the number and diversity of participants (approximately thirty faculty members in attendance from more than fifteen different Indiana University schools and departments), the consistency of attendance, and the level of enthusiasm (Environmental Literacy Seminar Minutes 2003). At the conclusion of the series, the participants decided to remain committed to it for an additional two semesters.

Designing the Seminar

The most significant challenge in advance of launching the seminar was to design its sessions so that experts from diverse disciplines would remain interested in the core project, sustaining them to produce ambitious but practical recommendations for making a significant impact on student learning and campus practices. The most important orientation in the design was the expertise and creative capacity of the seminar participants, and the key mode was *inquiry.* Acknowledging the complex and interdisciplinary nature of the interrelated social, economic, and environmental challenges of twenty-first-century society, the seminar focused on two questions: What should an environmentally literate person know? and, What teaching and learning strategies are most effective in promoting that knowledge campus-wide? The core format of the seminar was designed to leverage local experts to take up that inquiry in ways that would create locally viable educational solutions.

The seminar meetings were both voluntary and meant to be cumulative. Each ninety-minute session was organized over a light lunch of sandwiches from the local food cooperative, which helped to ensure a broad and inclusive participation (everyone needs to eat lunch!).

Each of the first seven meetings began with an expert speaker or roundtable presentation. The presenters were asked to do three things: recommend a background reading to focus participants on key concepts and issues for the session at hand; submit a short essay identifying key aspects of environmental literacy motivated by their area of expertise, including applications to everyday life choices; and create a five-minute presentation encapsulating their environmental literacy recommendations. Readings were posted on the web two weeks before each session to facilitate advanced preparation.

After the speaker or roundtable presentation, the instructional consultant facilitated a breakout session, in which participants broke into groups of approximately five to address the guiding seminar questions: Given all we have heard so far, what should all students know about this topic in order to be considered environmentally literate? And, what teaching and learning strategy would foster this knowledge?

The breakout groups allowed participants to discuss and develop environmental literacy recommendations on the session's topic. Their notes were written on flipchart paper, which allowed them to be captured by the seminar coordinators and shared with the reconvened seminar participants toward the end of each session. The graduate student project assistant posted the breakout summaries regularly on the web. This reporting activity insured that ideas were documented for use as the seminar progressed and available for compiling for various reporting purposes.

The semester's meetings were divided into two sections—content and pedagogy, each preceded with a Scholarship of Teaching and Learning program keynote speaker publicized to a campus-wide audience. David Orr (Oberlin College) kicked off the content section with a presentation focused on the rationale for environmental literacy, titled "Environmental Stewardship and Sustainability for the 21st Century: The Role of Education." The topics of the content section included Population and Environment (Emilio Moran, Ben Brabson, Sue Grimmond), Environmental Toxins and Biotechnology (Diane Henshel, Roger Hangarter), Institutions and Policy (Elinor Ostrom), Ecological Economics (Christine Glaser, of St. Mary of the Woods College), Sense of Place (Scott Sanders), Environmental Justice (John Applegate), and Religious World Views (David Haberman).

Christopher Uhl (Penn State) introduced the pedagogy section with a presentation titled "Teaching and Practices to Awaken Ecological Consciousness." The pedagogy-focused topics included three roundtable sessions. Experiential Learning Roundtables focused on the Indiana Environment (Keith Clay, Victoria Meretsky) and on Active Learning in the Large Lecture Model (Craig Nelson), Service-learning (Claire King), and Place-based Learning through the Five Senses (Matt Auer). An Educational Media Roundtable focused on web, video, and campus orientation formats (Jim Capshew, Jeanne Sept, and Ralph Zuzolo).

The first year's meetings concluded with the leadership team (Heather Reynolds, Eduardo Brondizio, Doug Karpa, and Briana Gross) presenting a report that offered a synthesis of the year's discussions for comments by the participants.

Gauging Success

The seminar had multiple outcomes and ripple effects that continue to suggest a high degree of impact. One of the significant indicators was that the seminar remained responsive to the input of participants while maintaining the facilitation structures designed by the leadership team. In particular, interest was so great that the series was extended for two additional semesters, with high attendance throughout. During the second semester, the participants developed the work of the first semester into a core strategy for promoting environmental literacy and sustainability on the Bloomington campus of Indiana University, "A Pedagogical Approach to Greening IU" (appendix). The core strategy recommended creating a multi- and interdisciplinary environmental literacy initiative through service-learning and other experiential teaching and learning opportunities that would serve to "green" the Bloomington campus, thus integrating the "shadow curriculum" of the campus environment with the traditional academic curriculum. The core strategy was presented to the campus's most senior academic officer, Chancellor Kenneth R. R. Gros Louis. Based on the encouragement of the chancellor and the commitment of the participants, the seminar was extended for a third semester. During this final semester, the seminar participants invited additional campus staff and student representatives into their discussions to explore the potential for implementing this core strategy.

The number of partnerships that the seminar established indicates a great degree of relevance in the way it was framing issues. For example, the formal outgrowth of the Environmental Literacy and Sustainability Initiative from the now-defunct Council for Environmental Sustainability suggests that faculty recognized the potential in bringing ELSI's pedagogical goals together with CFES's broader membership and mission. In addition, the third, more informal semester of the seminar focused mainly on building coalitions with students and staff on campus, including with student government, the residence halls, purchasing, and the physical plant.

In an additional outcome, the seminar participants realized that their discussions could serve as a model process for reaching across disciplines toward a common goal of environmental literacy and sustainability. Work on the present edited volume proceeded apace. A few additional chapter authors were solicited in order to fill in disciplinary coverage. In further discussions, the seminar leadership team clarified the audience for the book, deciding to speak primarily to a broad range of university educators who may also be grappling with environmental literacy and sustainability issues.

The seminar participants also realized that their goals would be most effectively accomplished through a more robust institutional structure in support of environmental literacy and sustainability. A working group was designated at the end of the third semester to develop recommendations for an institutional structure for an Environmental Literacy and Sustainability Initiative on the Indiana University Bloomington campus, aimed at implementing the core pedagogical strategy developed earlier. The proposal to the administration recommended

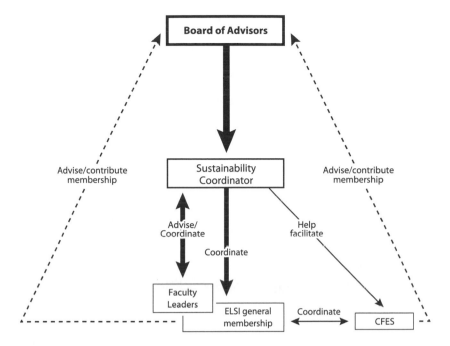

FIGURE PART 1.1. Proposed institutional structure in support of campus environmental literacy and sustainability.

adding a full-time sustainability coordinator position to the campus staff, one that would build and coordinate campus environmental literacy and sustainability activities (figure part 1.1, table part 1.2).

In a separate but related initiative in 2006, members of ELSI joined other faculty, staff, and students in petitioning the university provost to establish a campus-wide task force on sustainability. In 2007, the university's vice president announced the formation of an Indiana University Task Force on Campus Sustainability, the membership of which drew significantly from faculty and staff involved in the Environmental Literacy and Sustainability Initiative. Drawing on the reports and findings of ELSI as a component of its own extensive research, the more than one-hundred-person task force recommended designating a new campus sustainability coordinator, establishing an internship program and other activities directly involving students, and creating a website (http://www.indiana .edu/~sustain). Moreover, in fall 2008, the Dean of the Faculties initiated two new internal grant competitions to support the development of the teaching of sustainability. The $8,000 Sustainability Course Development Fellowships are designed to support "innovative approaches to instruction of complex, interdisciplinary topics at both undergraduate and graduate levels of instruction.

Table Part 1.2. Proposed ELSI Leadership and Advisory Bodies

Sustainability Coordinator	A full-time professional staff member with primary operational responsibility for coordinating and facilitating the main activities of ELSI and for supervising staff. This person will also coordinate Council for Environmental Stewardship (CFES) meetings and activities either directly or through a graduate assistant and in conjunction with the CFES chair.
Board of Advisors	Faculty, high level administrators, and representatives from the constituencies of ELSI and CFES. The Board of Advisors will periodically meet with the Sustainability Coordinator.
CFES Chair	A faculty member, staff member, or graduate student with primary responsibility for facilitating CFES meetings and the direction of CFES.
CFES Graduate Student Coordinator	A part-time graduate student coordinator who will assist the CFES chair in managing the day-to-day activities and monthly meetings of the CFES.
ELSI Faculty Leaders	A core group of ELSI faculty. The Faculty Leaders will receive course release time that enables them to take lead responsibility for specific environmental literacy projects.
Staff	Two graduate assistants and two undergraduate assistants who will support the production of public events (such as a speaker series), facilitate tasks associated with the greening projects, and support grant and report writing.

Service-learning courses and those that involve application of principles of sustainability to the IU Bloomington campus are of particular interest" (http://www.indiana.edu/~sustain). The $30,000 Indiana University Sustainability and Environmental Literacy Leadership Award supports an interdisciplinary or intradisciplinary team "proposing a new teaching and learning initiative that promises to have a sustained impact upon sustainability research and education and that could serve as a model for the development of academic programs with sustainability-related themes on the [Indiana University Bloomington] campus" (http://www.indiana.edu/~sustain).

Conclusions and Connections

The notion of a "campus conversation" that is based on inquiry and designed to align teaching goals and methods with learning objectives emerged in the 1990s in the context of scholarship of teaching and learning initiatives spearheaded by the Carnegie Foundation for the Advancement of Teaching. At Indiana University, a Scholarship of Teaching and Learning (SOTL) program was established under the auspices of the Dean of the Faculties as an interdisciplinary community in support of faculty inquiry into undergraduate learning (Robinson and Nelson 2003). Advocating a scholarly, visible, inquiry-based stance toward establishing context-sensitive relationships between teaching and learning, the Indiana University environmental literacy seminar became the first sustained, multidisciplinary example of topic-specific inquiry on campus that was informed by the scholarship of teaching and learning. In keeping with the SOTL approach, the ELSI seminar asked faculty members to draw on the strengths of their disciplinary training—including their ability to ask precise questions, their specialized reserve of knowledge, their facility in particular methodologies for collecting and analyzing evidence, their experience with the signature pedagogical practices of their fields, and their understanding of diverse career opportunities for their students—to understand how and what students learn in response to particular teaching methods (Boyer 1990; Hutchings and Shulman 1999). Highly sustained and successful, it became an exemplar in garnering administrative support for other, subsequent inquiry-based discussions conducted by faculty and designed to close the loop between teaching and learning on issues of significant import (Nelson and Robinson 2006). And like other scholarship of teaching and learning projects, the seminar itself, in addition to its recommendations specific to environmental literacy and sustainability, can be considered a model worth testing and extending to other contexts so as to build viable change initiatives.

References

Boyer, E. 1990. *Scholarship Reconsidered*. San Francisco: Josscy-Bass.

Environmental Literacy and Sustainability Initiative. At http://www.indiana.edu/~elsi/elsi.html (accessed 5 December 2008).

Environmental Literacy Seminar Minutes. 2003. At http://www.indiana.edu/~elsi/elsi.html (accessed 1 December 2008; page no longer available).

Henshel, D. 2005. *Mold on the Indiana University Bloomington Campus: A Review of Conditions, Procedures, and Impacts*. At http://classwebs.spea.indiana.edu/dhenshel/v600-mold/Default.htm (accessed 5 December 2008).

Hutchings, P., and L.S. Shulman. 1999. "The Scholarship of Teaching: New Elaborations, New Developments." *Change* 31 (5): 10–15.

Indiana University Sustainability Task Force. At http://www.indiana.edu/~sustain (accessed 1 December 2008).

Lubchenco, J. 1998. "Entering the Century of the Environment: A New Social Contract for Science." *Science* 279: 491–497.

Nelson, C. E., and J. M. Robinson. 2006. "The Scholarship of Teaching and Learning and Change in Higher Education." In L. Hunt, A. Bromage, and B. Tomkinson, eds., *Realities of Educational Change: Interventions to Promote Learning and Teaching in Higher Education*. London: RoutledgeFalmer.

Reynolds, H. L., and Brondizio, E. 2002. "Cultivating Freshman Environmental Literacy—A Faculty Seminar." Proposal to the Multidisciplinary Ventures and Seminars Fund, Office for Academic Affairs and Dean of Faculties, Indiana University. At http://www.indiana.edu/~elsi/history.html (accessed 5 December 2008).

Robinson, J. M., and C. E. Nelson. 2003. "Institutionalizing and Diversifying a Vision of Scholarship of Teaching and Learning." *Journal on Excellence in College Teaching* 14: 95–118.

Overview

Heather L. Reynolds
Biology

"What should an environmentally literate person know?" Our group addressed this question from the perspective of environmental literacy as a basic competency for *all* graduates. We therefore sought to identify the core elements of environmental literacy (also referred to as ecological literacy, e.g. Orr 1990, 1994) and examine how these could be approached from a wide range of disciplines. Most definitions of environmental literacy emphasize the distinction between knowledge, skills, and motives (the latter is more often expressed as values or as affective goals) and a focus on environmental problem solving and sustainability (Orr 1990, Moseley 2000, Coyle 2005). Environmental literacy is also understood to encompass knowledge about the natural environment (e.g. laws of thermodynamics, ecological principles) as well as human economic and social systems (e.g. Berkowitz et al. 1997, Orr 1994, 2004), reflecting a growing appreciation that in a sustainable world, "the environment" cannot be separated from such social and economic concerns as human health, social justice, national security, and economic vitality (Lubchenco 1998). We merged these prior definitions of environmental literacy into one succinct statement (see box part 2.1), adding emphasis on personal actions motivated not only by information and skills, but by an ethics informed by a "sense of place" both natural and cultural, and over both space and time. This reflects our belief that citizens and their everyday life choices, rooted as they are in local communities and local ecological webs, but

---

Box 2.1

Environmental literacy: An understanding of the environmental, social, and economic dimensions of human–environment interactions, and the skills and ethics to translate this understanding into life choices that promote the sustainable flourishing of diverse human communities and the ecological systems within which they are embedded.

---

with connections that ripple out over the globe and to the future, are the foundation of a sustainable society.

With its strong emphasis on environment, society, and economy, environmental literacy is decidedly multi- and interdisciplinary. While this is appropriate given the college-wide literacy that we are aiming for, it also poses the special challenge of balancing breadth and depth. It has been argued that achieving detailed scientific, political, or economic understanding for all citizens is not possible, and that the focus should instead be on teaching critical thinking skills, such as the skill of evaluating the credibility of decision-making processes (Schneider 1997). Detailed expertise in all disciplines is certainly an unrealistic academic goal for an individual; thus critical thinking skills are key to ongoing assessment of emerging information and contexts. Indeed, the ability to integrate across disciplinary paradigms is itself a form of critical thinking increasingly demanded by the complex challenges faced in our globalized and multicultural twenty-first-century world. We propose a level of environmental literacy—both possible and desirable for all graduates—that integrates across disciplines the knowledge produced in specialized disciplinary domains. Every citizen can and should be equipped with this core level of environmental literacy in order to contribute to the healthy functioning of society.

At the Core: Three Central Organizing Themes

Multidisciplinary knowledge is by nature complex, but complexity can be made tractable with central themes by which diverse information can be organized, connected, and made sense of. We identified three central organizing themes for environmental literacy: ecosystem services, ecological footprint, and sustainability. We propose that, collectively, these three themes represent three essential elements of the human–environment interaction that every citizen should know: that humans ultimately *depend* on the environment for essential ecosystem services that support the human economy and social well-being; that the scale and scope of human activities makes humanity the dominant biological force on earth, and this domination must be appreciated at least in part for the risks it poses to the ecosystem services on which humans depend; and that a powerful alternate paradigm to domination is sustainability, through which human *alliance* with the environment can permit enduring and resilient human and natural economies. These three themes have a parallel in the three fundamental stages of ecological consciousness identified by Uhl (2004): awe, alarm, and empowerment. Uhl makes a compelling case that people must first be grounded in the wonder and awe of earth and its ecological systems in order to have the strength to face the alarming extent of damage that humans are causing to these ecosystems, and to then be empowered by the hope that humanity will be able to create socially just economies that work with earth's ecological systems to create sustainable societies.

Ecosystem Services: Human Dependence on Ecosystems

Ecosystems, or "natural capital" (Constanza and Daly 1992), provide an array of resources, processes, and conditions essential to human life and well-being. Collectively, the many benefits provided to humans by ecosystems can be characterized as ecosystem services (Millennium Ecosystem Assessment 2005). From the air we breathe to the water we drink, from the raw materials for our economy to the landscapes that nourish our spirit, ecosystem services are the foundation for human life and civilization (Daily et al. 1997). Familiar services provided by ecosystems include food production, recreational and aesthetic experiences, timber, and pharmaceuticals such as the cancer-fighting drug Taxol, derived from the bark of the Pacific yew tree. For the most part, the value of these services has been well integrated into our economic systems, and society readily attaches dollar values to them.

Less obvious but just as fundamental are the many other life-supporting services that ecosystems provide, from the supply of fresh air and water to climate regulation, UV protection, pollination of food crops, storm water control, the generation and maintenance of soil fertility, and the decomposition of waste. These services are either entirely unrecognized or taken for granted by the average citizen, and are not well-integrated into our economic markets (Daily et al. 1997), although the new field of ecological economics is attempting to assign dollar values to such services. One estimate, published in the journal *Nature*, put the dollar value of approximately twenty ecosystem services at nearly twice the global GNP (Constanza et al. 1997).

Accepting that the human economy is embedded within and dependent on nature's economy represents a paradigm shift for many people. Perhaps the most basic level of environmental literacy is thus an appreciation of ecosystems and the fundamental life-supporting processes arising from them. From dead zones in the ocean to global climate change, it is clear that current modes of human activities on earth are degrading natural capital and its services, threatening our own well-being and that of future generations (Vitousek et al. 1997; Millennium Ecosystem Assessment 2003). Literacy about ecosystem services is thus becoming more and more critical, and no student should graduate from college or university without a basic understanding of the ecological infrastructure that underpins human society. We cannot value and protect what we do not know to be valuable and worth protecting. Indeed, ecological scientists have concluded that sustaining a projected population of eight to eleven billion on earth over the next century hinges in large part on public understanding of humanity's dependence on ecosystem services (Palmer et al. 2004).

The concept of ecosystem services often raises justifiable concern over expressing the value of nature in utilitarian, economic terms. If the value of nature is solely identified with the services it provides, then what happens when technology (e.g., a water treatment plant) seems able to replace nature (e.g., a wetland) in providing a needed service (e.g., water purification)? Or when no agreed upon "service" can be identified with an obscure species of bird, plant, or insect? Or when humans, recognizing the value of ecosystem services, begin to create "designer ecosystems" (Palmer et al. 2004) that manipulate services to provide maximum human benefit?

Alone, information about human dependence on ecosystems may do little to protect biodiversity and promote the sustainable flourishing of humans and nature. This does not argue for avoiding the theme of ecosystem services. Rather, the ultimate dependence of humans on ecosystems, as an unalterable fact of life, is a necessary but not sufficient aspect of environmental literacy. The other two core themes, of human domination (ecological footprint) and human alliance with nature (sustainability) are essential. Furthermore, students must have the opportunity to engage these themes with all three aspects of knowledge: information, skills, and ethics.

Ecological Footprint: Human Domination of Ecosystems

In practical terms, an understanding of human dependence on ecosystem services mattered little in the so-called "empty world," when human population size was small and our technology limited (Daly 1996). But in a "full world" approaching seven billion people equipped with the power of the agricultural, industrial, and information revolutions, humans are in a position to threaten the provision of the very ecosystem services upon which we rely. Environmentally literate citizens need to understand the origins and extent of this threat. At heart, such an understanding involves knowledge of the connections between population, consumption, and environment.

The concept of ecological footprint gained currency as a way to quantify a given population's demands on natural capital by expressing that population's needs to consume resources (e.g., food, fiber, oil, building space, water) and assimilate waste (e.g., carbon dioxide, toxic emissions, sewage) in units of productive land and water area required to meet those needs (Wackernagel and Rees 1996). Recent estimates suggest that under current modes of operation the human ecological footprint is larger than the productive area of the earth (Wackernagel et al. 2002). The scale and scope of the human endeavor is resulting in habitat destruction, rising greenhouse gases and other changes to global biogeochemistry, and biotic changes such as exotic species introductions that are in turn resulting in major changes in the diversity and functioning of ecosystems from local to global scales (Vitousek et al. 1997). Repeated warning calls have largely gone unheeded. In 1992, over fifteen hundred of the world's top scientists, including most Nobel laureates in science, issued an eloquent appeal for humanity to join in ceasing environmentally damaging activities, or risk "vast human misery" and "irretrievable mutilation" of the biosphere (World Scientists' Warning to Humanity 1992). Yet more than a decade later, the world's leading scientists have concluded that nearly two-thirds of critical ecosystem services, from supply of fresh water to the maintenance of biological diversity, are being degraded or used unsustainably (Millennium Ecosystem Assessment, 2005). While an awareness of the unsustainable size of the human ecological footprint can lead to what Uhl calls the "despair" stage of ecological consciousness, such awareness is an essential antidote to the hubris of human domination and an essential starting point for change.

An important feature of human resource use in today's world is the loss of connection between the consumer and the environment. Aldo Leopold (1966) famously alluded to this loss when he said: "There are two spiritual dangers in not owning a farm. One is the danger of supposing that breakfast comes from the grocery, and the other that heat comes from the furnace." The "disconnect" between consumer and environment is particularly extreme in the heavily industrialized societies of the more developed world (Moran 2006). The ecological footprints of such societies are vast, reaching into all areas of the globe for the raw materials, labor, and even waste assimilative capacities that drive comfortable, consumer-centered lives. Such globalization of resource use creates a loss of local accountability that hinders citizens from living economically, ecologically, and socially responsible lives (Berry 1999). In industrialized countries, the biggest consumers are those with the economic means to make responsible choices, and the main limitation is education. This is why we have identified an understanding of ecological footprint—the connections and feedbacks between population, consumption, and environment—as the second of three key central organizing themes for environmental literacy.

Sustainability: Human–Environment Alliance

Sustainability is meeting current human needs without compromising the ability of future generations to meet their needs (World Commission on Environment and Development 1987) and manifests the "hopeful" stage of ecological consciousness (Uhl 2004). Our society has been operating on the myth of an environment that is separate from, and often incidental to, our economic and social concerns. Sustainability offers a new paradigm that explicitly recognizes and honors the interrelationships between environmental integrity, social health and justice, and economic vitality (figure part 2.1). Sustainability is conditioned on an environmentally literate society; one that, as we have defined it, has the understanding, skills, and ethical motivation to take action aimed at reconciling the ecological, social, and economic dimensions of human–environment interactions.

Sustainability is shorthand for "sustainable development"—human economic and social improvement without use of resources or production of wastes beyond the regenerative and assimilative capacities of earth's ecosystems (Daly 1996; Merkel 1998). The concept was developed as a way to resolve the urgent need for continued development in the "less developed" world with the equally urgent need to avoid the unsustainable patterns of resource consumption and waste production already established in the "more developed" world (Newman and Kenworthy 1999). Ideally, the new paradigm of sustainability will allow abandonment of the unsustainable features of the first industrial revolution to the sustainable practices of a new ecoindustrial revolution (McDonough and Braungart 2002), such as ecological economics, sense of place and social equity, and ecological design.

Approaching Environmental Literacy from Multiple Disciplines

The chapters in part 2 of this book offer perspectives on teaching the three core themes of environmental literacy across a range of disciplines. Given these core themes and their own area of expertise, contributors were asked to identify and discussthe key types of information (e.g., facts, concepts, principles), skills (e.g., critical thinking, action skills), and ethics (e.g., social, ecological, global, local) that are essential for basic competency in environmental literacy. In addition,

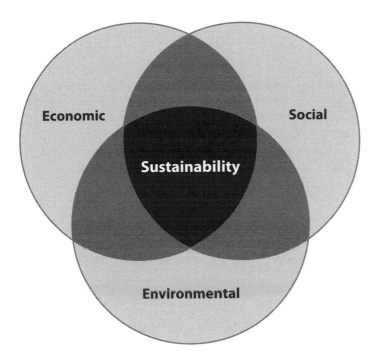

FIGURE 2.1. Sustainability integrates economic vitality, social health and equity, and environmental integrity.

contributors were asked to identify connections between those key areas and everyday life choices. The target audience was identified as a national audience of university educators. The resulting chapters provide a rich sampling of perspectives on the content of environmental literacy that is accessible across disciplines.

Using forests as a charismatic and familiar case study, biologists Keith Vogelsang and Eric Baack focus on the fundamentals of ecosystem services, considering the impact of past and present land use decisions, such as removing or restoring forests, on human well-being. Their place-based approach provides a powerful framework for addressing ecosystem services in the context of both ecological footprint and sustainability, while cultivating students' ethical and emotional connections to the land.

Anthropologist Emilio Moran provides an introduction to ecological footprint through discussion of its two basic components, population and consumption. Moran's contrast of lightly versus already heavily industrialized countries contributes a strong ethical dimension to the topic. As a brief overview of the connection between population, consumption, and environment, Moran traces the "empty-to-full-world" trajectories of global human population, resource consumption, and global change over time. These trajectories are both striking and sobering, and all citizens should be familiar with their form, meaning, and implications. Moran's discussion of feedbacks, including mechanisms such as product pricing, "green labeling," and local economies, that can begin to restore lost feedbacks between individual choices and the environment, emphasizes the connections between ecological footprint and our day-to-day lifestyle choices.

As a physicist, Brabson addresses both ecological footprint and sustainability from an energy perspective, arguing that the physical aspects of energy use cannot be understood in isolation from their social and economic dimensions. Citing the unsustainability of the growing world population, the increasing energy use per person, and the finite supplies of fossil fuels, he urges a transition to sustainable energy sources that will enable not only human survival but human equity and well-being in a diverse world. He suggests ways in which a university campus can function as a site for learning about these interconnections, at both local and global scales. Such an integrative education, he says, would enable students to make choices and decisions that support sustainable energy use.

Economist Christine Glaser addresses the economic dimension of sustainability. She demystifies markets, showing that they are what we make of them, reflecting human perceptions and values. Her essay addresses a basic flaw in the conventional capitalist market system: the failure to acknowledge that the human economy is contained within the biosphere and ultimately dependent on the natural environment as the source of all energy and matter. Glaser shows how the ecological economics view of the economy as a subset of the environment paves the way for an honest accounting of the costs and benefits of economic activity, allowing markets to become positive forces for environmental and social good.

Awareness of new facts, concepts, and principles, and the skills to think critically about and to act on this information are essential aspects of environmental literacy. But the motivation for action does not come solely from intellectual grounds. There is an equally critical ethical dimension that is informed by a sense of place, or sense of connectedness to the environment and the community of life. English professor Scott Russell Sanders beautifully articulates this feeling of connectedness to place—from the "bone deep familiarity" with local landscape to a sense of belonging within the whole earth system, or biosphere, and even the cosmos beyond. Sanders offers that it is this deep-seated connection to place, in space and time—from rock, tree, and creek, to ancestors and cultural history, and to the larger biosphere and cosmos—that most inspires its fierce protection.

Law professor John S. Applegate describes how this relationship between sense of and protection of place gave rise to the U.S. environmental movement and to the first pollution control laws. Applegate notes that a sense of place is fundamental to the recognition of threats to the integrity of place (environmental harms), to the subsequent protection of place (environmental remedies), and to the equitability with which harms are distributed and remedies are applied (environmental racism and environmental justice). Environmental inequities can result from environmental racism, the more frequent placement of environmental harms within low income or minority neighborhoods. Applegate discusses three types of environmental justice, the most promising of which— procedural justice—emphasizes democratic environmental decision-making processes that depend on well-developed environmental literacy among citizens —including a strong sense of place. On the face of it, environmental justice is about the "have-nots," but Applegate notes that the lifestyle choices of the "haves," at least under our current industrial paradigm, are key drivers of environmental injustices.

Philosophy professor Lisa Sideris affirms the importance of sense of place, in local communities and in the larger economy of nature, as fundamental to the attachment to and defense of place. She explores the role of wonder as a virtue essential to fostering a sense of place, a virtue that opens us to the surrounding world, engendering humility in the recognition of one's place in a vast scheme of nature that begins with one's backyard and local community. Sideris observes that colleges and universities tend to emphasize a rootless "life of the mind" reinforced by a nationally drawn faculty, and as such need to work harder to allow students to root themselves in place and community.

Phaedra Pezzullo, professor in the Department of Communication and Culture, establishes the central role of rhetoric and communicative frames in public discussions of the environment. She argues that the study of environmental communication should be a cornerstone of an environmental literacy curriculum because the symbolic constructions that we use in talking about the environment contribute to shaping our understanding of and relationship to it, and how we might act in response. Moreover, by engaging students directly in the study of controversy, she prepares them to negotiate the rhetoric deployed in environmental debates they will encounter in the future so that they can make informed, ethical decisions.

"What should an environmentally literate person know?" These chapters demonstrate how the themes of human dependence on, domination of, and alliance with nature can be approached through multiple disciplines to foster understanding of the interdependency of the environmental, social, and economic dimensions of human well-being, and the skills and ethical stances to act on that understanding.

References

Berkowitz, A. R., M. Archie, and D. Simmons. 1997. "Defining Environmental Literacy: A Call for Action." *Bulletin of the Ecological Society of America* 78: 170–172.

Berry, W. 1999. "Back to the Land: The Radical Case for Local Economy." *The Amicus Journal* Winter: 37–40.

Constanza, R., and H. E. Daly. 1992. "Natural Capital and Sustainable Development." *Conservation Biology* 6: 37–46.

Constanza, R., R. d'Arge, R. de Groot, S. Farber, M. Grasso, B. Hannon, K. Limburg, S. Naeem, R. V. O'Neill, J. Paruelo, R. G. Raskin, P. Sutton, and M. van den Belt. 1997. "The Value of the World's Ecosystem Services and Natural Capital." *Nature* 387: 253–260.

Coyle, K. 2005. *Environmental Literacy in America: What Ten Years of NEETF/Roper Research and Related Studies Say About Environmental Literacy in the U.S.* Washington, D.C.: The National Education and Training Foundation.

Daily, G. C., S. Alexander, P. R. Ehrlich, L. Goulder, J. Lubchenco, P. A. Matson, H. A. Mooney, S. Postel, S. H. Schneider, D. Tilman, and G. M. Woodwell. 1997. *Ecosystem Services: Benefits Supplied to Human Societies by Natural Ecosystems.* Issues in Ecology 2, Ecological Society of America, Washington, D.C.

Daly, H. E. 1996. *Beyond Growth: The Economics of Sustainable Development.* Boston: Beacon Press.

Leopold, A. 1966. *A Sand County Almanac.* New York: Ballantine Books.

Lubchenco, J. 1998. "Entering the Century of the Environment: A New Social Contract for Science." *Science* 279: 491–497.

McDonough, W., and M. Braungart. 2002. *Cradle to Cradle: Remaking the Way We Make Things.* New York: North Point Press.

Merkel, A. 1998. "The Role of Science in Sustainable Development." *Science* 281: 336–337.

Millennium Ecosystem Assessment. 2003. *Ecosystems and Human Well-being: A Framework for Assessment.* Washington, D.C.: Island Press.

———. 2005. *Living Beyond Our Means. Natural Assets and Human Well-being. Statement from the Board.* Washington, D.C.: Island Press. At http://www.millenniumassessment.org/en/Reports.aspx (accessed 23 March 2009).

Moran, E. F. 2006. *People and Nature: An Introduction to Human Ecological Relations.* United Kingdom: Blackwell.

Moseley, C. 2000. "Teaching for Environmental Literacy." *The Clearing House* September/October: 23–24.

Newman, P., and J. Kenworthy. 1999. *Sustainability and Cities: Overcoming Automobile Dependence.* Washington, D.C.: Island Press.

Orr, D. W. 1990. "Environmental Education and Ecological Literacy." *Educational Digest* 55: 49–53.

———. 1994. *Earth in Mind.* Washington, D.C.: Island Press.

Palmer, M., E. Bernhardt, E. Chornesky, S. Collins, A. Dobson, C. Duke, B. Gold,

R. Jacobson, S. Kingsland, R. Kranz, M. Mappin, M. Luisa Martinez, F. Micheli, J. Morse, M. Pace, M. Pascual, S. Palumbi, O. J. Reichman, A. Simons, A. Townsend, M. Turner. 2004. "Ecology for a Crowded Planet." *Science* 304: 1251–1252.

Schneider, S. H. 1997. "Defining and Teaching Environmental Literacy." *Trends in Ecology and Evolution* 12: 457.

Uhl, C. 2004. *Developing Ecological Consciousness: Path to a Sustainable World*. Lanham: Rowman and Littlefield.

Vitousek, P. M., H. A. Mooney, J. Lubchenco, and J. M. Melillo. 1997. "Human Domination of Earth's Ecosystems." *Science* 277: 494–499.

Wackernagel, M., and W. E. Rees. 1996. *Our Ecological Footprint: Reducing Human Impact on the Earth*. Gabriola Island: New Society Publishers.

Wackernagel, M., N. B. Schulz, D. Deumling, A. Callejas Linares, M. Jenkins, V. Kapos, C. Monfreda, J. Loh, N. Myers, R. Norgaard, and J. Randers. 2002. *Tracking the Ecological Overshoot of the Human Economy*. Proceedings of the National Academy of Sciences 99: 9266–9271.

World Commission on Environment and Development (Brundtland Commission). 1987. *Our Common Future*. New York: Oxford University Press.

World Scientists' Warning to Humanity. 1992. At http://www.ucsusa.org/about/1992-world-scientists.html (accessed 1 November 2008).

Keith M. Vogelsang and Eric J. Baack
Biology

When human societies adopt an extractive relationship with nature, the native vegetation and natural contours of the land give way to satisfy the short-term needs of a developing society. As important as economic developments are in meeting the needs of a community, some of their costs are shifted elsewhere, either in space or in time. For a devegeted landscape, these costs may include eroded hillsides where the native forest once held soil in place. Or, these costs may increase stream flow variability in a forest that once regulated the flow of water over and through a landscape. The retention of soil and regulation of water flow are two examples of ecosystem services, defined here as the benefits that humans obtain from ecosystems. Ecosystem services include the provision of raw material (e.g., fish or timber), the regulation of natural processes (e.g., flooding or climate), essential supporting services (e.g., oxygen in the atmosphere due to photosynthesis and the formation of soil), and cultural services (e.g., recreational opportunities or aesthetic gratification) (Millennium Ecosystem Assessment 2003).

Human societies have always altered ecosystems: too often, those changes have been made without an understanding of the consequences. In the past century, ecologists have traced the myriad connections between different ecosystems and the processes essential to human life. As the ability of human societies to alter the earth intensifies, it is increasingly important to understand the services that ecosystems provide as a way to offset or prevent losses that threaten our long-term social and economic prospects. In this chapter, we discuss a place-based approach to introducing students to ecosystem services.

Many environmentalists are uneasy about a focus on ecosystem services and attempts to place a value upon them. Placing a more sophisticated price tag on nature suggests a continuing willingness to buy and sell, and a failure to see value in non-economic terms. Despite these concerns, we view the lens of ecosystem services as one useful perspective, a productive addition to historical valuations of ecosystems based on what could be extracted from them. Many Americans may question whether preserving wetlands for their rich biological complexity is worth the cost—but these same individuals will likely agree to wetland preservation if doing so offsets property damage from flooding or fees for building a higher levee.

Our focus on the forests of southern Indiana emerges from several concerns. First, ecosystem services in the abstract can become an unappealing litany of complex processes. When teaching environmental literacy, we strive to engage our students with the local landscape, teaching ecological concepts along with (we hope) a love of place. We thus offer our home landscape—Indiana's forests— as a model for how to embody the abstractions of ecosystem services in the history of the natural communities of a particular area. In other places, the native landscapes might be dominated by sagebrush, ponderosa pines, arboreal cacti, or perennial bunchgrasses, and thus our attention would turn to the particulars of these ecosystems. When choosing our focus, we first look for changes that are dramatic, and so readily apparent to students regardless of their formal background in ecology or natural history. Deforestation fits these cause and effect requirements: ancient Greek and Roman writers noted the prompt effects of deforestation with the erosion of soil and the drying of springs. If we were examining the loss of prairies, we would start with the erosion that accompanied the conversion of perennial grasses to annual crops. After capturing student interest, we could then move on to other important consequences of prairie conversion, such as the loss of carbon storage in the soil and its connections to global climate change issues. Finally, our choice of forests reflects a deliberate effort to provide a message of hope. Environmental educators must necessarily increase student consciousness to the grave challenges facing humanity without being seen as the voices of fear and despair. The regeneration of forests in Indiana and elsewhere testifies to the resilience of the natural world, and to the importance of understanding the conditions under which ecosystem services can be restored. Elsewhere, we might turn to the rebirth of rivers following the Clean Water Act of 1972, the rapid recovery of riparian areas following fencing from livestock, or the success of prairie restorations. We believe that teaching students to see the changes in their landscape, wherever that might be, is the best place to begin. Curiosity about the ecological consequences of those changes would then be more likely to inform a student's consciousness.

Deforestation and Ecosystem Services

Deforestation provides one a vivid example of the value of intact ecosystems to human societies. Deforestation of a watershed can occur over just a few years, making the environmental consequences readily apparent. The resulting erosion and increased flooding are obvious indicators of the lost ecosystem services once provided by a functioning forest. In Indiana, the deforestation caused by the first wave of European settlement led to stark ecological and economic consequences.

Prior to European settlement, mature hardwood forests covered most of Indiana. Trees often exceeded a meter in diameter at their base, and some species such as sycamore were known to exceed four meters across and fifty-one meters high (Sieber and Munson 1992). For European settlers who began arriving in earnest during the early nineteenth century, these forests were appreciated for their timber and the abundant acorns that could feed pigs, but for little else. Most settlers wanted to farm, and this meant clearing land for crops and pasture. These early settlers and land speculators often relied on the presence of sugar maple, walnut, and cherry trees to indicate high quality farm land with productive soils (Whitney 1994). The trees that were in the way were sometimes cut for lumber, but often simply logged and burned. Thus, these settlers understood the importance of good soil but failed to recognize the soil building and protection services offered by the hardwood forests.

In northern Indiana, the deep soils that remained after the forests were removed have proven productive thus far for corn and soybeans. In southern Indiana, however, farming was less successful. The steep ridges and gullies rapidly lost the thin soil that had accumulated in the forests. Settlers throughout southern Indiana had a special name for many of the upland ridges that were deforested for agriculture: ten-year land. These ridges were so designated because after a mere ten years of tillage, enough topsoil had eroded away to make farming too expensive (Sieber and Munson 1992).

The rapid degradation of farmland was readily apparent, as were other negative consequences to society and the larger ecosystem. By the early twentieth century, deer and wild turkeys were extinct in Indiana. Rivers in the southern part of the state often ran brown due to the extensive erosion on the surrounding hillsides. Local farm economies collapsed, and much of this social and environmental upheaval could be linked directly to ill-conceived land use decisions that undermined the natural services of intact forests. In the early part of the twentieth century, the state and federal government took steps to restore forests due in part to the negative effects incurred by their loss.

Forests and Ecosystem Services

A short hike in a forest on a summer's day can reveal many of the services provided by this functioning ecosystem. Perhaps we notice the diversity of life present here. We harvest oyster mushrooms and chanterelles while the dog startles a turkey into flight and then chases a deer. A pileated woodpecker drills into a tree ahead of us, and in the process, creates habitat for various other forest animals that thrive in tree cavities. Jewelweed and woodland sunflowers are nearly in bloom. As we enter the shade of the forest, the temperature drops. Forests create their own microclimate: in cities, trees can help to balance out the heat trapped by pavement. Our buildings and paved surfaces absorb solar energy throughout the day, creating "islands" of radiating heat that can be as large as our biggest cities (USEPA 2003). On hot days, this stored heat causes us discomfort that we address using air conditioners, which are typically powered by burning fossil fuels to generate electricity. At the individual scale, trees provide shade and thus reduce the total heating by the sun in their immediate environment. With the cumulative effects of shading, heat transferred back into the air from our cities is reduced, thus reducing heat island misery for urban dwellers. The deciduous trees of Indiana work especially well in our cities by providing needed shade in the summer, and then allowing solar gain in the winter when leaves have dropped. Trees further cool the air by evaporating water from their leaves, which can reduce peak summer temperatures by as much as 9°F (USEPA 2003). Wind velocity can be slowed by trees, and thus augment our efforts to regulate comfortable building temperatures or prevent the undesirable effects of wind on farm fields, parks, and other areas of open space.

In addition, forests can alter the climate of a region. Trees transport water from the soil to their leaves, where it evaporates and later falls as rain. On a broader scale, forests play a role in the short-term regulation of the earth's climate by absorbing carbon dioxide from the atmosphere and storing it in soil, roots, leaves, and branches. Carbon storage is recognized as a critical component to offsetting CO_2 emissions and the risks from accelerated climate change (IPCC 2007). A recent economic analysis suggests that storing carbon in our nation's forests is one of the most cost-effective strategies for dealing with the climate crisis, and that a mix of policies promoting this ecosystem service could remove atmospheric carbon for as little as $25 per ton (Stavins and Richards 2005). In fact, reviving forests throughout Europe, China, and North America already sequester nearly a third of humanity's historical carbon emissions, much of which was released when the original forests were cut down. With the burning of fossil fuels such as coal, oil, and natural gas adding to the carbon liberated from human land use, we urgently need forests to continue storing carbon.

A hike in the forest during a thunderstorm also teaches a great deal. At the forest's edge, the heavy rain is washing away topsoil from a cornfield, carrying with it nutrients such as nitrogen and phosphorous. Once in rivers, lakes, or the ocean, these nutrients will feed algal blooms which will then sink, decay, and consume much of the available oxygen, creating "dead zones" where no fish can survive. In contrast, soil and its nutrients remain in a functioning forest, held in place by the many roots and sheltered from the heaviest rains by the layer of leaf litter (Daily et al. 1997; Millennium Ecosystem Assessment 2003). Nutrient cycling maintains soil fertility, and intact forests cycle nutrients such as nitrogen and phosphorus more efficiently than over-harvested or degraded forests, with the nutrients remaining in the forest rather than flowing into streams and lakes. These nutrients—some of which form the mass of animals and their excrement— would likely be designated as "waste" from our anthropocentric perspective, but in a well-functioning ecosystem, one organism's waste is another's meal. Fungi, plants, animals and microorganisms are linked in interdependent food webs where energy from one form or another is converted into living tissue. These efficient webs of nutrient cycling benefit all watershed users by maintaining good water quality and regenerating soil fertility, thus improving the productive capacity of the forest itself.

The summer thunderstorm reveals a third key service. At the forest's edge, the rain and hail beat down and runnels of water move quickly into drainage areas. Inside the forest, the leaves slow the falling rain, and the water sinks into the loose soil on the forest floor. Rather than flowing quickly into streams and rivers, carrying away soil, the water percolates through the landscape more slowly. The forest soil releases the water into streams and rivers over days and weeks, rather than hours, reducing the drying up of streams long after the rain has passed. The movement through the soil also filters out impurities in the water, leading to higher quality habitat for fish and cleaner drinking water for humans.

The forest soil provides an additional service: flood control. In an average year, healthy forests may allow less than half an inch of runoff out of approximately forty inches of precipitation received. Severe storms that drop four inches of rainfall in twenty-four hours, a one-in-ten-year occurrence in central Indiana, still result in just half an inch of runoff from forested land (Frankenberger 2000). A field of corn allows 1.1 inches of runoff each year on average; although in a severe storm half the precipitation runs off. Suburban houses function much like cornfields in terms of the absorption of rainfall. A much more serious problem is posed by commercial developments with extensive paving that blocks infiltration and increases the speed and volume of runoff, thus washing our leaked automotive and industrial chemicals into our waterways. A severe four-inch rain leads to nearly four inches of runoff from a typical commercial development, compared to 1.1 inches from residential areas. The slowing of runoff due to forests is a vital ecosystem function—and one that is expensive to replace.

Ecosystem Services and Human Well-Being

The value of ecosystem services becomes clearest when they are gone. In southern Indiana, forests were lost and the soils soon followed, leaving behind impoverished rural communities, remnants of which can still be seen today. In many parts of the world, the loss of forests near villages leads to increasingly long treks for firewood. In addition, the loss of forests can promote erosion, leading to diminished food production.

If we consider the interaction between the vegetation and the soils, we see evidence that forests contribute to local and regional water cycles. The Caribbean island of Hispaniola provides a case study. The prevailing winds come mostly from the east, which brings more rain to the Dominican Republic side of the island than to Haiti on the western portion of the island. Historically, however, the differences in rainfall did not matter much to the economic prospects of the indigenous Taino farmers. With abundant forests, the rains were reliable and farming was sustained throughout the island for many generations prior to the arrival of conquering Europeans. The French conquered Hispaniola in the west and the Spanish conquered Taino tribes in the east, with persistent socioeconomic and political effects that are still with these post-colonial Caribbean nations (Wucker 1999). Haiti generally lacks extensive forest cover with only 1 percent of its trees remaining. The citizens of this impoverished nation continue to convert their forests to fuel wood. About 28 percent of the forests remain in the Dominican Republic (Diamond 2005). The differences in forest cover between these two nations are sufficient to alter the regulation of their water cycles (Diamond 2005). Haiti is much drier now than it was historically when forests were abundant, because trees allow soil moisture to remain in circulation with the atmosphere by drawing moisture up through their roots and allowing it to evaporate through their leaves (Daily et al. 1997). In Haiti, the flooding effects of seasonal storms are generally more intense than they were historically, and this is largely due to the inability of the degraded landscape to absorb rain and buffer against wind. In contrast, living standards in the Dominican Republic are much better than they are in Haiti, and these standards are linked in part to the ecosystem regulating functions of the Dominican Republic's remaining forests (Diamond 2005).

The expensive replacement costs of diminished ecosystem function help to convey a sense of the value of what is being lost. Indianapolis, like many American cities that grew up along rivers, is often threatened by floods. In 1998, the city of Indianapolis began a $12 million project to prevent flooding in Pogues Run, a small urban stream that drains thirteen square miles of the city. Tunnels beneath the city would flood during intense storms and allow millions of gallons of runoff to mix with the raw sewage system, all of which would then empty into the White River. Engineers modified parks and created wetlands upstream from downtown in an effort to slow runoff (Webber 2005). The millions of dollars spent on restoring water retention in a corner of Indianapolis give some indication of the value of preserving flood plain forests. Lost flood plain forests must be replaced in the form of higher levees, increased water treatment facilities, and deeper wells to tap a depleted water table. The costs for these replacement services run into the millions for one city, with spending commitments to continue for the next two decades to prevent the harmful effects of flooding-induced sewage spills.

Beyond regulating climate and water, forests provide other benefits that are less easily quantified. Forests shade streams and rivers, maintaining cooler water temperatures that favor fish (and likewise fishermen). Riparian forests also provide corridors for migrating wildlife, especially songbirds. Forests shelter native pollinators that visit orchards and farms, a particularly important service now that European honeybee populations are in decline. These services are more difficult to put a price tag on since it isn't clear how they can be replaced.

The services provided by Indiana forests are not unique: every ecosystem provides some mixture of services that human societies value. Every ecosystem contributes to biodiversity by protecting the species already present and facilitating the evolution of new traits and species. Plant cover reduces soil erosion throughout the world. Students may see this most clearly in a comparison of a fragment of the intact ecosystem with the modified landscape around it. In any region, inviting students to examine historic photos alongside contemporary ones can unleash curiosity. Tall-masted ships in harbors that are now shallow wetlands illustrate how quickly California's coastal hillsides could erode once cattle and agriculture were introduced. In New England classrooms, we might ask how photos or paintings of New England's nineteenth-century agrarian landscapes compare to its forests today. Other scales, human landscapes, and ecological processes are relevant, too. For example, how do hedgerows on a farm alter ecosystem services? What happens when native species are planted or allowed to flourish along highways? Teaching and research tools are increasingly available for this kind of approach. For example, the time-series of aerial photographs available for many parts of the United States as part of the soil surveys provide an accessible starting place for students to begin exploring these changes.

A Forest Reborn: Restoration in
Southern Indiana

The failure of farms in southern Indiana by the early twentieth century provided an opportunity for forest regeneration and ecosystem restoration. It was during the 1930s that the state of Indiana began acquiring degraded land for use as state forests, and the federal government purchased land to be designated as national forest. It is interesting to note that the Hoosier National Forest marks the boundaries of some of the most severely eroded land in Indiana, according to a 1935 soil survey (Sieber and Munson 1992). Farmers eager to sell exceeded the public budget to purchase land. The Hoosier National Forest, which now stands as a 200,000-acre monument to nature's inherent limits, also demonstrates nature's resiliency when society changes course and actively promotes ecosystem restoration. Various state and federal programs planted trees on the degraded land, and state agencies raised and released deer and turkeys in the new forests (Hasenstab 1997). Now, seventy-five years later, forests have become a new source of wealth in southern Indiana. Each autumn, tourists swell the roads to view forest colors, and hunters come in search of the abundant turkey and deer. Students can explore similar socioeconomic histories of their own landscapes. For example, what connections exist between the shifting economic fortunes and the historic land use decisions of their home ecosystem? What conditions are necessary for land to rehabilitate? And how does restoration influence economic opportunities and the return of ecosystem services?

The challenge for citizens is to begin to see the essential services played by diverse ecosystems and to understand that when those ecosystems are disrupted, those services must be replaced. All too often, the beneficiaries of ecosystem destruction have simply shifted the full cost of their economic enterprise to the rest of society: a landowner clearing away extensive forest cover will capture all of the short-term economic benefits of this land-use change, but society as a whole will pay the costs associated with the resulting floods, nutrient-enriched streams, or climate feedbacks from the liberated CO_2. For the many replacement services that are provided by local, state, and federal government agencies, it is often far more economical to preserve intact ecosystems than to try to re-engineer their services. This fact is abundantly clear to the city of Indianapolis, as flood plain forests gave way to paved development and then had to be re-engineered at great expense.

As environmental educators, we hope that students will embrace the value of nature for reasons beyond human self-interest. However, we believe that all students must develop a deep understanding of the services that we have taken for granted for centuries. Our current global realities include widespread

land degradation and accelerated climate change. These realities require immediate solutions that won't necessarily wait for the next generation to solve. It may
not be enough, for example, to simply end unsustainable forest practices; many
parts of the world need active forest restoration. There is a general consen-
sus that an education curriculum that emphasizes ecological concepts, natural
processes, and environmental literacy would contribute meaningfully toward
better land stewardship. Education by itself, however, might still fall short if we
premise our collective action on a wholly economic, utilitarian view of nature.
We need to develop a land ethic grounded in our shared history that forms a
covenant with future generations. We need genuine affection for our landscapes
—and so we hope that letting the local landscape teach students will provide the
seeds of this love. Viewing nature as merely a collection of services delivered for
human well-being is narrow and misses much that astonishes and delights.
However, when sober economic analysis and love of place both push for the
preservation and maintenance of functioning ecosystems, we have more reason
to hope.

References

Daily, G. C., S. Alexander, P. R. Ehrlich, L. Goulder, J. Lubchenco, P. A. Matson, H. A.
Mooney, S. Postel, S. H. Schneider, D. Tilman, and G. M. Woodwell. 1997. *Ecosystem
Services: Benefits Supplied to Human Societies by Natural Ecosystems*. Washington, D.C.:
Ecological Society of America.

Diamond, J. 2005. *Collapse: How Societies Choose To Fail Or Succeed*. New York: Viking
Penguin.

Frankenberger, J. 2000. *Land Use and Water Quality*. Purdue University Cooperative
Extension Service.

Hasenstab, L. D. Sr. 1997. "History of Public Conservation in Indiana." In *The Natural
Heritage of Indiana*. Ed. M. T. Jackson. Bloomington: Indiana University Press..

IPCC. 2007. *Climate Change 2007: The Physical Science Basis*. New York: Intergovernmental Panel on Climate Change.

Kremen, C., N. M. Williams, and R. W. Thorp. 2002. "Crop Pollination from Native Bees
at Risk from Agricultural Intensification." Proceedings of the National Academy of
Sciences 99: 16812–16816.

Millennium Ecosystem Assessment. 2003. *Ecosystems and Human Well-being: A Framework for Assessment*. Washington, D.C.: Island Press.

Sauer, L. J. 1998. *The Once and Future Forest: A Guide to Forest Restoration Strategies*.
Washington, D.C.: Island Press.

Sieber, E., and C. A. Munson. 1994. *Looking at History: Indiana's Hoosier National Forest
Region, 1600 to 1950*. Bloomington: Indiana University Press.

Stavins, R. N., and K. R. Richards. 2005. *The Cost of U.S. Forest-Based Carbon Sequestra-
tion*. Arlington, Va: Pew Center on Global Climate Change.

USEPA. 2003. Cooling Summertime Temperatures: Strategies to Reduce Urban Heat Islands. Washington, D.C.: United States Environmental Protection Agency.

Webber, T. 2005. Flooding Just Part of Nature—Development Doesn't Help But Isn't All to Blame. *Indianapolis Star*, January 30: B1.

Whitney, G. G. 1994. *From Coastal Wilderness to Fruited Plain: A History of Environmental Change in Temperate North America, 1500 to the Present.* Cambridge: Cambridge University Press.

Wucker, M. 1999. *Why the Cocks Fight: Dominicans, Haitians, and the Struggle for Hispaniola.* New York: Hill and Wang.

Bennet B. Brabson
Physics

In their comprehensive article on sustainability, Thomas Prugh and Erik Assadourian (2003) introduce the general the idea of development, followed by the more specific idea of sustainable development. "All people and cultures try to improve their lives and conditions: this process is often called development." They then paraphrase the Brundtland Commission's (1987) definition of sustainable development as "roughly, the ability to meet our needs without compromising the ability of future generations to meet theirs." Immediately, this definition raises the question of what future generations need. Though it would be presumptuous for us to decide what they need, they will, no doubt, want more than to simply survive. Like us, they will want choices; they will want to thrive.

Since our lives are so extensively shaped by the consumption of energy, it is likely that these future generations will also want substantial energy. Of course, this presents an intriguing dilemma. The world population, now greater than 6.7 billion people, is growing and projected to reach 9 billion by 2050. At the same time, we are rapidly depleting our nonrenewable fossil and nuclear fuel resources to meet our own energy needs. How, then, can we reconcile our own enormous and growing appetite for energy with this concept of sustainable development and the evident energy needs of our children? Clearly, energy must enter our discussions of sustainability and sustainable development.

Sustainable development can be viewed as the integration of three key categories of human needs: economic (material goods and services), environmental ("natural capital," including clean air, clean water, biodiversity, and raw resources), and social (education, collaboration, quality of life . . .) (Prugh and Assadourian 2003). From this perspective educational institutions provide a microcosm of the world. Just as the long-term economic, environmental, and social health of the world depends on our choices and decisions about energy, so also does the health of an educational institution. Environmental literacy at the university scale, then, includes an understanding of the economic, environmental, and social consequences of energy use at local and global scales and, perhaps more importantly, learning how to make choices and decisions about energy use during this intense period of student learning.

Sustainability and Our Energy Supply

Just how much fossil fuel energy do we have? Environmental literacy must surely address this question. The university students of today will be making most of the future decisions about energy. It is critical that these decisions be informed ones, based on an accurate assessment of the world's available energy.

Human beings are greatly resourceful. Replacing physical labor by harnessing external energy sources has a long and auspicious history. While renewable resources such as wind, water, and wood have been used for several thousand years, the last four hundred years have witnessed the rise and recent dominance of the use of the nonrenewable fuels, coal, oil, natural gas, and uranium. During the twentieth century the consumption of these relatively plentiful nonrenewable resources grew exponentially, mainly because our unbounded human ingenuity found so many ways to use them. At this moment in our human story, both the energy use per person and the population itself continue to grow. For both of these reasons we are rapidly drawing down the world's nonrenewable fuels, both fossil and nuclear. The history of U.S. oil resources serves to illustrate this point. The United States was self-sufficient in oil until 1965. Since that time we have been obliged to import oil. In spite of new oil from the Alaskan north shore, U.S. annual oil production peaked in 1970 and has been in decline since that time. Remarkably, the amount of oil we consume each year continues to grow. At present we in the United States consume some five times more oil per person than the world average and are obliged to import the majority of the more than seven billion barrels we consume each year. As our own oil resources dwindle, we find ourselves turning to our unrivaled military strength to protect our external oil supply lines.

A more detailed analysis predicts that a finite resource like oil will be produced and consumed according to a bell-shaped curve called the Hubbert curve (Hubbert 1971). According to this model, when first discovered, the production of a resource such as oil grows rapidly as new uses for the resource are found. The resource is relatively plentiful and production easily keeps up with rapidly growing consumption. As the resource becomes more difficult to extract, for example, through mining or drilling, the production levels out and eventually drops away; hence the falling production on the downward slope of the Hubbert curve. U.S. oil production reached its peak in 1970 and has diminished, following the Hubbert curve with uncanny accuracy for the past thirty-five years. Year on year, as our oil appetite continues to grow and as our own oil production falls, we in the United States depend more and more heavily on imported world oil resources.

More importantly, the world oil resources follow their own Hubbert curve. Where, then, are we on the world oil production curve, and when will we feel the pain of not having enough? At this writing it is likely that we are still on the upward slope of that bell-shaped production curve. Both the production and consumption of oil continue to grow world-wide. That said, we are approaching the point of maximum production, from which point world oil production must decline. Predictions for the number of years to peak production vary from zero (now!) to twenty years in the future (Campbell 2008, World Energy Outlook 2008). Unfortunately, the painful moment comes several years before peak production, when the world's rapidly rising need for oil exceeds the more slowly rising world production. By the time the production of oil has reached peak, the rapidly rising demand has been constrained for several years. Several pieces of information indicate that we have reached or are rapidly approaching this point. The first is a persistent lack of excess capacity in the world oil extraction rate, with a corresponding price rise. Second, the amount of new oil extracted per foot of oil well drilled continues to decrease. And third, an increased year-by-year demand for oil is coming both from the developed world, the United States included, and lately from the developing world, China and more recently India. Considerable efforts are being made by both the United States and China to "lock in" their future oil supplies from the oil exporting countries. All oil-importing countries are concerned about the onset of this new era of insufficient oil.

A Sustainable Economy and Energy Use

The gross domestic product, or GDP, is often used to measure a country's economic strength. Historically, the per capita gross domestic product of most nations has been closely correlated with their per capita energy use. In a nutshell, rich countries with affluent citizens consume more energy per person than do poor countries. For example, with a GDP/person some five times the world average, each person in the United States consumes energy approximately five times faster than the world average. That is, GDP per person is directly proportional to energy per person by a constant I call the economic energy efficiency, or EEE, the amount of GDP produced per unit of energy consumed. In the form of a simple equation,

GDP/person = GDP/energy used × energy/person = EEE × energy/person   (1)

This empirical relationship brings energy use to center stage in the discussions of a sustainable economy. It suggests that to raise the world's per capita GDP, we may choose to increase EEE or to increase the world's per capita energy use. The latter is difficult to imagine. To bring all countries up to U.S. per capita energy would require an enormous increase in energy production and a corresponding rapid depletion of the world's fossil and nuclear fuel resources. Two recent developments help to mitigate this dismal outlook. First, the EEE in the United States has been increasing slowly as we learn how to generate wealth with less energy. Information technology has no doubt helped to accomplish this. Second, a number of western European countries have achieved a higher per capita GDP than ours while using half our energy per person. That is, their economic energy efficiency is more than double our own, an encouraging precedent and valuable example. From these developments we find that high per capita energy use is not a requisite for a vibrant economy. In summary, others have demonstrated that energy use can be effectively decoupled from the economy. How, then, does energy use relate to our ultimate goal of sustainable development?

Thirty years ago Holdren and Ehrlich (1974) identified a simple relationship between environmental degradation (pollution, etc.) and consumption in society:[1]

environmental degradation = population × consumption/person × damage/unit consumption   (2)

The degradation of the environment is directly proportional to the population, to the amount each of us consumes, and to the environmental damage created by each unit of consumption. At present our energy use in the United

---

1. A parallel relationship (Barker 2002) and one of the most broadly recognized is I = PAT,
I [impact] = P [population] x A [affluence] x T [technology].

Here, I, impact, is related to the environmental degradation, A, affluence, to the per capita consumption, and T, technology, to damage per unit of consumption in Holdren and Ehrlich. As an example in building construction, replacing wood or steel with aluminum requires substantially more energy and produces considerably more pollution.

States is growing faster than our population. That is, our energy use per person in the United States is growing, this in a world fully aware of diminishing fossil fuels and uranium. The coupling between Holdren's and Ehrlich's consumption and our energy use is sufficiently strong that I find it useful to write in analogy with their relationship the following:

environmental degradation = population × energy/person × damage/unit energy use

$$(3)$$

The motivation for this relationship comes from the heavy dependence of the United States on nuclear and fossil fuels (92 percent of our total energy) and from the environmental degradation that arises from their use. The environmental degradation manifests itself not only as pollution from the use of energy through transportation, heating, manufacturing, and electricity production, but also as warming of the earth's surface from fossil-fuel-produced CO_2. Following the guidance provided by equation (3), reducing environmental degradation requires:

> reduction in population and/or
> reduction in per capita energy use and/or
> reduction in the environmental damage done
>   per unit of energy consumed.

The first term requires serious consideration of all population limiting behaviors and policies. The second term requires an actual decrease in per capita energy use. From our earlier discussion and equation (1), the [energy/person] = [GDP/person] / [EEE]. To reduce our energy use per person and at the same time increase our GDP/person, we must dramatically increase our economic energy efficiency. While U.S. economic energy efficiency has been increasing slowly, it has not been sufficient to accomplish an actual decrease in per capita energy use. An actual change in energy consuming behavior is essential. Brian Czech (2002; 2003) makes a related point: "If biodiversity, ecological integrity, and economic sustainability are good things, then frugality, thrift, and conservation are virtues." The parallel statement here identifies frugality, thrift, and conservation of energy as virtues in our efforts to reduce environmental degradation. In a nutshell, we, like our European colleagues, must simply use less energy.

The third term reminds us of the value of moving away from fossil fuels toward essentially any of the renewable fuels that are carbon neutral, such as wind, solar, biomass, and geothermal energies. Their impact both on chemical pollution and on climate change is far less than the fossil fuels. The third term also reminds us of the need to take into account all of the environmental consequences of a potential expansion of our consumption of nuclear energy. Unlike the world's large coal resources, the world supply of economically extractable uranium is close to that of oil, a relatively small resource. While extensive scientific research has been dedicated to problems of disposal of radioactive waste and to safer reactor designs, with some success, continued use of nuclear energy exposes humanity to the unsettling threat of the proliferation of nuclear weapons, as we are learning from recent experience with North Korea and Iran. The potential environmental damage per unit of energy consumed is enormous.

At present, maximizing economic growth is a central policy goal for the United States and other countries (Czech 2002; 2003). Historically, this goal has been achieved through increased population and/or increased per capita GDP and corresponding consumption. There are those who believe that increased technological efficiency alone can compensate for the increased environmental degradation from increased population, per capita energy use, and damage per unit energy. Ecological economists generally doubt this proposition, and argue that our society must embrace a new paradigm of a steady-state economy (Czech 2002; 2003). The analysis presented here would agree that a new paradigm is needed, but would argue for a system of steady-state energy use and one that moves rapidly away from the environmentally degrading fossil and nuclear fuels to renewable energy resources. Interestingly, the present U.S. energy policy stresses both the finding of new energy resources and the efficiency of energy use, but essentially never encourages the most effective means of reducing environmental degradation, namely reduced per capita energy use. This strategy is central to the western European successful energy policy.

As part of their (and our) environmental literacy, students who will be making future energy decisions must grapple with the questions raised by the tight-knit web of relationships among GDP, affluence, per capita energy use, and environmental degradation. The university campus provides a microenvironment for these studies. The dormitory floor or small businesses nearby can become the economic units of interest. How much energy is being consumed? Are there trends in this use? How much does this energy cost? What energy-saving alternatives exist and what are the economics of the proposed change? In caddition, a number of powerful analysis techniques are available, including ecological footprint analysis (Chambers, Jenkin, and Lewis 2005). An ecological footprint is the earth's surface area required to provide the goods and services for an individual. Whether a system is sustainable can be determined by comparing the total human footprint with the earth's available natural resources.

A Sustainable Climate and Energy Use

Part of environmental literacy lies in making the connection between energy generation and environmental degradation. As mentioned above, they are tightly coupled. The sheer magnitude of our fossil fuel use has created daunting problems of environmental degradation and pollution. The prospect of substantial growth in our fossil fuel consumption adds an additional level of concern. And, if this were not sufficient to challenge our ingenuity, we find that burning fossil fuels adds directly to the CO_2 content of the atmosphere. Recent climate warming is not only our concern but also largely our doing (IPCC 2007a). Environmental literacy includes both understanding these connections and developing critical thinking on the anvil of these difficult problems. The recently published second volume of the 2007 IPCC Report (2007b) gives an overview of the impacts of climate change coming from our extensive use of fossil fuels.

Climate change serves as a prototypical example of a situation where unfettered energy use results in environmental damage through the production of carbon dioxide. Several universities in the United States and Europe have established centers for the reduction of carbon (Carbon Reduction Strategy 2005). These centers serve as a fruitful source of experiments and projects in this aspect of environmental science. They work with local institutions, including businesses, schools, and governments, to identify innovative ways to reduce carbon emissions. Interesting projects include new and refurbished low-carbon buildings on university campuses, the use of renewable energy for water heating, photovoltaic panels for electric generation, natural lighting and ventilation schemes, the use of biofuels, and energy-efficient vehicles. Carbon reduction extends well beyond technical innovation to consumer decision-making, technological and social innovation, and zero-waste economies (Rogers and Munk 2005).

Sustainability and Social Justice: Energy Disparities in the World

Returning to Prugh and Assadourian (2003), "Extreme inequity—immense disparity between rich and poor—has grown in the past half-century, within countries as well as among them, and now threatens the well-being of countless communities." Often, large gradients in wealth or in quality of life across borders lead to instabilities, tensions, aggravations, and even war. Energy, like many of our valuable resources, is not equitably distributed among the peoples of the world. This is particularly true of the nonrenewable resources such as oil, coal, and gas. Fortunately, sunlight, the major source of renewable energy, is more equitably available to the world's population. A collaborative effort on the part of the developed world to insure that the developing world has full access to the use of this energy treasure would begin the process of reducing energy disparities. Reduced disparities and the concomitant reduced tensions between nations bode well for sustainability.

At present, the developed countries of the world are living a highly unsustainable model, one that depends on a constant flow of resources from the developing countries. The large energy consumption in the developed world is often due to the large per capita energy use associated with their high rates of consumption. Are the equatorial countries in a position to "leapfrog" over these unsustainable development strategies and go straight to sustainable development? The equatorial countries begin with the potential advantages of greater renewable energy resources (solar, wind . . .) and low per capita energy use. Are they positioned to develop highly energy-efficient transportation systems, energy-efficient dwellings, and renewable energy sources from the start? Fresh ideas from enthusiastic and energetic students are essential in addressing this question. Universities bring together students with vastly different experiences from countries representing all levels of development, wealth, and energy. Exchanging these experiences in a classroom setting can be a start toward an understanding of inequity. Environmental literacy includes an understanding of these inequities and their consequences.

The Transition to Sustainable Energy

Consuming nonrenewable energy resources such as oil, gas, coal, and uranium is automatically unsustainable. Fortunately for us, these nonrenewable resources are available in sufficient quantities to give us "breathing room" while we figure out how to reduce our energy use and to switch our energy dependence to the renewable energy sources. Solar energy in its many forms (wind, photovoltaics, hydroelectric . . .) provides an essentially unlimited supply of energy.

We are obliged to pay attention to this patently unsustainable part of our future by considering both energy conservation and renewable energy sources. Conservation of energy on a university campus leads directly to a host of studies, projects, and service-learning opportunities extending from the replacement of incandescent bulbs by energy-saving fluorescents to recycling projects, to installation of energy saving windows in buildings, to a revamping of the entire heating and electricity system of the university through various geothermal and co-generation schemes. Not surprisingly, our future energy sources on campus will be largely renewable ones. In this regard it is worth keeping in mind the vast sizes of our renewable energy resources. Imagine, for a moment, the entire fossil fuel supply on earth, including all the fuels we have already used and all coal, oil, gas, tar sands, and shale oils still in the ground. The amount of sun's energy striking the earth's surface delivers this much total energy every ten days! This helps to encourage us to get about the business of moving from our rapidly depleting fossil fuel sources, presently 85 percent of our total energy use, to the renewable sources.

Of course, some of our energy is already coming from renewable sources. Hydroelectricity accounts for some 7 percent of our total energy use in the United States. Enlarging this percentage in this country is unlikely to occur. We have already exploited most favorable sites. What, then, are the most likely renewable resources to enter our energy mix, and how is environmental literacy on campus to be affected by these new resources? Fortunately, wind energy, one of the forms of solar energy, is already a competitive source of electricity. Since 2002, major wind farms have been constructed in the United States. Energy companies are already buying up "wind rights" from large expanses of the windy states (Texas, Oklahoma, North and South Dakota, Nebraska, Minnesota, Wisconsin . . .). In a head-to-head comparison with electricity from coal, for example, wind is competitive. It is less expensive than nuclear electric generation.

With much talk of automobiles powered by hydrogen fuel cells, what are we to make of the so called "solar/hydrogen revolution?" Solar energy (wind, photovoltaics, direct solar with mirrors . . .) will be used to generate electricity, electrolyzing water to hydrogen and oxygen. The hydrogen will serve either as fuel for fuel-celled cars or it will be used as a replacement for natural gas for heating buildings and industrial processes. A good deal of science and engineering effort is being spent in this direction. This highly attractive picture of our future energy from renewable sources requires a couple of significant qualifiers. First, this picture depends on the development of far less costly fuel cells than those available today. Estimates put this as much as twenty years into the future. Second, hydrogen is often presented in the popular literature as a ubiquitous new source of energy readily available from water. Unfortunately, this is not the case. The energy you get from burning hydrogen is equal to the energy it takes to electrolyze it from water. That is, hydrogen is not a primary source of energy.

Sustainability and Environmental Literacy

How, then, do university students enter into these discussions, and can they carry out projects on campus that focus on the transition to renewable fuels? Perhaps two examples will help. In the Netherlands, photovoltaic tiles have been installed on the roofs of extensive apartment complexes. The cost of such tiles is rapidly falling with economies of scale. Exploring this technology, an environmental physics student at Indiana University carried out a study of the installation of photovoltaic tiles on bicycle parking sheds on campus. He addressed both the scientific and economic questions about the provision of electricity from this project. As another example, like many universities, Indiana University recently decided to undertake a full-fledged examination of the potential sustainability of its present use of resources. The extensive project includes not only the major uses of energy (heating, lighting . . .) but also building design, food, recycling, resource use, land use, and education. Two hundred students responded to a note asking if they would like to help with the study and dozens carried out research! The result of their work is on display at: http://www.indiana.edu/~ sustain/.

Energy is, of course, only one contributor to the larger issue of sustainability. As Prugh and Assadourian (2003) discuss, "sustainability means not only human survival but also the development of a fully biologically diverse world, one where human equity and quality of life are paramount." Energy discussions must take place in the context of these larger goals.

If my original premise is correct, that educational institutions provide a microcosm of the world, then the potential for environmental literacy in the university setting is unbounded. It expands to include the economic, environmental, and social health of the university and by analogy the world. In summary, environmental literacy at university is mastering the basis for decision-making that will provide an invaluable lifelong perspective for our students and a sustainable future for the earth.

References

Barker, J. F. 2002. *I = PAT: An Introduction, Human Population Growth and International Migration*. At http://www.population-growth-migration.info/essays/IPAT.html, and references therein.

Campbell, C. 2008. Association for the Study of Peak Oil and Gas. Newsletter96-December. At http://www.aspo-ireland.org/contentFiles/newsletterPDFs/newsletter96_200 812.pdf (accessed 29 April 2009).

Carbon Reduction Strategy (CRed) 2005. Low Carbon Innovation Centre, School of Environmental Sciences, University of East Anglia. At http://www.cred-uk.org.

Chambers, N., N. Jenkin, and K. Lewis. 2005. A resource flow and ecological footprint analysis of the southwest of England. At http://www.steppingforward.org.uk/index .htm (accessed 26 March 2009).

Czech, B. 2002. "The imperative of macroeconomics for ecologists." *Bioscience* 52(11): 964–966.

—— 2003. "Technological Progress and Biodiversity Conservation: A Dollar Spent, a Dollar Burned." *Conservation Biology* 17(5): 1455–1457.

Holdren, J. P., and Ehrlich, P. R. 1974. "Human Population and the Global Environment. *American Scientist* 62(3): 282–292.

Hubbert, M. K. 1971. "The Energy Resources of the Earth." *Scientific American* 225(9): 60–70.

IPCC, 2007a. *Climate Change 2007: The Physical Science Basis*. Contribution of Working Group I to the Fourth Assessment Report of the Intergovernmental Panel on Climate Change. Ed. S. Solomon, D. Qin, M. Manning, M. Marquis, K. Averyt, M. M. B. Tignor, H. L. Miller, Jr., Z. Chen. Cambridge: Cambridge University Press.

——. 2007b. *Climate Change 2007: Impacts, Adaptation, and Vulnerability.* Contribution of Working Group II to the Fourth Assessment Report of the Intergovernmental Panel on Climate Change. Ed. M. L. Parry, O. F. Canziani, J. P. Palutikof, P. J. van der Linden, C. E. Hanson, Cambridge: Cambridge University Press.

Prugh, T., and E. Assadourian. 2003. "What is Sustainability, Anyway?" *World Watch Magazine* 5: 10–21.

Rogers, S., and D. Munk, eds. 2005. "Heat: How Global Warming Is Changing Our World." *The Guardian* June 30: 3–34.

Trauger, D. L., B. Czech, J. D. Erickson, P. R. Garrettson, B. J. Kernohan, and C. A. Miller. 2003. "The Relationship of Economic Growth to Wildlife Conservation. *Wildlife Society Technical Review* 03(1). The Wildlife Society, Bethesda, Md. 22 pp.

World Energy Outlook. 2008. International Energy Agency. At http://www.worldenergy outlook.org/ (accessed 6 December 2008).

Emilio F. Moran
Anthropology

Understanding the dynamic interaction between population, consumption, and environment is fundamental to environmental literacy. Population size and distribution in space and time have very large impacts on the planet—and so does the consumption of natural resources. A population's environmental impact, or "ecological footprint," is proportional to population and per individual consumption. For this reason, it is possible for a small population to have very large impacts on the environment through very high consumption habits, as is evident today in western Europe and North America, while elsewhere, where consumption is low but population densities are very high, comparably high impacts on environment may occur. The impacts of high population size and high population density tend to be seen in the immediate environment where people live and thus are quite visible to any observer. In contrast, the impacts of high consumption by small, affluent populations may be spread out over very distant parts of the planet through the consumption of imported goods: logs, coffee, grain, and other items, brought from across the planet. In other words, high consumption societies export their immediate environmental impacts to other places. Even emerging consumerist societies now do this: for example, China imports soybeans and beef from Brazil and is developing close relations with several nations in Africa to ensure provisioning of its people while reducing environmental consequences at home. This chapter provides a global perspective on population, consumption, and environment, contrasting their feedback dynamics in countries experiencing various degrees of industrialization.

Population and Its Distribution

When one thinks of population's impact on environment, it is usually the sheer numbers of people that are the consideration. Surely, numbers of people play an important role, but in fact population has hardly ever been distributed evenly across the land. When agriculture was the chief mode of production, people clustered in areas, such as fertile river valleys, where better soils and plentiful water for agriculture were located. Those areas were more highly impacted, and many of them ended up degraded due to salinization and overuse, resulting in the collapse of those economies and societies. Industrialization favors the congregation of people (many of whom are low wage workers) and resources needed for production in urban areas, which tend to be sited within easy access to raw materials (such as iron ore, bauxite, copper) and channels of transportation. We can see this process taking place today in China at unprecedented rates. Urbanization results in changing drainage due to asphalting of the land surface and construction of buildings, in high levels of local pollution, and in great differences in quality of life compared to rural areas. Thus both numbers of people and their location matter in population–environment interactions.

An interesting example of this is observable in Brazil. Following the first oil shock of 1973, when OPEC was created and oil prices spiked, the Brazilian government launched an ambitious national ethanol development program (PROALCOOL) linked to economic development goals. The idea was to produce ethanol from sugarcane in areas of northeast Brazil, which were historically where poverty has been concentrated. However, as the program got going it was clear that the bulk of vehicle consumption of fuel was to the south, in São Paulo state, with up to 85 percent of the total gasoline consumed there. In a couple of decades what we see is the transformation of the land use of São Paulo from pasture and other crop commodities to sugarcane crops and ethanol plants. The practice of burning sugarcane before harvest, along with fertilization and effluents associated with vast areas of sugarcane, resulted in air and water pollution in many parts of São Paulo. This land use change also changed employment and ownership patterns of land.

Consumption

When one thinks of consumption, one thinks mostly of the consumption of natural resources by factories and large industrial producers—and indeed they account for a lot of consumption. But this consumption comes from the demand by consumers in particular places willing to pay a given price for a given consumption item. It is our daily use of goods that is responsible for the growing pressure on the planet: from the time we get up in the morning, we are using goods from throughout the world. Typically, orange juice comes at least in part from Brazil, our coffee from Brazil, Mexico, Sumatra, or Hawaii. In winter, the fruits in our cereal here in North America come from Central America, Chile, or Ecuador. As we get dressed, our clothes will have labels telling us that they come from Bolivia, Sri Lanka, or China. A backpack is likely to be made overseas too, as will our jogging shoes and computers—mostly in Asia. Because these items come from far away, one may worry less about their environmental and social costs, which over time has grown into a significant problem. Whereas in Europe it is hard to go very far in any metropolitan area without seeing sophisticated recycling bins that separate glass, paper, metal, and organics—such separation is hardly ever found in American cities. The good news is that this consumption coming from global sources is not having a huge local impact on the physical environment of consumers, and it is providing employment to persons far away. The bad news is that consumption of these global items is having a very large impact on that far-away country's physical environment in the form of resource use and air and water pollution, and that those are jobs that are no longer available to people in our country. Very large sectors of American society have lost jobs to the global economy as a result of a preference in our society for cheap goods without a concern for its consequences for local employment.

History of Population and Consumption

The impact of population and consumption on the environment takes many forms: energy consumption, emissions of greenhouse gases, loss of soil nutrients, and changes in water quality and in the amounts of food production. These impacts have taken place since human beings first appeared on the planet. However, they were barely measurable during our long history as hunter-gatherers and can only begin to be observed with the domestication of plants and animals about ten thousand years ago, during the Neolithic revolution. Even then, the impacts did not reach levels with measurable consequences on the planetary scale; their effects were local or regional. With the arrival of the Industrial Revolution and the use of fossil fuels in industrial production, one begins to see a measurable impact through rural-to-urban migration and the emission of gases from the combustion of fossil fuels. Yet three hundred years ago, when this process started, the number of places that had industrial capacity was very limited and, again, the impacts were highly local (air pollution in London) rather than national, much less planetary. Europe's mercantilist (from the sixteenth century) and colonial (from the nineteenth century) expansion led to the development of an increasingly interconnected world economic system, involving the flow of people and goods and featuring boom and bust cycles, that impacted forests, soils, water, and regional populations (e.g. slavery).

Over the past three hundred years, human population size and industrialization, including the application of fossil fuels in agricultural production, spread worldwide. While this process was slow and gradual over this period, it increased exponentially following World War II (figure 3.1).

Consequences

Thus, in the second half of the twentieth century, we are able to observe a process with no previous analogy: a continuous and exponential increase in greenhouse gases and other human-induced changes in the atmosphere (figure 3.2, panel d), such as had not occurred in 450,000 years (figure 3.3). Levels of greenhouse gases are now higher than anything we know of and are at levels where we cannot even predict what might be the impacts to the functioning of the planet. Among other impacts, we have seen acceleration in nitrogen fixation rates, increased species extinctions, and rising global surface air temperatures (figure 3.2, panels a–c). Such data offers good evidence, in concert with much other support, that exponentially increasing populations combined with industrialization have led to unprecedented per-capita human impact on the earth.

Will the earth system collapse? We are currently operating outside the known boundaries of the way the planet has ever operated before. Central to these considerations is the concept of thresholds or tipping points for ecosystem functions. In figure 3.4, we can see the sudden tipping point of a system that was reset at a different equilibrium point following years of stress. Following such a sudden shift, the system resettles at a very different equilibrium point, but as a system with different characteristics.

There is evidence already that climatic anomalies, such as El Niño and La Niña events, are now taking place with greater frequency, and result in more frequent extreme events worldwide: floods, droughts, collapse of fisheries, and hurricanes. There is also growing concern that weather patterns are changing due to shifts in the circulation of warm and cold ocean currents. These changes could result in parts of the planet no longer having a viable agricultural sector due to reduction in warm days, drastic drops in precipitation at key moments in the agricultural

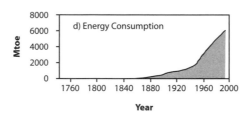

FIGURE 3.1. Rate of increase in many spheres of human activity for the last 300 years: a) population (U.S. Bureau of the Census 2000); b) world economy (Nordhas 1997); c) motor vehicles (UNEP 2000); and d) energy consumption (Klein, Goldwijk, and Battjes 1997). Reproduced by permission from W. Steffen et al. *Global Change and the Earth System* (New York: Springer-Verlag, 2004), 5.

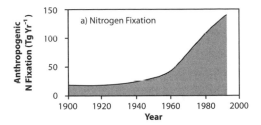

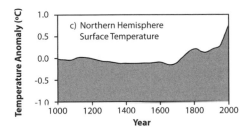

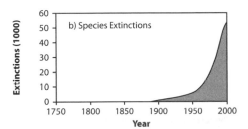

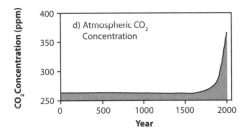

FIGURE 3.2. Responses of the earth system to increasing pressure from human activities: a) nitrogen fixation (Vitousek 1994); b) species extinctions (Smith 2002); c) northern hemisphere surface temperature (Mann et al. 1999); and d) atmospheric CO_2 concentration (adapted from Keeling and Whorf 2000). Reproduced by permission from W. Steffen et al. *Global Change and the Earth System* (New York: Springer-Verlag, 2004), 6.

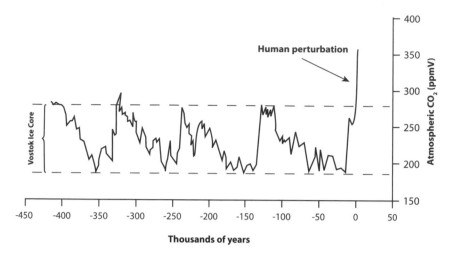

FIGURE 3.3. The Vostok Ice Core provides the best current record of atmospheric CO_2 for the past 450,000 years. Reproduced by permission from J. R. Petit et al., "Climate and Atmospheric History of the Past 420,000 Years from the Vostok Ice Core, Antarctica" (*Nature* 399 [1999]):429–436.

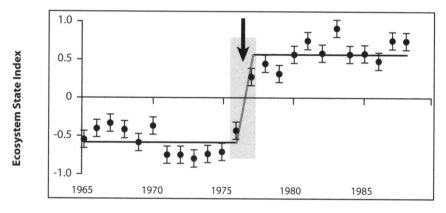

FIGURE 3.4. Small climatic changes led the ecosystem of the North Pacific in 1977 to shift in its equilibrium—an example of positive feedback and system restructuring when a threshold or tipping point was reached. Reproduced by permission from S. R. Hare and N. J. Mantua, "Empirical Evidence for North Pacific Regime Shifts in 1977 and 1989" (*Progress in Oceanography* 47 [2000]):103–145.

cycle, or shifts in some ecosystems from tropical moist forest to savanna as a result of climatic shifts (see figure 3.5).

Yet there is very little evidence that major industrial nations, such as the United States, Japan, Russia, and China, are facilitating policies that can effectively reduce emissions of carbon dioxide, methane, and other greenhouse gases. Indeed, evidence is that some of these highly industrial and populous countries are increasing their emissions rather than beginning a process of reduction. The size of their population and/or their strongly consumerist economies means that they account for a large proportion of the emissions. Western Europe has taken a different course from other countries, advocating reductions of carbon dioxide emissions systematically to 1992 levels, and they appear to have done so without reductions in the quality of their standard of living. This stands in sharp contrast to the reluctance of the United States to engage with the Kyoto Protocol agreement and the Intergovernmental Panel on Climate Change and its preference to rely on voluntary measures by corporations rather than setting government-mandated targets. By any measure, these voluntary approaches have not worked across industrial sectors, and now even some major corporations have begun to ask government to start mandating targets so that the corporations can more systematically set their plans for future building and product standards.

Feedbacks

As the price of oil was rising in 2008, there was a return to questioning whether it makes sense for goods to travel across the country and across the world to supply our consumption, or whether it would be preferable to return to local production of items and a recognition of the value of eating according to the seasons and cycles of nature locally. This is a good example of negative feedback (system responses that dampen the magnitude of the original forcing factor).

In affluent, highly industrialized societies consumption, more than population, has a particularly dangerous impact on the environment, because it does not tend to give clear evidence to the consumer of the impact of his or her consumption decisions. Villagers in populous India who cut trees for fuel to heat their small houses immediately feel the impact of that action: soon enough when they go out to get fuel, there will be no trees. They must either plan ahead and plant trees (which will take years to grow), or they will have to go much farther to get enough fuel to heat their homes. Under those conditions, they are more likely to just cut branches, and leave the trees to produce more branches to be harvested later. In addition, there is likely to be some effort to adjust consumption of fuel to match the modest quantity of branches that can be harvested in a sustainable manner—otherwise the people would be forced to move from their village.

Savanna   Forest

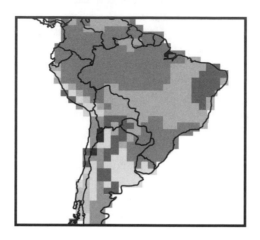

2000 Amazon Biomes

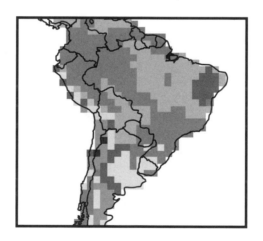

2100 Amazon Biomes

(note the reduction in forested area)

FIGURE 3.5. Is a collapse of the Amazon Forest imminent? Reproduced by permission from M. D. Oyama and C. A. Nobre, "A new climate–vegetation equilibrium state for tropical South America" (*Geophysicial Research Letters* 30[23] [2003]):2199.

In contrast, when consumers in a less populous but wealthier society buy a home, they tend to buy far more square footage than they really need (note the contrast between the 1,500-square-foot home with a one-car garage, the standard for a middle class family of five in 1960, with the 3,800-square-foot homes with up to three-car garages being built today), which requires year-round energy to heat and cool.

Such a family sees no trees cut for all the wood floors and cabinetry put into the home, sees no oil rigs near their home pumping the petroleum required to produce the energy required to heat and cool the house, and does not see all the other raw materials extracted from all over the world for the materials in the house. This family may even imagine themselves to be very "green" and ecologically minded. Why? Because they have not received any environmental feedbacks as to the consequences to people and the environment in all the places from which those items came. And as long as people do not know that their choices to consume a given item have had a corresponding impact on the environment, they feel unconstrained to keep from consuming.

As another example, when a consumer buys a pound of coffee, there is very little information on where that coffee came from, whether people were displaced to produce it, or whether they have even the most minimal of living conditions—and certainly no information on how sustainable the plantation is. At the same time that U.S. consumers were paying three dollars for a cup of latte, farmers in Brazil and Mexico were getting only twenty-nine cents a pound for their coffee. This low price fueled, for example, heavy migration from coffee regions of Mexico to the United States. Efforts to develop fair trade certified coffee are built on the notion that providing minimum economic conditions for coffee workers would improve their lives and help reduce the pressures to migrate. However, very few consumers are willing to pay the few additional cents that such certified coffee implies. On the other hand, in Europe there has been a much stronger campaign to educate consumers on what fair trade coffee does, and a willingness to support it.

What may be required to change the current and dangerous conditions of our planet? Environmental education and literacy about population, consumption, and ecological footprint is one first and necessary step. Without understanding the consequences of each action one takes, there is little motivation to act responsibly. First, then, all citizens must understand the real condition of the planet or earth system, and the exponential processes occurring simultaneously, and at unprecedented magnitudes. Second, people must grasp the complexity of the population issue, including an understanding of both population numbers and distribution of population. Third, people must understand in clear and unequivocal terms how feedback operates, and how our consumption footprint matters.

And last, there is considerable value in rethinking the demands that one places on the planet. Moving toward at least part of our consumption being local would go a long way toward putting us back into contact with our environment and would serve to teach us very important lessons on how to take care of both our local and our global environment.

Christine Glaser
Economics

Economics is perceived by many as being about money, about numbers (like Gross Domestic Product, GDP), and about graphs (such as demand curves). Economists are often seen as being cold and calculating, supporting profits and markets—which are frequently identified as the main culprits in the destruction of the environment. But at its most basic, economics is about values. It is about scarcity of resources, and about ways in which humans deal with that scarcity. Economics, in my view, has a lot to teach about how we interact with the environment, why we are destroying the environment, and what can be done to change that. Instead of idealizing or demonizing the market, a program of teaching environmental literacy will teach students that:

· The human economy is nested within nature's economy, and economic activity must therefore ultimately be constrained within the biosphere's finite capacity to regenerate resources and assimilate wastes.

- Markets do not have a life of their own but are the reflection of the market participants' values, desires, perceptions, knowledge, and ignorance, all of which can change. Obviously the college experience could play a major role in questioning and shaping the values, desires, and perceptions of students, and in relieving ignorance about the state of our environmental life support systems and the social and economic systems that depend on them.
- People respond to incentives, and therefore markets, and the price signals they send can become a useful tool for changing behavior, if prices reflect environmental and social costs and are allowed to act as incentives for sustainable practices and disincentives for unsustainable ones. In such a market environment, profits cannot be made from destroying life support systems or from increasing social inequity. Large institutions like universities also often set price signals. Consider parking fees, and how they may encourage or discourage driving. Or purchasing practices, and how they may encourage or discourage fair labor.
- Markets do not exist in a political vacuum; they are interwoven with the political realm—the realm of collective action. The college experience could offer opportunities for students to develop the skills and the knowledge they need to be successful advocates for social equity and for policies designed to achieve a sustainable scale of economic activity within the limits of the biosphere.

Environment, Economy and People

RESOURCES, SCARCITY, PROFITS, AND LOSSES: HOW MARKETS WORK

Most introductory economics courses start out talking about the scarcity of resources, which may surprise some, since the earth's limitations don't seem to get much respect from the economies we are familiar with. Resources are defined as human services of various kinds (labor); services and materials provided by nature, including minerals, water, forests, etc. (land); and produced factors of production, like machines and factory buildings (capital). These resources are seen as limited (scarce), compared to the seemingly unlimited wants of humans. It may sound strange to speak about scarcity in the country of big-box retail and giant malls, where shelves are overflowing and someone is always begging you to buy their stuff. Scarcity as defined by neoclassical economists is not poverty or lack, it is simply the contrast between the available labor, capital, and land resources and seemingly unlimited wants, with no distinction between survival needs and luxurious indulgences. In the neoclassical view, as a consequence of the scarcity of resources, we compete for those resources and for what they are capable of producing, and we have developed ways to ration those scarce resources. Rationing means deciding what the limited resources are used for, and by whom. In the market, the questions of what resources will be employed in the production process, what will be produced, and who gets it are settled by who is willing and able to pay, and how much. Neoclassical economists tend not to see resource limits or the complexity of natural systems as an issue of concern, because they assume that humans will always find substitutes and new ways of doing things if they run into limitations.

Over the last thirty years, ecological economists have widened the focus from the neoclassical, relative concept of scarcity, to include a much more in-depth and careful analysis of the goods and services natural systems provide to humans, of how economic activity affects these systems, and how the impairment and destruction of these systems in turn impacts economic activity. As a result of this analysis, ecological economists are prepared to accept that economic growth cannot go on indefinitely, and that ultimately economic activity needs to respect an absolute kind of scarcity that is the consequence of biophysical limitations.

NOT EVERYTHING THAT IS VALUABLE HAS MARKET VALUE

Markets, employing the self-interest, ingenuity, and creativity of market participants, are extremely successful in providing an abundance of marketable goods and services. In a market system, you better yourself (make more goods and services available to yourself), by putting effort into providing goods and services that others value more highly than the resources used up in the process of production. Markets give incentives for entrepreneurs to find and fill just about any niche of buyers' desires, and the rate of innovation and of so-called "progress" in provision of goods and services is truly astounding. Entrepreneurs are making sure to offer us endless new ways of satisfying our wants. The environment suffers in the process—when we extract needed resources, when we manufacture products, distribute them, advertise them, use them, and throw them away. While markets have been driving the expansion of production of goods and services beyond the carrying capacity of our biophysical environment, ironically they increase scarcity as defined by neoclassical economists, regardless of how efficiently we produce things. This is because the more prosperous people become, the more they become aware of things they don't have yet, but can now afford to buy. Wants increase with prosperity, unless we as individuals make a conscious decision that there is something like "enough." As studies have shown, satisfaction, happiness, and contentment do not increase with increased prosperity after a certain level of income is reached that guarantees that basic human needs for food, shelter, clothing, and healthcare are met. This certainly begs the question of why we wreck our life support systems for more stuff that doesn't even make us any happier. It also shows that an economy that respects biophysical limitations and produces less doesn't have to mean an impaired quality of life, if quality of life is measured by satisfaction and happiness. This should not be a big surprise, since traditional wisdom has taught mankind for millennia that happiness is something that comes from within.

For the market to protect species diversity and the integrity of our natural life support systems, their value to us has to be communicated through price signals. Let us look at a tropical rain forest, for example. This forest provides livelihood for traditional peoples (foods, shelter, medicines) who do not participate in the market economy. Now this rainforest is auctioned off to lumber companies by the government of the country. The companies bid on the right to log the forest based on the money they can earn on the lumber. Suddenly that rainforest has monetary value. Although the forest is vitally important to its inhabitants, they are unlikely to be able to make a counteroffer and outbid the logging companies to preserve their livelihoods. Therefore the market ignores the value of the forest to them. In the context of the market economy, the forest could, however, be preserved if some entrepreneur, or even a nonprofit organization, would value the standing forest highly enough to be able to outbid the logging companies. Let's say the owner of an eco-tourism firm is convinced that the value of the forest (in terms of future profits) as a tourist destination is higher than the value from logging. Consequently he can make an offer to the logging companies that is more lucrative than what these companies can make by logging. The rainforest could also be preserved by environmental groups in the United States who appeal to their members to donate money for the purchase of the rainforest land. Enough money to purchase that forest land (or to purchase the right to develop or log it) may be raised if people see value in preserving the rainforest, and if they value rainforest preservation more than other things they could buy with their money, such as tickets to a football game. They may or may not intend to ever travel to see that rainforest. Note that the only basis for value in these cases is that some humans have the interest and the money to protect that forest, and the market or the nonprofit sector offers them opportunities to express those values and make them felt in the economy. In markets, the value of anything and everything is derived from, in the last analysis, what we find it worth spending our money on.

A landowner may find it advantageous to turn her land into an organic farm. Or, she could make her land available for dumping of toxic wastes, fully knowing that all other uses of the land are destroyed for generations to come, and then use the money earned in the transaction to go gambling in Las Vegas. The market has no capability to distinguish between decisions that destroy our life support systems and others that don't. It doesn't sound any alarm bells when life support systems are destroyed for plastic toys that end up in the trash after being used once. In the context of the market, what actually happens on a piece of land is determined by what market participants value and are willing to pay for.

MARKETS FAIL TO ACCOUNT FOR EXTERNALITIES AND BIOPHYSICAL LIMITS

What often limits the ability of the market to protect our life support systems is that market participants pay for goods and services only insofar as someone has a property right on them, and they can be apportioned into marketable units, like kilowatt-hours of electricity. The electricity belongs to the power company, and it sells the electricity by the kilowatt-hour to anyone willing to pay. Contract law and property rights back up the power company's claim to be paid for the electricity it produces and makes available for purchase. On the other hand, the air that the power company uses as a repository for its wastes is not officially owned by anyone. We don't usually sell out waste deposit space measured in cubic feet of air above our land to the highest bidder. The power company does not make contracts with land owners for permission to deposit coal dust, or to drop acids on forests and lakes. Landowners do not have a right to be free of coal dust or acid rain. Nor does the power company have to contract with individuals living around the coal plant for permission to infiltrate their lungs with chemical waste products. If individual landowners had the right to keep pollution off their land and out of their lungs, the market would show how much people value their clean lungs compared to the money the company offers them for the right to pollute. This value could be expressed through the market. However, since such rights are not established, the use of air, lakes, and lungs becomes free and is not reflected in the price of the product, and thus prices don't indicate: Attention, something valuable has been used up! The reduction in property value and imposition of health costs not accounted for in market prices are called externalities. And anything that doesn't cost anything is likely to be used liberally and without much second thought.

The delineation of rights (rights to pollute or to be free of pollution) happens, for the most part, in the realm of collective action; that is to say, it involves laws, regulations, the courts, and the political process. This doesn't mean it is not influenced by market interests. Obviously those with economic power and money have a greater say in how rights are delineated than those with little or no power and money. It is important for students of economics to understand the interplay between the market and collective action. Collective action doesn't only set the framework for restrictions on pollution; it can also limit resource extraction, such as mining and fishing, or protect biodiversity. National parks and wilderness areas, and laws protecting endangered species, are the result of collective action, not of market activity.

MARKETS FOCUS OUR ATTENTION ON HUMAN ARTIFACTS

Entrepreneurs offer us our human-made, antiseptic, air-conditioned world of grocery stores, office complexes, drive-ins and suburban homes. Living in this man-made world, it is hard for us to notice the changes that we impose on our environment and life-support systems. We probably experience nature more often on a screen, in a magazine ad, or driving through it at sixty miles per hour talking on the cell phone than as active and knowledgeable observers. For us to prosper and succeed in our modern, human-created world, we don't really have to know what is going on in our natural environment. It is much more important that we log on to the internet and find out about new developments in the stock market. And as long as we are ignorant and seemingly unaffected by changes in our environment and life support systems, we are unlikely to attach any value to them, nor are we willing to sacrifice much to prevent their deterioration and destruction.

How Can Change Happen?

With an appreciation of the fundamental limits to growth imposed by the finite nature of the biosphere and a well-developed sense of ethics as prerequisites, conscious choice, market incentives, and truthful national accounting can emerge as powerful mechanisms for change.

CONSCIOUS CHOICES

Change can happen when increasing numbers of people consciously decide to consider the environmental consequences of their actions. In our multiple roles as homeowners, parents, students, managers, employees, investors, administrators, entrepreneurs, to name just a few, we have multiple opportunities to act in ways that have a positive effect on the environment. More and more people embrace those opportunities, for example, by buying organically grown food or investing only in companies with a good environmental track record. More and more people are committed to finding ways to reduce their consumption of fossil fuels, knowing that they contribute to global warming. Companies respond by offering products and services that are less damaging to the earth's life support systems. But these voluntary efforts may not be enough.

GETTING THE PRICES RIGHT

In order to induce more widespread changes in behavior, we can employ the help of the market incentives by taxing products that impose large environmental burdens, or by imposing cap and trade systems that put limits on pollution or resource extraction, all of which would make environmentally destructive activities more expensive. A carbon tax, for example, would lead to higher prices for gasoline, heating oil, natural gas, and electricity (which is mostly produced from coal); this would provide incentives to seek out alternative sources of energy and to reduce consumption of the higher-priced (highly polluting) fossil fuels. Some of these adjustments could happen very quickly, like turning thermostats down in the winter and up in the summer, and cutting unnecessary trips with better trip planning. In the long run, people could make larger adjustments, both in homes and workplaces, such as moving closer to work to reduce commuting distance, buying cars with better gas mileage, or retrofitting buildings to reduce heat loss.

Nothing else will set that in motion as effectively, broadly, and promptly as millions of limited budgets confronted with significantly increased prices for products that involve large externalities. When it costs $60 instead of $25 to fill a gas tank, that speaks loudly, and is more persuasive and compelling than any appeal for voluntary action. Suddenly, whether people care about the environment or not, they are confronted with an uncomfortable choice—if they keep on driving as they did, they'll have to give up something else, like going to the movies or eating out, because they can't afford to do both. Each person will have to decide how to respond, and where to cut expenditures, but there is a high likelihood that most will find some way to drive less and cut down their gas expenses as they adjust to the higher prices. For some people, the choice will not be between driving and movies, but between driving and eating, or between driving and buying needed medication. Any pollution tax program that involves drastic increases in prices should therefore be accompanied by measures that help the most vulnerable to cope with those changes.

To internalize external costs, those costs first have to be estimated. For example, for the carbon tax, we would have to estimate global warming-related damage that results from more severe storms, floods, droughts, and rising sea levels. The methods used to do that are sometimes controversial. But controversy is not the biggest obstacle.

Getting the prices right, so they can function as effective incentives and disincentives guiding behavior toward sustainability, usually requires political decisions. In the political arena there are many "players," often with conflicting interests, and agendas like "getting the prices right" don't promote themselves. They need advocates. For governments on the local, state, federal, and international levels to step in and make the necessary corrections to markets (internalizing externalities and respect for biophysical limits) there needs to be a broad constituency of active, watchful citizens who are well informed, concerned, and willing to act based on their convictions and values.

Internalizing externalities and raising the prices of highly polluting activities could work wonders. If you need any proof, just look at how quickly people responded to increases in energy prices during the 1973 oil crisis and, more recently, during the 2008 oil price spikes.

To "get the prices right"—that is, to ensure that markets reward sustainable practices and discourage unsustainable ones—we also have to take a close look at laws, regulations, taxes, and subsidies impacting a situation. Getting the prices right may require scrapping government subsidies for destructive practices. For example, if the U.S. Forest Service stopped subsidizing logging on national forests, prices for timber would rise, and more expensive timber would lead some people to buy less of it and turn to alternatives. Wood pulp is used in paper production. Paper from newly cut wood would be more expensive if it weren't subsidized, and recycled paper would become more competitive. Current income tax laws and federal subsidies for local highway building, as well as zoning regulations, have a role in promoting urban sprawl.

In analyzing a situation, it is important to look away from surface appearances and conventional wisdom that would tell us, for example, that people "just love their cars" and that is why they drive so much. By looking instead at incentives and disincentives that impact peoples' choices, we find out what promotes the "love," and that this "love" isn't something deeply innate or absolute; rather it is the result of choices that are based on benefits (incentives) and costs (disincentives) and available alternatives. Do Europeans drive less because they don't "love" their cars as much as Americans, or do they drive less because they have good public transportation, extensive bike trail networks, and much higher gas taxes?

TRUTHFUL NATIONAL ACCOUNTING

We are used to seeing growth of the GDP as an indicator of our economic progress and national well being. Looking at the growing GDP, we conclude that we are doing better and better, year after year. Better and better—that means: more goods and services are produced and consumed. But there are some serious defects in the way we calculate the GDP: some of that "growth" we supposedly experience comes about because the GDP adds goods and services produced solely for the purpose of dealing with the negative consequences of pollution and damage to natural systems.

The GDP celebrates increased expenses for ecosystem restoration, toxic waste cleanup, and medical services to treat pollution-related illnesses the same way it counts increased expenses for vacations, books, or for a second home: as growth. It doesn't distinguish between growth that benefits the rich and growth that benefits the poor, and it ignores that a current increase in production of goods and services may leave future generations with highly polluted groundwater, reduced agricultural productivity, and otherwise diminished and impaired life-support systems. The more that is produced and consumed now, the better for the GDP, no matter what the consequences later. Actually, dealing with the consequences in the future could add more "growth." Global warming brings more storms: Great, that means the construction industry has more work. According to the GDP, that is "growth."

The Genuine Progress Indicator (GPI), a creation of the public policy think tank Redefining Progress, was developed as an alternative to the GDP. The GPI deducts environmental damage repair costs, resource depletion, and social costs from a nation's income and therefore gives a more truthful picture of how well the national economy, and we, as members of that economy, are doing. Many countries with high GDP growth rates actually show much lower or even declining GPI growth rates. For the United States, for example, the GPI started declining during the 1980s, while the GDP continued to grow. The public discourse on growth will certainly change when we start taking an honest look at what it is that is actually growing, and whether our economic activity provides us with more goods than bads. Growth that is uneconomic (saddles us with more bads than goods, or higher costs than benefits) cannot be defended on economic grounds.

Considering the negative environmental and social impacts of growth and the failure of the GDP to reveal them, students need to explore the reform of national, state, and local policies that are currently geared toward stimulating GDP growth, including, for example, fiscal, monetary, and trade policies. Students also need to understand that in an economy that produces within the long-term carrying capacity of the earth, an increase in individual or national income and wealth comes with a reduction in income and wealth for someone else. This brings to the forefront the issue of distribution of income and wealth and considerations of justice and social equity.

Environmental Literacy

How can these insights from the discipline of economics be incorporated into Environmental Literacy Programs?

- Students must be introduced to the concept of biophysical limits—that our finite planet, while permitting unlimited development (i.e., greater social equity, stronger community ties, and other qualitative changes that improve human well being) can sustain only a finite amount of economic growth (as defined by increased physical throughput of resources).
- College professors should awaken their students to how powerfully economic incentives move large numbers of people to do things that seem perfectly rational to them individually, but, when taken together, lead to the destruction of our life support systems and to social inequity. Conversely, students need to know that, when properly informed by an

appreciation of ecological limits and of ethics, market incentives can be a positive force for environmental health and social equity. Students do not just need to know this in a general way; they need to be trained to put on their economic thinking caps and examine real-world examples with the goal of detecting what makes people do the things they do. For example, students may learn that tax laws and federal government subsidies for building local highways have something to do with sprawl, or that virgin paper sells for less than recycled paper because of federal logging subsidies. Students need to learn to not just accept conventional wisdom like "Americans love cars," but to dig deeper and discover what promotes that "love." Externalities are usually covered in introductory textbooks, and professors should seize the opportunity and provide examples that show the serious consequences from externalities impacting our life support systems. Political science has a role in teaching students about the political process that shapes incentives and disincentives and the delineation of (property) rights. The political arena is the sphere of action where externalities are corrected, and where destructive government regulations and subsidies can be addressed. To become successful advocates for the environment and for social equity, students need to learn how to engage with that process.

- Students do not only need the analytical skills to examine what incentives and disincentives are at play, they also need to be able to write and speak clearly and persuasively about their insights. Journalism, political science, writing, and public speaking courses could build these skills, and also include opportunities for practicing and sharpening the analytical skills taught in economics courses.
- The communities that host universities often provide opportunities for students to get engaged with environmental and social issues, to develop and practice their writing and speaking skills, and to effectively communicate through various media. This engagement should be encouraged through service-learning programs and course assignments. The university itself should give students opportunities to get actively involved in "greening" their campus. Besides exploring and experiencing sustainable alternatives to current practices of building, heating, cooling, lighting, landscaping, growing food, etc., students could develop research, communication, teambuilding, outreach, and organizational skills, as well as experience in dealing with sometimes reluctant, not always transparent, and often slow bureaucratic institutions. In examining what incentives and disincentives drive the relevant decisions of the university administration, they can further sharpen their analytical skills.

- Educators of all disciplines can encourage their students to search in themselves for what truly brings them happiness, satisfaction, and joy, and to discover their highest aspirations for themselves and the world. This will eliminate a lot of mindless activity and consumption, and will help students develop the inner freedom and strength to define for themselves what it means to be successful and useful members of society. Some disciplines may offer more opportunities for such explorations than others. I can see this happening especially in courses on ethics, philosophy, religion, and economics. Awakening to, acknowledging, and courageously following our highest aspirations and hopes is not a selfish pursuit. Our highest aspirations connect us with each other and the universe.

References

Czech, B. 2009. "Ecological Economics." In *Encyclopaedia of Life Support Systems (EOLSS)*. UNESCO-EOLSS Publishers, Oxford, UK. At http://www.steadystate.org/Files/Czech _Ecological_Economics.pdf (accessed 9 August 2009).

5
A Sense of Place

Scott Russell Sanders
English

In a speech delivered in 1952, Rachel Carson warned: "Mankind has gone very far into an artificial world of his own creation. He has sought to insulate himself, in his cities of steel and concrete, from the realities of earth and water and the growing seed. Intoxicated with a sense of his own power, he seems to be going farther and farther into more experiments for the destruction of himself and his world."

Carson voiced these worries before the triumph of television or shopping malls, before the advent of air-conditioning, personal computers, video games, the Internet, cell phones, cloning, genetic engineering, and a slew of other inventions that have made the artificial world ever more seductive. Unlike the earth, the artificial world is made for us. It feeds our bellies and minds with tasty pap; it shelters us from discomfort and sickness; it proclaims our ingenuity; it flatters our pride. Snug inside bubbles fashioned from concrete and steel, from silicon and plastic and words, we can pretend we are running the planet.

By contrast, the natural world was not made for our comfort or convenience. It preceded us by some billions of years, and it will outlast us; it mocks our pride, because it surpasses our understanding and control; it can be dangerous and bewildering and demanding; although it supplies every atom of our bodies and nourishes us so long as we live, it will reclaim us when we die. We should not be surprised that increasing numbers of people choose to live entirely indoors, leaving buildings only to ride in cars or airplanes, viewing the great outside, if they view it at all, through sealed windows, but more often gazing into screens, listening to human chatter, cut off from "the realities of earth and water and the growing seed."

By comparison with nature, the world presented by the electronic media is disembodied, stripped down, anemic, and hasty. The more time we spend in the "virtual" world, the more likely we are to forget how impoverished it is. A screen delivers us a patch of something to look at, and speakers or earphones deliver sounds to us from a couple of locations. Compare the experience of walking through a woods or a town square: not only do visual impressions and sounds come to us from all directions, but also smells, textures, tastes, sensations of wind or mist or heat against our skin, and the kinesthetic sensations from the movement of our body. In a woods or a town square, we are also surrounded by fellow creatures, our own kind or other species, and these, too, are centers of perception. We evolved to learn from and be stimulated by the full range of our senses. By comparison, the world given to us by television, video games, or computer screens is depleted—like a diet of bleached flour. To compensate for that impoverishment, the virtual world must become ever more hectic and sensational if it is to hold our attention. The actual world, the three-dimensional array of sights and textures and tastes and sounds that we find in a vibrant city or landscape, needs no hype in order to intrigue us.

This retreat into the manufactured world has practical as well as moral implications. It deludes us into thinking we can substitute our own inventions for the intricate, ancient, and essential processes of nature. It hides from us the consequences of our actions. It tempts us to think exclusively of our own personal needs, or at most those of our human contemporaries, without regard to the needs of other species or future generations. By spreading toxins, altering climate and ocean currents, loosing engineered organisms into the biosphere, destroying wild habitat, and disrupting natural processes in countless other ways, we endanger every species on the planet, and not merely our own. By fouling air and water and soil, squandering irreplaceable resources, and driving millions of species to extinction, we are handing on to our descendants a severely diminished legacy.

The more time we spend inside human constructions, the more likely we are to forget that these bubbles float in the great ocean of nature. A decade before

Carson issued her warning, Aldo Leopold in *A Sand County Almanac* recognized this danger as the central challenge facing the conservation movement: How do we nurture a land ethic in people who have less and less contact with land? How do we inspire people to take care of their home places if they feel no sense of place?

"We abuse land," Leopold wrote, "because we regard it as a commodity belonging to us. When we see land as a community to which we belong, we may begin to use it with love and respect." Leopold employs the word *belong* here in two radically different ways. The first is economic, legal, and abstract; it's about claiming ownership and power. When I say that a city lot, a field, or a mountainside belongs to me, I set myself apart from the land, asserting my right to treat it as raw material for my own designs. The second use of *belong* is moral and emotional; it's about claiming kinship. When I say that I belong to this town or watershed or region, I'm declaring membership, as in a family, and I'm acknowledging my obligation to behave in a way that honors and protects the whole of which I am a part. The first use of *belong* is about grasping, and the second is about being embraced. The choice we make between these rival meanings will dramatically influence how we treat the land.

The land does not belong to us; we belong to the land. Conservation begins from this plain and simple fact. Understanding this truth not merely in our minds, but in our bones, will require us to venture outside the human bubble and pay attention to a given landscape season after season, year after year, until we become true inhabitants of our place, taking it in through every doorway of the body, bearing it steadily in heart and mind. Only those who achieve such bone-deep familiarity with a place are likely to care for it as they would care for their children or parents or lovers.

If we aim to nurture a practice of conservation, we need to cultivate this intimacy with land in ourselves and we need to encourage it in others, especially in the young people who pass so quickly through our schools. For teachers, this will mean poring over maps with our students, asking them to read the history and lore of our region, taking them outside to learn the animals and plants and terrain, setting them tasks in service to the community and the local landscape. To do this, teachers need not be experts in natural history. They can recruit birders, gardeners, rockhounds, farmers, foresters, and other knowledgeable people from the community, or they can recruit colleagues who teach biology, geology, history, folklore, and other relevant subjects. They can enlist the help of librarians to identify poets, essayists, and novelists who have written about the place, as Willa Cather wrote about Nebraska or Wendell Berry writes about Kentucky. They can enlist art historians to identify painters and photographers who have recorded impressions of the place, as T. C. Steele painted southern Indiana or Ansel Adams photographed California.

Even as our students are gaining a deep local knowledge, we need to help them understand their lives and their homes within the great web of winds and waters and weather, animal migration, glacial history, continental drift, and cosmic evolution. Here, for example, are a few questions that students might ask about the place where they spend their college years. What is the local bedrock, and how did it form? What are the principal soils, and how did they form? What forces of geology, glaciation, erosion, and human activity shaped the local topography? How much precipitation does the region receive each year, and where does the water flow, through what creeks and rivers, to what gulf or ocean? What are the boundaries of the watershed? What kinds of vegetation, from mosses and grasses to wildflowers and trees, are native to this region? What kinds of animals? How have the varieties of wildlife and patterns of vegetation changed over time? What do we know about the earliest humans who lived here? Do their descendants survive, and, if not, what imprint have they left behind? What do we know about the first settlers of European, African, or Asian descent, and what do we know about how they fashioned communities and changed the land? What do we know of the people who came here as immigrants or slaves? How have people made a living here? How have they entertained themselves? How have they worshipped? What sort of buildings have they erected, out of what materials? How is this place bound to other places—through climate, for example, through migration of birds, through the flow of water and people? What scholarship, what literature, what art has this place inspired?

Such questions might be addressed through writing assignments, through photography or other forms of art, through interviews, through research at historical societies, through volunteer work with local service organizations or land trusts, through outings with environmental groups, through exhibits or activity fairs, through field trips or campus walks. By finding answers to questions about the place where they are attending college or university, our students would come to feel less like tourists, just passing through, and more like inhabitants of an old, storied, and continuing place. Having tasted what it's like to be at home somewhere, they're more likely to fully invest themselves wherever life may take them after graduation.

We need far more citizens who know and care deeply about the place they share with neighbors and other animals, and not merely about their private circumstances. We need citizens who recognize that their own well-being is inseparable from the well-being of the human and natural communities to which they belong. We need citizens who are devoted to creating and nurturing, rather than to getting and spending. The dominant media in our society proclaim that happiness, meaning, and security are to be found through piling up money and buying things. Whatever troubles us, shopping can fix it; whatever hollowness we feel, shopping can fill it; whatever questions haunt us, shopping can provide the answers. A recent billboard for a brand of cigarettes used the slogan, "Get More Stuff," and that might serve as the motto for our entire commercial culture. Responding to these relentless exhortations, Americans, while constituting less than 5 percent of the world's population, presently account for a quarter of the world's annual consumption of oil and other nonrenewable natural resources and produce about 20 percent of the world's energy-related carbon dioxide.

If we aim to foster a shift from this culture of consumption to a culture of conservation, we'll have to work at changing a host of things, from ads to zoos, from how we put food on our plates to how we imagine our role in the universe. Out of all these necessary changes, one crucial need is to recover an intimate knowledge of, and affection for, our home ground. Every neighborhood, every watershed, every wild land needs people who feel responsible for that place, who know its human and natural history, who speak resolutely on behalf of it. Whatever else our students may learn from us, they should learn the pleasure and value of such belonging.

John S. Applegate
Law

Environmentally literate persons should understand that environmental harms and environmental regulation operate at two different levels: national or widely shared effects and rules, and local or narrowly felt effects and rules. Perhaps the most apparent and most important differences between the national and local are the burdens and benefits of environmental degradation and environmental regulation on specific places. Both environmental harms and remedies help some people and hurt others. A polluting factory economically benefits its owners, employees, and the local community, but it hurts its downwind or downstream neighbors.[1] Pollution control helps the neighbors (who may overlap with the owners, employees, and community), but it can also encourage the shifting of

---

1. These issues are explored in Richard J. Lazarus, *Pursuing "Environmental Justice": The Distributional Effects of Environmental Protection*, 87 Nw. U. L. Rev. 787 (1993). For a more general treatment of environmental justice issues, see Kenneth A. Manaster, *Environmental Protection and Justice: Readings on the Practice and Purposes of Environmental Law*, 3rd ed. (LexisNexis, 2007).

pollution from one form and location to another, as when water pollution is treated to become solid waste that is transported to another location, or when a factory's operations move to another locality. Environmentally literate persons should be sensitive to disparities in environmental benefits and burdens, and they should also understand that identifying and justly managing disparate effects involve complex factual and philosophical issues. They should be able to analyze claims of consequences and assess their moral and political significance. These considerations should affect individual lifestyle choices; more importantly, they should affect individuals' social and political commitments and involvement in the governance processes of the places where they live.

Place and Environmental Law

The environmental movement in the United States began as a heightened sense of place. The movement to create the Yellowstone and Yosemite national parks drew its inspiration from the obvious specialness of those places, their vistas, plants, animals, and geological marvels. The pioneering works of the ecologist Eugene Odum and conservation biologist Aldo Leopold—two founders of modern environmentalism—concentrated on the complex and interrelated workings of the organisms and inanimate environment of particular places. Likewise, many of the earliest pollution control laws (anti-smoke, anti-dumping, etc.) were, in essence, specific instances of the centuries-old law of nuisance, which deals with the interference by the owner of one specific piece of property with a neighbor's property. Environmental harms and environmental remedies, in other words, expressed and protected people's sense of particular places.

As environmental law moved from concern with large-scale, readily observable phenomena, like protection of wilderness or prevention of smog, to a concern with the effects of chemicals on human and ecological health, the sense of place diminished. Rachel Carson, perhaps the preeminent founder of modern environmentalism, focused less in her masterpiece, *Silent Spring*, on particular places than on chemical harms that are ubiquitous, operate invisibly (her favored term was "sinister"), and affect all human beings, plants, and animals in similar ways. (It is no accident that, while she opened *Silent Spring* with a "parable" about a town where "no birds sing," that town was imaginary, not a real place.) The concern that Carson sparked in American environmental law resulted, accordingly, in new legal standards (national ambient air quality standards, technology-based water pollutant discharge permits) that were based on general chemical effects and were applied to specific places almost as an afterthought.[2]

---

2. Congress typically retained standard setting in national institutions, like the Environmental Protection Agency, and left the permitting and enforcement work to the states.

Concern with place and with large-scale effects never entirely disappeared, of course. The foundational National Environmental Policy Act is primarily used to address placed-based environmental effects, such as those involved with highways and forest management. Nevertheless, until recently, it was generally assumed that the uniform application of national standards would improve everyone's environment, and so a more finely tuned, locally oriented analysis was unnecessary.

This assumption was challenged in a series of protests and studies that revealed apparent disparities in the siting of hazardous waste landfills. The protestors—neighbors of these landfills—claimed that landfills and the like (known as locally undesirable land uses, or LULUs[3]) are more often located in predominantly poor and minority neighborhoods than in wealthier and "whiter" areas. Moreover, those who suffer the environmental harm rarely enjoy its economic benefits. In litigation that drew national attention, the poor African-American residents of St. James Parish, Louisiana—who live in the corridor of chemical plants along the lower Mississippi River known as Cancer Alley—told of sitting on their porches, facing the fences of the chemical plants and breathing the plants' emissions, while the white employees of the plants drove by on their way to and from work. These complaints, under the rubric of environmental racism or environmental justice, caused a major reconsideration of the relationship of environmental regulation to the sense of place. The appalling response (or *lack* of response) to Hurricane Katrina in New Orleans highlights the gulf between rich and poor and black and white in the distribution of environmental and social amenities.

Scholars, activists, and regulators have come to recognize that environmental harms are not evenly distributed among places and populations and, further, that environmental remedies may help some places and populations but not others. For example, some places are "toxic hotspots." Either through siting choices or just unlucky meteorology or hydrology, they suffer the cumulative impacts of many different sources of pollution. Conversely, the benefits of environmental protection can be unevenly distributed. The level and strictness of enforcement activity can vary considerably among different places and populations. Moreover, some environmental controls, evenhanded on their face, in effect transfer risks from one population to another. For example, the pesticide laws that responded to *Silent Spring* led to the phasing out of persistent, low-toxicity pesticides in order to protect the public who consumes the treated food; however, the replacement chemicals, high-toxicity pesticides that break down rapidly in the environment, place agricultural workers at a much higher risk of acute and long-term poisoning.

---

3. The category includes environmental hazards, as well as socially beneficial facilities like halfway houses.

These differences in impacts of both environmental degradation and regulation become apparent only when one moves from the national to the local. A sense of place brings into focus the particular effects of environmental harm and the efforts to remedy or prevent the harm. It is no coincidence that the re-examination of the distribution of environmental impacts and protections was sparked by the siting of landfills, a strikingly place-based concern. Interestingly, the recent concern with global warming shares these characteristics. The scale of the environmental problem is, obviously, worldwide, the immediate causes are a relatively uniform increase in the levels of carbon dioxide (and other greenhouse gases, or GHGs) in the atmosphere, and the underlying cause (carbon dioxide and GHG emissions) is essentially the same throughout the world. Yet with global warming we simultaneously have an acute sense of the *differences* between places. While climate change will be universal, the nature of the changes in temperature and precipitation will be quite particular. Coastal areas and small island states will, of course, be affected especially severely. Likewise, the politics of global warning has made us all aware that efforts, uniform on their face, to address emissions will have very different impacts on the developing world, which is struggling to rise out of poverty, and the industrialized world, which has heretofore been the source of most emissions. Two particular places, China and India, pose the very particular situation of making industrialization choices that set them on a course to outpace the emissions of the United States and Europe. Even a global environmental problem, then, is pervaded by a sense of place.

Place and Environmental Justice

Having found inequities, the next question that will occur to the thoughtful observer is how they might be remedied. This is not as simple as it might seem. Taking the practical problems first, deciding how to define impacted places and populations has proven quite difficult. Neighborhoods or other distinct areas are relatively easy to recognize on an intuitive basis, but they become devilishly difficult to define in a rigorous and consistent way. Most studies of environmental equity, for example in the siting of hazardous waste landfills, have serious methodological problems that derive from this and other difficulties. Where does a neighborhood end? At what point do the emissions become too dispersed to matter? Is *concern*, without a demonstrated health effect, enough to justify rejection of a facility or activity? Absent some evidence of a purpose to target a particular place for locating LULUs or to withhold environmental protection, it is also very difficult to establish that the reason for uneven distribution is not the result of chance, of the application of conventional siting criteria used by city or county planning authorities (access to utilities, transportation, customers, etc.), or, most frequently, of the price of land. Finally, it is very difficult to measure environmental harms in any but subjective terms. Quantitative health risk estimates are uncertain, incomplete, time-consuming, and expensive. The offsetting benefits, if any, of the LULU—economic development, for example—are often uncertain and highly controverted.

These difficulties challenge our ability to identify and remedy environmental disparities. Behind the practical problems, however, are conceptual ones. What does justice or equity mean in these situations? Three kinds of justice are often identified: corrective, distributive, and procedural.

The easiest case—and the one that gave "environmental racism" its name—is the deliberate selection of a particular population for disproportionate exposure to environmental harm.[4] The most egregious case, of course, is where that population is particularly vulnerable or has been historically discriminated against, i.e., racial or ethnic minorities. This was the gist of the siting complaints that launched the environmental justice movement. Activists claimed that poor African-American communities were targeted for landfills, especially hazardous waste landfills. For example, the decision to locate a landfill for toxic waste in Warren County, North Carolina, one of the poorest and most predominantly African American counties in the state, sparked a local protest that gained national attention.[5]

It is quite clear that in such situations *corrective* justice demands a remedy. However, intentional discrimination is extremely difficult to prove. There are commonly many nondiscriminatory reasons for placing a LULU in a particular location. For example, a landfill operator might choose a location based on proximity to highways and the low price of land. These characteristics are frequently associated with low-income and minority populations, but they are perfectly sensible considerations to rely upon. Moreover, the LULU can point to offsetting benefits (employment, for example) which make it difficult to portray the situation as calling out for correction. These difficulties are to a large extent built into the legal standards that govern equal protection claims under the U.S. Constitution. They require proof of discriminatory intent and have thwarted virtually all attempts to obtain relief under the civil rights laws.

Distributive justice is less restrictive. Instead of focusing on a distinct wrong that demands correction, distributive justice looks to the situation as we find it—

---

4. A very pointed study of environmental justice as it relates to hazardous waste, and a classic of the field, is Robert D. Bullard, *Dumping in Dixie: Race, Class, and Environmental Quality* (Westview, 1994). A skeptical view can be found in Christopher H. Foreman, Jr., *The Promise and Peril of Environmental Justice* (Brookings, 1998).

5. The story is told in *Toxic Wastes and Race in the United States* (United Church of Christ Commission for Racial Justice, 1987) and Demographics of People Living Near Waste Facilities (U.S. General Accounting Office, 1995). Both studies also include broader demographic analyses.

for example, have some persons been placed at greater risk than others. The evidence for intentional discrimination is rare, but it is relatively straightforward and nontechnical. Proving maldistribution, by contrast, raises all of the difficulties of proof mentioned above: defining the place, defining the impacted population, characterizing and quantifying the burdens and benefits, and so on. Moreover, maldistribution is necessarily a relative thing, because obviously neither every place nor every person can be made subject to exactly the same type and amount of environmental benefits and burdens, and there no single, objective, widely accepted metric that would permit direct comparisons of the "packages" of benefits and burdens across places and people.

Both corrective and distributive justice also challenge our ability to develop appropriate and effective remedies. Some decisions, like a discriminatory decision to place a landfill in a particular location, can be simply reversed. But then the landfill operation will have to go somewhere else—where? Even if new locations are considered in a nondiscriminatory manner, what positive guidance can we give for selecting the new place? One model is dispersion, that is, LULUs of a certain type must be kept at a certain distance from each other. Another is fair share, in which particular zones (in the New York City version of this, the five boroughs are the units of measurement) are to receive equal benefits and burdens. The difficulties and impracticalities of these approaches are obvious. Even setting aside the measurement problems described above, they ignore differences in community needs and resources, comparability of LULUs, and the special locational needs of the LULUs, to name a few. And, at the end of the day, it is extremely unclear whether dispersion or fair share regimes will last beyond the amount of time it takes for those who can afford it simply to move away. To the extent that housing and industrialization patterns are driven by land prices (which is a very large extent, by any reckoning), dispersion and fair share regimes seemed doomed to fail in the long run.

Given the difficulties of developing a credible, effective scheme for equitable distribution, many observers have chosen to focus their efforts on a third kind of justice. *Procedural* justice means adopting processes that will assure that all persons, including poor and minority communities, have a meaningful voice in environmental decisions. Such procedures would include, at a minimum, giving all community members notice of a proposed decision, access to relevant information, and a forum for seeking to persuade decision-makers to be moved by their concerns. Additional procedures might include helping the general public to understand technical issues or requiring the issuance of a formal decision stating facts and reasons. The familiar requirement to generate environmental impact statements, especially ones that examine impacts on subgroups or particular places, is a step in the direction of procedural justice. While impact statements do not mandate a particular result, they do permit affected parties to make informed arguments. Similarly, provisions in the recent Food Quality Protection Act require the Environmental Protection Agency to study the effects of chemicals in food on specific subgroups of the population. Procedural remedies avoid the problem of defining in advance what constitutes distributive fairness, or even of determining whether an injustice has been done. Rather, they provide an opportunity to consider claims of maldistribution in advance and on an individualized basis that is tailored to the needs and characteristics of a particular situation. Indeed, procedural justice embodies, in this way, a sense of place.

Place, Justice, and Environmental Literacy

Most aspects of environmental literacy are intended to encourage people to make daily lifestyle choices more deliberately and with a better appreciation of the consequences of their choices. For most college students, therefore, environmental literacy should inform practical, personal choices, like whether to drive or take public transportation, whether to buy a large or a small car, whether to use disposable or washable utensils, whether to maintain a meat or vegetarian diet— all of which have profound environmental implications. For many college students, these are choices in the special environment of a residential institution that is open to and encourages such choices. For them, environmental literacy will be the foundation for thoughtful decisions after college, when they have a wider range of choices to make and the good decisions will often be harder to make. For college students living off campus, however, environmental literacy will be of immediate relevance to the lives that most Americans lead, with the familiar difficulties of reconciling housing patterns with public transportation, overpackaged and overprocessed products with time demands, an electricity-dependent lifestyle with coal-fired power plants, and the needs of other family members.

Why is environmental justice an important subject for *all* college students? First, it offers an opportunity to make informed, analytical, and ethical judgments. Environmental justice is most often about the lives and quality of life of people who do not have the opportunity to attend a college or university, and who do not have that range of choices and opportunities. Choices by college students or college graduates can improve or worsen the situation of such individuals, and so those choices offer an important opportunity for students to exercise their analytical (How will my actions affect others?) and ethical (What should I do?) faculties as educated citizens in a democratic society. Second, in our society, as in all societies, the haves exercise power in a myriad of obvious and subtle, direct and indirect ways over the have-nots; in a decent, democratic society, the haves should recognize and act on the needs and just demands of the have-nots. A basic sense of empathy demands that we recognize that, just as we have a strong sense of attachment to the places we love and our homes, others have a similar sense of attachment to their places. A just and sustainable society cannot flourish where the comfort and enjoyment of some comes at the cost of harm to others. We will be better people and citizens, and our society more just, if we see and understand the situation of others, especially others who are otherwise invisible to us. Third, the lifestyles of the haves depend on patterns of consumption that generate environmental injustice. From broad inequities in consumption to the pollution of industries that meet demands for goods and services, personal behavior and everyday lifestyle choices reinforce the injustices that we have been discussing. Fourth, even injustices with only a very indirect connection with individual choices have a great deal to do with personal political and social commitments, such as support for environmentally damaged communities, opportunities for volunteerism, and involvement in national and local political processes. While some environmental inequities seem to "just happen" (that is, they are the result of broad market and social forces that resist incremental or short-term solutions), many result from affirmative public decisions—for example, the zoning, permits, and development subsidies that are the staples of local government—which allow for the involvement of active citizens.

There is much work to be done to define the contours of environmental justice to the point that it can be enforced on a consistent, principled basis, and instilling an understanding of environmental justice can begin, and end, with a sense of place. Justice in general and environmental justice in particular are subject, and properly so, to analysis in terms of the larger philosophical, legal, and scientific frameworks—How do corrective and distributive justice differ and what do they mean in the environmental setting? How would one prove an injustice, and what should be the consequence of unequal distribution of environmental goods and bads? What do we know about the impact of pollution on persons and the environment? All of these perspectives have been brought to bear on the problem of environmental justice, and they provide the basis for a multifaceted and educationally invaluable exploration of this problem. A sense of particular places can add depth in several ways. At the beginning of the analysis, it draws the student into the issue; it attaches persons and places to the issue, providing both familiarity and urgency. As the philosophical, legal, and scientific issues are being considered, place offers an integrative opportunity. While each perspective has its own integrity and validity, in actual operation they combine in application to particular settings. A place offers a concrete opportunity for interdisciplinary learning. Finally, a place can offer an opportunity for service learning or a lasting commitment to a particular community or to similar communities that face these issues. A sense of place can infuse the consideration of environmental justice with a concreteness and a passion that inspires not only the student but also the citizen.

Lisa H. Sideris
Religious Studies

A newspaper cartoon that hangs outside my office door depicts two elderly men engaged in a fireside chat. One old curmudgeon remarks to the other, "I remember when there was no damn environment." The humor of this observation plays upon a distinction between the environment as a modern concept—frequently, an *issue* or *problem*—and the environment in the quaint old sense of nature, the great big world out there. Rachel Carson is someone to whom we are deeply indebted for our concept of the environment in the former sense of the word. But Carson would have urged us never to lose sight of the environment in the latter sense—the natural world in all its magnificence and wonder, its immediacy and visceral impact. In educating ourselves and others about environmental problems and solutions, we should not forget to cultivate an attachment to the very entity that inspires our concern in the first place. With Carson's life and work as a touchstone, this essay explores the important role a sense of wonder can play in fostering and sustaining environmental virtues and love of particular places, and in energizing interdisciplinary approaches to environmental problems and their solutions.

Rachel Carson and Nature Study

Rachel Carson was born in 1907 in Springdale, Pennsylvania, a small, bucolic community near the Allegheny River and not far from the heavily industrialized and polluted environs of Pittsburgh. Carson's keen sense of the beauty of her immediate surroundings may well have mingled, at an early and impressionable age, with an equally acute awareness of the manmade threats edging ever closer to her little farm (Lear 1998: 392). Many years later, Carson would begin *Silent Spring* with a fable about a small rural community whose backyards, fields, and streams were mysteriously silenced and stilled by careless chemical assaults: "The people had done it themselves" (Carson 1962: 3).

As a young girl, Carson's passionate interest in the natural world was reinforced at home and in school. The informal education Carson acquired during her solitary wanderings in the woods and streams near her home was formalized in the nature-study curriculum widely used in the early twentieth century. Embraced by Cornell botanist Liberty Hyde Bailey and his colleague Anna Botsford Comstock, as well as Indiana native Gene Stratton-Porter and many others, nature-study sought to put children into direct contact and lifelong "sympathy" with nature (Bailey 1911). To describe nature-study as formal, however, is perhaps misleading: nature-study advocates chafed against the formal, dry, mechanical teaching of biology and natural history. In place of learning facts and memorizing names, they encouraged education via the senses and the emotions. They understood their curriculum to be distinct from science education, not in the sense that it was unscientific but in that it sought to lay the foundation and provide the moral framework for later scientific knowledge. "Nature study is not the teaching of science," Bailey argued. "Its intention is to broaden the child's horizon, not primarily to teach him how to widen the boundaries of human knowledge" (Bailey 1911: 30). Nature-study was seen not as an additional program to be added to a pupil's list of daily lessons but a way of looking at the world that could be combined with virtually any of his subjects. The claim we hear today that all education is environmental education has roots in the nature-study tradition.

While cultivation of the proper orientation, the proper virtues, was part of the overall goal, nature-study achieved this goal indirectly. Rather than preach the injunction "Thou shalt not kill," Bailey explained, "I should prefer to have the child become so much interested in living things that it would have no desire to kill them" (1911: 31). A common thread running through Carson's writings is that cultivating a sense of wonder is the best way of curbing destructive impulses toward the natural world. "The more clearly we can focus our attention on the wonders and realities of the universe about us, the less taste we shall have for destruction" (Carson 1998: 163).

The nature-study curriculum of a century ago was motivated by many of the same concerns that animate current environmental education and literacy programs—concerns not only about threats to the natural world but also threats to the psychological and emotional well-being of young people exposed to unprecedented urbanization and rampant technology. Richard Louv describes the hallmarks of what he terms nature-deficit disorder among young people today: "diminished use of the senses, attention difficulties, and higher rates of physical and emotional illnesses" (Louv 2005: 34). The modern trappings of youth—computer games, internet communities, DVDs, cell phones, and so on—make the indoors a place that competes as never before with the enchantments of the outdoors. "I like to play indoors better," one young boy explains, "'cause that's where all the electrical outlets are" (Louv 2005: 10). Nature is further marginalized by education that acquaints young people with the environmental crisis—what Uhl calls "a depressing litany of environmental woes"—without having first bonded them to the natural world they are supposed to want to protect (2003: xvii). Most young people today can recite a list of global threats, but fewer and fewer have sustained physical contact with the world of nature. Writers ranging from Rachel Carson to Richard Louv and Christopher Uhl agree that instilling a sense of wonder at nature is the first step toward cultivating environmental responsibility.

Defining a Sense of Wonder

What is a sense of wonder and how might it be linked to environmental consciousness? Advocates of environmental education, past and present, and theorists of the sense of wonder more generally, tend to agree on one thing: to cultivate a sense of wonder, start early and work on it often. Wonder in response to the world is characterized simultaneously as an almost instinctive childlike sensibility (Bennett 2001) as well as an enormously complex intellectual, emotional, ethical, and aesthetic capacity that can be cultivated through experience and daily "practices" (Uhl 2003). That wonder can rightly be described as something both innate and cultivated, both basic and complex, makes sense: education that cultivates wonder is like other forms of moral education that seek not to "go against the grain" of the child's basic nature but to expand on and correct "some natural inclination(s) they have" (Hursthouse 2007: 161). Thus environmental education and cultivation of wonder can build upon what the sociobiologist E. O. Wilson has called a biophilic impulse that dwells somewhere in all of us and manifests itself so strongly in young people: an innate affinity for and attachment to nature, a fascination with life processes.

Wonder is often understood to exist alongside a set of virtues or dispositions that include generosity, gratitude, humility, restraint, and appreciation of difference or otherness. Often it accompanies a sense of mystery, an awareness of something that lies just beyond our comprehension. At the same time wonder is often characterized as the starting point for knowledge, a driving force behind science (Fisher 1998). Like the category of the sublime, wonder may contain an element of fear or be akin to fear in certain ways (fear is also a response to something surprising or sudden or mysterious). Wonder can transfix as well as transport us. The ability of wonder to transport us is crucial because were we to remain merely transfixed, we might respond too passively or in a purely contemplative way. A stunned mind cannot pursue anything very far, so ideally wonder activates some response or behavior. We are motivated by wonder, not just intellectually but *ethically* (Bennett 2001). Moreover, wonder may create or reinforce a sense of our own insignificance in relation to the object of wonder, perhaps a sense of loss of the self. A sensed loss of the self and/or an awareness of something much larger than ourselves is, of course, one of the links between wonder and experiences often termed *religious*, as theorists such as William James have noted (James 1982). But loss of self, and other responses that may flow from it—including ethical impulses to generosity or humility—need not themselves be, or be considered, religious. And finally, because of its connection to novelty and surprise, wonder is frequently seen as the prerogative of youth. Indeed, some theorists argue that wonder necessarily decays or declines with age and experience (Fisher 1998). This is a rather depressing conclusion and one that, in my opinion, is not necessarily warranted.

Regarding its practical applications, wonder is often distinguished from curiosity. The latter falls within standard operating procedure and accepted frameworks while wonder gropes beyond those frameworks. That is, curiosity motivates a focused search for a particular answer to questions that crop up in the course of ordinary life or within normal scientific and technical contexts (Opdal 2001). While this form of "frame-directed" inquiry remains extremely useful, wonder can facilitate forms of inquiry that question the frames themselves (Opdal 2001: 332). One reason wonder is strongly associated with youth is that children's questions are often of the frame-questioning variety. As any parent knows, children question the rules and categories themselves. But there are more mature (that is to say, adult) forms of the same general phenomena, and in scientific research, wonder and the creative and critical inquiry it fuels may produce profound new insights, even a wholesale change in perspective. I return to this point below.

Not surprisingly, there are areas of disagreement regarding definitions of wonder. For example, some doubt that memory can play a direct or important role in experiences of wonder, given that these experiences seem firmly rooted in the novel and unexpected. A few theorists exclude memory entirely from the realm of wonder (Fisher 1998). Others contend that some experiences we might label as wondrous "could not be described at all convincingly in terms of response to the surprising and novel" but arise instead from "the linking of present experience with memory-traces of very early experience" (Hepburn 1984: 135). Emotional impressions from childhood or youth may lend new life, renewed excitement, to sensory experiences in later adulthood that might otherwise affect us very little. Even our awareness of the large temporal gap between this moment and our remote past contributes to the feeling of wonder (Hepburn 1984).

The understanding of wonder as "renewable" throughout life has been central to educational programs that aim to instill a sense of wonder at (and later, responsibility toward) the natural world, ranging from the nature-study movement of the early twentieth century to modern-day environmental education programs. Intense sensory and emotional engagement with nature at an early age may have a lasting impact, even after maturity replaces the child's sense of the magical with a more rational, even scientific, understanding of nature and its processes. Certainly, Carson's account of nature education fits this mold. The "emotions and the impressions of the senses are the fertile soil" of childhood, she writes in *The Sense of Wonder* (1965: 56). Children and indeed all of us need a "sense of wonder so indestructible that it would last throughout life, as an unfailing antidote against the boredom and disenchantments of later years, the sterile preoccupation with things that are artificial, the alienation from the sources of our strength" (1965: 54). Given the close, primal link between the senses—particularly the sense of smell—and memory, it seems plausible that wonder has a great deal to do with what Carson calls the remembered delights of childhood.[1] Accounts such as these cast doubt on the pessimistic conclusion that wonder necessarily decays as we leave childhood behind.

Carson believed strongly in "the lifelong durability of the sense of wonder" (1965: 106). Her understanding of wonder closely allies it with an appreciation of mystery, and she saw no reason why perception of nature's mysteries should be rendered obsolete by adult or rational forms of knowing. This is not to say that Carson endorsed deliberate obfuscation of things that can be clearly understood through science, nor that she applauded states of ignorance. She was more convinced that mystery could never be drained away from nature than she was concerned about adding it back in. Long before she even thought of writing a book about the dangers of indiscriminate pesticide use, she was primarily a biographer of the sea. Raised in a landlocked region, Carson developed an early enchantment with ocean waters she had imagined but never seen. It is

---

1. Carson writes of "the rush of remembered delight that comes with the first scent" of the sea at low tide. "For the sense of smell, almost more than any other, has the power to recall memories and it is a pity that we use it so little" (*The Sense of Wonder*, 83).

evident from her sea writings that a sense of wonder and enchantment meant to Carson a sense of mystery that scientific inquiry and explanation could aid but never exhaust.

Carson had enormous respect for science and its wonder-enabling qualities, but she also understood it to have definite limits. Her writing frequently evokes a sense of some ineffable and elusive quality in the natural world that science glimpses but never quite explains or explains away (Carson 1951). One of Carson's favorite childhood authors, Gene Stratton-Porter, wrote that scientific investigation "reaches the hearts of things we want to know, how matter and life originated"; yet at a certain point it invariably reaches "a granite wall . . . and there science may search, climb, and batter until it is worn out, but the answer never comes" (Stratton-Porter 1909: 68). Carson might not have put the point quite so emphatically, but she embraced the mystery that continually outstrips science and is at the same time the inspiration for further research. Carson writes that the natural scientist is never bored by her studies because "every mystery solved brings us to the threshold of a greater one" (Carson 1998: 159).

Wonder as an Environmental Virtue

I teach environmental ethics, a discipline engaged in locating the appropriate (religious and secular) ethical frameworks that govern or ought to govern the human–nature relationship. Some students may not even realize that they hold any particular perspective or set of values with regard to nature. One of the perennial challenges in teaching environmental ethics is thus to help students see that their own (or their cultural or religious tradition's) perspectives on the human–nature relationship came from somewhere, and that cultural and religious world views vary significantly in their understanding of this relationship.

Virtue ethics has recently come to the fore in both secular and religious discourse about the environment, and wonder plays a central role. Along with environmentalists and writers such as Aldo Leopold and Henry David Thoreau, Rachel Carson is often identified as a key figure in this discourse (Cafaro 2005). Attitudes of humility and wonder—and related "green" virtues such as restraint, courage, gratitude, and hope—are particularly conducive to caring for the natural world, while vices such as shortsightedness, apathy, and greed are especially problematic. Certain core vices seem to aggravate others. For example, pride and vanity make us less willing "to acknowledge our greed, self-indulgence, shortsightedness, and lack of compassion"; dishonesty, in the form of self-deception, "enables us to blind ourselves to relevant facts and arguments and find excuses for continuing as we are" rather than implementing needed change in habits and lifestyle (Hursthouse 2007: 157).

Wonder appears to be an important keystone virtue that may counter such vices. Though it sometimes has religious overtones, the sense of wonder can emanate from either religious or secular-scientific worldviews. It is also a response found across numerous cultures and religious traditions, and this is what we would expect if, as Wilson maintains, positive, biophilic responses to nature are virtually universal. With regard to its virtuous dimensions, wonder is fundamentally decentralizing: it tends to enhance a sense of our relative insignificance in salutary rather than dispiriting ways. That is, wonder creates openness to the world around us, an increased receptivity to beauty, and feelings of gratitude for such beauty. The recognition of one's place in something much vaster—the expanded horizon so often alluded to in accounts of wonder—helps to instill a sense of humility and modesty, a sense of caution about our interventions in the natural forces around us. Carson's indictment of the attitudes that often attend chemical control of nature provide a good example of the link between virtues such as humility and cautious intervention in nature. "These practitioners of chemical control," she writes in *Silent Spring*, "have brought to their task no 'high-minded' orientation, no humility before the vast forces with which they tamper" (1962: 297).

As Aristotle observed long ago, whether or not a particular disposition amounts to a virtue rather than a vice depends on correct orientation; thus, anger felt in the right amount, at the right time, at the right things or the right person, may be a virtue, just as fear felt in the right degree and in the right situations contributes to the virtue of courage. By the same token, I would argue that a correctly oriented form of wonder—wonder properly directed at natural processes over and above, say, wonder and awe at our own achievements and creations—amounts to an important virtue. One might say that Carson's early writings, including of course *The Sense of Wonder*,[2] took the first form of (virtuous) wonder as a central theme; *Silent Spring* was, among other things, a critique of the latter kind of (vicious) wonder, what Carson saw as a dangerous enchantment with ourselves and our powers. Of course, learning to experience wonder in appropriate ways, toward the right objects, for the right reasons, in the right manner, etc., and then learning to act in accordance with it, is a complex task. Precisely for this reason, wonder needs to be instilled at an early age, as part of children's moral and emotional education, and cultivated throughout the course of one's entire life. Loss of direct contact with nature and immersion in overly specialized and balkanized disciplines create a narrowness of vision that is the antithesis of wonder. Thus, depending on how education is designed, wonder can be cultivated or deadened through learning.

---

2. *The Sense of Wonder* originated as an essay in 1956 in *Woman's Home Companion*, titled "Help Your Child to Wonder," and was published as a small book posthumously in 1965.

The Sense of Wonder and a Sense of Place

While it may be true that *Silent Spring* dealt with environmental and human harms whose effects were large-scale and ubiquitous rather than place-specific, as John Applegate points out in his chapter in this volume, Carson's message sparked concern at very local levels. Along with figures such as Leopold and Thoreau, Carson "cultivated strong ties to particular places and worked to protect them" both through her writing and through direct community involvement (Cafaro 2005: 37). In *The Sense of Wonder,* Carson observes that one way of activating this sense is to ask yourself, "What if I had never seen this before? What if I knew I would never see it again?" (1965: 67). For readers of *Silent Spring,* the question "What if I knew I would never see it again?" took on new meaning. Carson's portrait in her opening fable of a spring devoid of bird or insect voices, of apple trees blooming without a bee in sight, of vacated backyard birdfeeders and empty streams, resonated strongly with average Americans. *Silent Spring* captured readers' attention because it spoke to a tragedy unfolding, potentially or actually, in their own backyards. Carson appealed to commonly held values, to readers' love of familiar places and simple things, some of which we may easily take for granted, such as birdsong in spring. An important part of Carson's legacy is her empowerment of citizens: she depicts environmental harms as a violation of basic rights and assumes that readers share her sense of civic duty as well as her sense of outrage. "If the Bill of Rights contains no guarantee that a citizen shall be secure against lethal poisons distributed either by private individuals or by public officials," Carson argues, "it is surely only because our forefathers . . . could conceive of no such problem" (Carson 1962: 13).

People will often defend places they know and love, but first they must become attached, they must *become native* to the places they already inhabit, in the favorite phrase of bioregionalists. One of the great ironies of environmental education at the college level is that a typical classroom contains many students who do not hail from the town in which the university is located, often receiving environmental instruction of one sort or another from a professor who is likewise almost certainly not a native of the area but landed there following a nationwide job search. By and large, college professors belong to one of the most "rootless" professions. For most job openings in the academic world, "nonnative status" is considered an "implicit qualification for employment" (Zencey 1996: 18). Professors may be acclimated to the so-called life of the mind, accustomed to membership in a world that allegedly embraces a certain kind of cosmopolitanism over parochialism, geographic or otherwise—a "boundless world of books and ideas and eternal truths" (Zencey 1996: 16). But most students need something less abstract from their education, something that satisfies their greater need to belong to something more tangible. Many students seem to find their own way to local community involvement, even if their university is not in or near the place they call home, but universities can do more to help students inhabit more fully the place where they live.

Wonder has a role to play in this context as well, because awakening the sense of wonder contributes to awakening a stronger sense of place, and vice versa. If a student spends her college years—typically the most intellectually intense and active period in a person's life—largely oblivious to the natural community in which the university exists, she may never learn to make connections between her chosen career, her own livelihood, and the natural world that makes all livelihoods possible. It might appear that the expanded vision of the sense of wonder, that sense of being part of something vast and ancient, is at odds with an emphasis on a more rooted and localized education, but this is not the case. Developing a sense of wonder begins with paying close attention to the place where you find yourself; it is "largely a matter of becoming receptive to what lies all around you" (Carson 1965: 67).

The skills involved in learning to inhabit the places where we live are, like the sense of wonder itself, renewable and transferable. Even if most students do not remain in their university town after graduation, they should graduate with the understanding that all communities and their economies exist first and foremost within a natural community and a natural economy. In towns such as my own, where the university students comprise half of the town's population (and thus a large part of its ecological footprint), it is particularly important that those students feel more like natives and less like transient laborers. University programs that connect students with local issues and local history, with social action and volunteer opportunities, have important environmental implications even if environmental issues are never addressed directly in the curriculum. Universities can contribute immeasurably to creating "competent citizens living in solid communities, engaged in and by their places" (Orr 1996: 234). That sense of belonging to a community is something students and professors alike need to cultivate precisely because university life may so easily work against it.

Interdisciplinarity: Wonder at the Bigger Picture

Nature-study advocates such as Bailey argued that children are by nature "generalists" and should not be forced to become "specialists" too soon. We might say the same about college students. Carson arrived at college with a clear vision of who she was and what college education was all about, but she soon felt pressured to decide between the subjects she loved most: biology and literature. In essays she wrote shortly after arriving at college, Carson described her love of nature—"I love all the beautiful things of nature, and the wild creatures are my friends"—and her vision of college as a "spiritual adventure" (Lear 1998: 32–42).

Initially an English major, Carson later switched her major to biology, believing she had left writing behind forever. Eventually she understood something that did not occur to her as a student, namely that her decision to major in science did not mean abandoning writing at all. It meant that she had found something compelling to write about. "What surprises me now," she remarked years later, "is that apparently it didn't occur to any of my advisors, either" (Carson 1998: 149).

It is surely significant that some of the most influential and inspiring environmentalists are people who managed, like Carson, to bridge the "two cultures" (too often without encouragement from others). Today's college students may not have the luxury of seeing their college years as an adventure, spiritual or otherwise —certainly many students I meet are overburdened with a full load of courses, part-time jobs to support their education, and anxieties about job prospects. But there is a dawning recognition in modern universities of the importance of interdisciplinary studies. Today's universities make it more feasible for a student, at least at the undergraduate level, to combine her interests. But students also need to find teachers whose own interests and expertise bridge disciplinary divides.

In *Silent Spring*, Carson takes aim at overly specialized and compartmentalized disciplines—particularly in the sciences. Often when I speak to scientists about Carson's critique of specialization, they respond angrily that we would not know anything were it not for the intense focus that specialization allows. But I think this misses the point of Carson's critique. It is precisely because we know so much that we need to talk with one another, and this is especially the case with environmental problems. Otherwise, knowledge of nature threatens to become too compartmentalized and self-contained, and solutions to our problems may elude us. Carson understood the pesticide problem to be largely a problem of poor communication not only between scientists and society but also among researchers working in distinct but related fields. Cut off from creative and vital exchange, the various branches of science turn moribund, and eventually the deadly effects show up in nature: "We allow the chemical death rain to fall as though there were no alternative, whereas in fact there are many, and our ingenuity could soon discover many more if given opportunity" (1962: 12). Carson envisioned a team of specialists from "the vast field of biology . . . all pouring their knowledge and their creative inspirations" into finding alternatives to chemical control of nature (1962: 279). She understood specialization to be a problem only insofar as it ignores or remains unaware of a bigger picture. This fragmentation of education is still lamented by environmental educators such as Orr, who writes that "after 12 or 16 or 20 years of education, most students graduate without any broad integrated sense of the unity of things" (Orr 1991). Carson had particularly high hopes for the (then) new field of ecology because it appeared to offer opportunities for holistic, integrated knowledge and cooperation among specialists. The interrelatedness of fields of study might come to mirror, and thus safeguard, nature's fragile interrelatedness, Carson hoped. Knowledge has its own ecology; nothing exists unto itself.

I have suggested that wonder at the natural world is a kind of prerequisite or supplement to other forms of education, particularly education focusing on environmental problems. In this sense, as Bailey believed, education for wonder is not quite the same as science education but offers a kind of framework for that education. But wonder also has a more direct role to play in research that aims to address environmental problems. That is, wonder might suggest an alternative methodology (Opdal 2001). As noted previously, curiosity is sometimes defined as operating in accordance with standard methods and procedures and within accepted frames, while wonder "points to something beyond the accepted rules," fostering greater critical and creative skills (Opdal 2001: 331). Just as wonder at the natural world often involves truly seeing and appreciating things we may normally take for granted, wonder as a form of inquiry may generate "a probing into the frames that so far have been taken for granted . . . critical examination of our basic concepts, ways of reasoning, and our fundamental assumptions" (Opdal 2001: 332) One of the virtues of interdisciplinary and collaborative work is that different disciplines do not necessarily share the same ways of reasoning, the same accepted frames and basic assumptions. In this sense, we might say that a certain type of methodological wonder frequently accompanies interdisciplinary approaches. When basic assumptions and frames are questioned, a wholesale shift in "perspective"[3] is more likely to occur. Approaches that combine different areas of knowledge might be more likely to find new solutions to environmental problems; at the very least, such an approach can generate a new research program.

Teaching Who We Are

In the opening pages of *Developing Ecological Consciousness*, Christopher Uhl describes his own painful discovery that, for better or for worse, we teach who we are. If we are primarily anxious and worried about environmental problems, our students will be also. If we teach only the depressing litany of environmental woes, without providing what Uhl and so many others describe as an initiation into the wonders of the natural world, students may leave the university more alienated from their environment than when they arrived. An initiation into (or

---

3. Opdal does not deal with interdisciplinary research, but his account of wonder and education seems relevant here. He defines a perspective as a "hierarchic structure, where some components occupy more central positions than others do . . . one belief can be the logical presupposition of another, and while some assumptions may be easily rejected, we stick to others as long as possible" (2001: 33).

reacquaintance with) wonder can provide a foundation for environmental education and environmental values; a sense of wonder may also help students—and professors—to become more at home in the places where they live, and to keep in mind the bigger picture, the interconnected web of knowledge, in which their own studies are situated. Instilling and cultivating a sense of wonder in ourselves and in others is a crucially important step in awakening environmental consciousness and envisioning solutions. For those who spend much of their lives thinking and writing about contemporary environmental issues, a sense of wonder is necessary in order to maintain perspective on these problems, to remain energized and hopeful that we can remedy them. As Carson put it,

> Those who dwell, as scientists or laymen, among the beauties and mysteries of the earth are never alone or weary of life . . . their thoughts can find paths that lead to inner contentment and to renewed excitement in living. Those who contemplate the beauty of the earth find reserves of strength that will endure as long as life lasts." (1965: 100)

References

Bailey, L. H. 1911. *The Nature Study Idea*. New York: Macmillan.

Bennett, J. 2001. *The Enchantment of Modern Life: Attachments, Crossings, and Ethics*. Princeton, N.J.: Princeton University Press.

Cafaro, P. 2005. "Thoreau, Leopold, and Carson: Toward an Environmental Virtue Ethics." In R. Sandler and P. Cafaro, eds., *Environmental Virtue Ethics*. 31–44. Oxford: Rowman and Littlefield.

Carson, R. 1956. "Help Your Child to Wonder." *Woman's Home Companion* (July): 24–27, 46–48.

———. 1962 [1994]. *Silent Spring*. Boston: Houghton Mifflin.

———. 1965 [1998]. *The Sense of Wonder*. San Francisco: HarperCollins.

———. 1998. *Lost Woods: The Discovered Writings of Rachel Carson*. Ed. L. Lear. Boston: Beacon Press.

Fisher, P. 1998. *Wonder, the Rainbow, and the Aesthetics of Rare Experiences*. Cambridge, Mass.: Harvard University Press.

Hepburn, R. W. 1984. *"Wonder" and Other Essays*. Edinburgh: Edinburgh University Press.

Hursthouse, R. 2007. "Environmental Virtue Ethics." In Rebecca L. Walker and Philip J. Ivanhoe, eds., *Working Virtue: Virtue Ethics and Contemporary Moral Problems*, 155–172. Oxford: Oxford University Press.

James, W. 1982. *The Varieties of Religious Experience*. Harmondsworth, UK: Penguin.

Lear, L. 1997. *Rachel Carson: Witness for Nature*. New York: Henry Holt.

Louv, R. 2005. *Last Child in the Woods: Saving Our Children from Nature-Deficit Disorder*. Chapel Hill, N.C.: Algonquin.

Opdal, P. M. 2001. "Curiosity, Wonder and Education Seen as Perspective Development." *Studies in Philosophy and Education.* 20: 331–334.

Orr, D. 1991. "What is Education For?" Context Institute, at http://www.context.org/ICLIB/IC27/Orr.htm (accessed 27 March 2009).

——. 1996. "Re-Ruralizing Education." In W. Vitek and W. Jackson, eds., *Rooted in the Land*, 226–234. New Haven: Yale University Press.

Stratton-Porter, G. 1909. *Birds of the Bible.* Cincinnati: Jennings and Graham.

Uhl, C. 2003. *Developing Ecological Consciousness: Paths to a Sustainable World.* Oxford: Rowman and Littlefield.

Zencey, E. 1996. "The Rootless Professors." In W. Vitek and W. Jackson, eds., *Rooted in the Land*, 15–19. New Haven: Yale University Press.

8

Teaching Environmental Communication Through Rhetorical Controversy

Phaedra C. Pezzullo

Communication and Culture

> The problem the environmental community has is they don't listen to their opponents. When I do my research, I spend more time studying the opposition argument because that's what I need to respond to.
>
> —FRANK LUNTZ

At the turn of the century, Frank Luntz is one of the most famous communication professionals in the United States. With an undergraduate degree in history and political science from the University of Pennsylvania and a doctorate in politics from Oxford University, he has taught at the University of Pennsylvania, Harvard University, and George Washington University. A Republican pollster

---

The epigraph is from A. G. Little, "And Now, a Word from Our Detractor: GOP Strategist Frank Luntz Argues Enviros Are Failing—and They're Mean to Boot." *Grist Magazine: Environmental News and Commentary*, 31 January 2007. At http://www.grist.org/article/luntz1/.

and communication consultant for a range of corporations, including MSNBC, CNBC, AT&T, Merrill Lynch, and Federal Express, Luntz's advice is epitomized in his best-selling book, *Words That Work: It's Not What You Say, It's What People Hear* (Luntz 2006). A pivotal moment in his career was in 2003, when a memo he wrote to the Republican Party was leaked on the Internet. There, Luntz advised—among other points—that the environment is the issue on which Republicans "are most vulnerable" and therefore needed to pay more attention (133–134). His solution, however, was not necessarily to change environmental policy, but to change how people talk about—or frame—environmental debates. Some of Luntz's more famous examples implemented by the George W. Bush Administration include "redefining labels," so that "drilling for oil" becomes "responsible exploration for energy," "logging" is labeled as creating "healthy forests," and "weakening the Clean Air Act" is renamed "Clear Skies" (142). In addition to suggesting language that plausibly will sound more positive to audiences who care about the environment, Luntz also provided advice on how to stall implementing policy that targets global warming through communication, including claiming the scientific debate remains open and calling for more "free and open discussion" for the American people (137).

Luntz's work and its popularity signal a new era for environmentalism. The environmental movement has been a success insofar as the majority of people in the United States claim to care about the environment when asked. We, therefore, no longer live in a time when most politicians, corporations, or other institutions will argue that the environment doesn't matter. Since at least 1988, all significant U.S. presidential candidates claim to care about the environment to some degree. Sales of "green" products are soaring. Even polluters pay billions a year in "green" advertising. Public discourse has thus shifted. Perhaps more than ever before, citizens must distinguish among a range of discourses that claim to promote environmental sustainability but may represent a wide range of agendas.

Within this context, it becomes clear that—in addition to learning about what science has established, the figures and events that historically have shaped our world, and the ways a sense of place within broader ecosystems matters—an environmental literacy curriculum should include *environmental communication* as a fundamental cornerstone. Communication studies professor J. Robert Cox, who is also three-term president of the Sierra Club, the oldest U.S. environmental organization, defines environmental communication as "the pragmatic and constitutive vehicle for our understanding of the environment as well as our relationships to the natural world; it is the symbolic medium that we use in constructing environmental problems and negotiating society's different responses to them" (Cox 2006: 12).

Environmental communication, therefore, involves not only acknowledging *how* we talk about the environment (e.g., with which words, through which media, in which tone, etc.), but also the understanding that our symbolic constructions about environmental concerns *profoundly shape* what we know and how we might act in response. Thus the field of environmental communication reflects the wide range of communication contexts in which the environment is negotiated, including through media, organizations, interpersonal interactions, public participation in decision-making processes, and social movements.

For purposes of this volume, I'll highlight two ways an awareness of the nuances of environmental communication may be incorporated in one's classroom to improve environmental literacy across the curriculum: engaging environmental rhetoric and enacting environmental debates. The overall argument I wish to emphasize in this chapter is that environmentally literate students must learn how to read, assess, and respond to environmental communication with a keen appreciation for the stakes of rhetorical controversies.

Engaging Environmental Rhetoric

In this section, I want to clarify some foundational perspectives and vocabulary that may help illustrate the significance of environmental communication. An ecological awareness reminds us that the environment is more than a "place," "scene," "context," or generic "space" per se. Rather, the environment is temporally and spatially dynamic, involving several interactive material elements, from the toxins we may breathe in from the paint on our walls to the nourishment we require from the food we eat. Human existence is predicated on our physical interactions with the environment (via breathing, eating, drinking, excreting, etc.). An ecological awareness, therefore, compels us to challenge attempts to divide humanity from the environment as somehow independent, isolated, or contained. We require the environment to live, let alone act.

As cultural studies scholar Raymond Williams further notes, "We have mixed our labour with the earth, our forces with its forces too deeply to be able to draw back and separate each other out" (Williams 1973: 83). Humans and the environment are materially inseparable not just because humans require certain environmental conditions to live, but also because we have transformed the environment in ways we still do not fully comprehend. Nature is managed. Drugs can induce birth. Death is prolonged by medicine. Human-made toxins are found in living creatures on every continent. Ice caps are melting at alarming rates.

Despite our interdependence and inseparability, the environment regrettably remains ignored in the majority of higher education curricula. Changing this pattern will require not only an increased appreciation for the environmental systems on which life depends and the ecological footprints we all make, but also *rhetoric, the symbolic discourses through which these systems and impacts are negotiated.* As Tarla Rai Peterson, Texas A&M University's Boone and Crockett Chair of Wildlife and Conservation, reminds us:

> . . . although nature is not inherently a rhetorical text, human actions and social structures associated with it function rhetorically . . . [and thus] environmental communication must maintain the integrity of both verbal and natural systems since both are essential: our existence depends on nature, and we use language to conceptualize and discuss the natural systems on which we rely. (Peterson 1998: 372)

With this understanding, an environmental communication perspective does not deny the material significance of the nonhuman; however, it does maintain that symbolic systems of humans are profoundly influential as well (Williams 1973; Nash 1982; Killingsworth and Palmer 1992; Cantrill and Oravec 1996; Herndl and Brown 1996; Muir and Veenendall 1996; Meister and Japp 2002). Communication is not neutral, a mere mirror held up to the world; rather, the discourses we choose and embody implicate specific values, judgments, and interpretations.

Consider the word "environment" itself. As others in this volume have emphasized in the introduction and throughout, a more sustainable future will need to engage the ways the environment, economies, and social equity are intertwined. Environmental literacy should therefore address natural systems, how humans interact with them, and how humans interact with each other. Likewise, our definition of "environment" should reflect this sense of interconnectedness. In concert with John Applegate's chapter in this volume, I believe the environmental justice movement has articulated a foundational definition of the environment that environmentally literate students would benefit from learning, because it offers a fundamental perspective that is vital to sustainability; namely, that the environment is defined as the places where we live, work, play, pray, and bury our dead (*Proceedings* 1991, DiChiro 1992, Higgins 1994, Novotny 2000, Pezzullo 2001, and Pezzullo 2007). "The environment," therefore, includes not only vacation destinations where human presence is relatively scarce (e.g., wilderness areas and national parks), but also our homes, prisons, workplaces, schools, sacred sites, cemeteries, and so on. Ultimately, this definition of the environment implicates anywhere we have been, are, or are going, because humans cannot exist absent an environment. In a profound sense, we also have come to the point, as Bill McKibben (2006) argues, that nature does not exist outside our impact. Therefore, creating a mutually exclusive binary between the environment and humanity in our language and our ways of imagining the two can shape our beliefs and actions about a range of issues in problematic ways, including whether or not people need this planet for survival, and whether or not people should feel accountable for environmental disaster. Thus, the rhetorical *naming* of a concept or place or person reflects our culture and shapes subsequent actions.

Beyond individual words, rhetoric constitutes the broader stories we do and do not tell ourselves. As noted in relation to Frank Luntz, a key rhetorical tactic of environmental communication is *framing*, or what people more popularly call a "spin" on an issue (usually referring to journalists or politicians). According to sociologist Christian Smith, "frames" are "interpretive formulas that assign meanings to events and issues by selecting out and organizing certain elements into packaged story lines" (1996: 238). In other words, rhetorical tactics (such as metaphor and synecdoche) are used to shape what issues receive more or less attention. Frames often inform how we name a person, place, or idea. Using Luntz's example mentioned above, a frame could influence whether we name a practice "oil drilling" or "responsible exploration for energy." The former highlights a fossil fuel and the damaging process by which we extract it from the earth; the latter highlights the reasonableness of looking for sources of energy, which we can assume we all use to some degree and, therefore, want. Framing oil drilling as a source of environmental degradation or as a source of energy sparks different constraints on discussion, as would alternative frames such as "reducing our dependence on foreign oil for national security" or "finding an alternative to our fossil fuel economy." Inventing new frames for specific contexts and audiences is a rhetorical skill that our students will need in the future not only to better assess the frames they face, but also to develop skills at imagining new ones.

Enacting Environmental Debates

As great communicators from Aristotle to Luntz (see epigraph) know, the position one advocates is improved by engaging those who disagree. Debate, therefore, is a vital skill for students learning environmental literacy across the curriculum, particularly in a time of rhetorical controversy. To be clear: I am *not* suggesting that engaging differing opinions should be taught as a way to arrest action or to hide behind a myth that a "balanced" curriculum is ideal, let alone achievable. Rather, I am suggesting that *debate*, or engaging arguments for and against one's own opinion, is a vital art of the humanities that helps students develop their rhetorical skills in a time when contingency and uncertainty abound. To debate, we must identify the primary tropes (or turns in an argument), which involves comparing and contrasting the language used and the frames at work in various positions. The goal is not to represent the liberal myth that there are two sides to every debate; rather, "the development of a respect for pluralism, tolerance, and free speech remains political valuable" and intellectually challenging (Greene and Hicks 2005: 121).

Although the United States was founded on debate, we cannot take for granted that our students appreciate its value. As former vice president and Nobel Peace Prize winner Al Gore writes, "Faith in the power of reason—the belief that free citizens can govern themselves wisely and fairly by resorting to logical debate on the basis of the best evidence available, instead of raw power—was and remains the central premise of American democracy. This premise is now under attack" (Gore 2007: 2). Gore traces his own career-long belief in the importance of fostering this type of political culture as far back as his senior undergraduate thesis on visual rhetoric's impact on political debates (which he jokes was perhaps too prophetic of his own career).

In my own undergraduate environmental advocacy classes, I like to vary the topics from local issues (for example, whether our university should run on coal, or whether a state-long highway should be built on new terrain) to issues that blur local and international boundaries (such as whether Wal-Mart can become sustainable and whether we need federal legislation to restrict concentrated animal feeding operations). I veer away from topics I think are no longer viable debates with credible voices questioning alternatives (e.g., although we might debate what to do about it, I wouldn't have students still debate whether or not global climate change is happening). Also, in my courses in a communication and culture department, I do not choose topics that a student could not assess from our class (e.g., I wouldn't have students debate the water quality on campus because I do not teach water sampling); rather, I emphasize that the goal of this assignment is to focus *on the arguments being made* so that we might better assess the cultural values, language, and frames involved. (If debates were used in other disciplines, different skills obviously could be developed.) Choosing contemporary topics of rhetorical controversy that require students to research varying positions helps provide a vital skill for their futures in and beyond the environmental classroom. Overall, I judge student debates on creativity, research, and overall coherence—each of which warrants elaboration.

CREATIVITY

The "debate" I am promoting is not a traditional "debate" insofar as I do not wish students to embarrass or "beat" each other. For this reason I assign groups to work together, so that what they are performing in class is an overall map of arguments circulating in the public sphere on a particular topic. I also assign students their oral positions, emphasizing that they may have to argue something to which they do not adhere; this allows a freedom, I believe, that is vital to an invigorated undergraduate curriculum in which students are required to appreciate why someone might disagree with them. This theory of pedagogy is influenced by a performance studies perspective, which, as Dwight Conquergood emphasizes, "privileges challenge, struggle, innovation, movement, and openness (Conquergood 1995: 338)."

Students, therefore, are encouraged to embody these controversies in the classroom in ways that aim to move their audiences and themselves. Teaching environmental communication involves a focus on not just what is said but *how*. This involves a variety of media, from experiential education outside the classroom to constructing media campaigns online. Emphasizing the range of rhetorical tactics involved in environmental advocacy fosters a more robust appreciation for the ways politics, society, and culture are shaped. I've had students dress up in character, use props (from store-bought maps to homemade picket signs), sing songs while playing guitar, show video clips, and more. They have shouted, whispered, called each other on cell phones in class, laughed, and given speeches behind podiums. The scenes they have evoked have included a radio show forum, a television game show, a "live" political debate between candidates, a graveyard where great figures of the past came to life, pitching two competing film scripts, and a Thanksgiving dinner debate among an extended family. A forum where students can bring their talents into the classroom and embody the material they have researched often allows them to develop a greater appreciation for the courage it takes to express an opinion, the value of listening to other's perspectives, and the many ways we communicate about environmental matters. More often than not, I find students become more opinionated by the end of these debates because they "make somebody else's words live as their own" and, as D. Soyini Madison observes, "they took ideas and reconstructed them through voice, movement, and staging to provide us with the opportunity to understand these ideas from other angles and with more felt-sensed insights" (Madison 1995: 316). The heightened sense of energy in the room on these days is palpable.

RESEARCH

Before each debate, I require individual papers so that no student comes to a group meeting without some research and feedback. Since most research occurs online, it is worth noting the error of assuming that since students use online technologies so much, they already know how to differentiate between credible and questionable sources. First, students need to learn the difference between primary, secondary, and tertiary sources online. For example, if someone wants an organization's or institution's opinion on a debate topic, that organization's or institution's website serves as a *primary* source, because it portrays their opinion unfiltered by another's interpretation; however, if someone finds that organization's or institution's website analyzed in an academic journal (which they'll also probably read online), that is a *secondary* source, which interprets original information. Going online goads many students to *tertiary* sources, which include

Wikipedia and other online resources. To evaluate these sources, I find that teaching students how to cite websites is a critical skill in pointing out whether or not one can verify the validity of a source. Before my classes, many students do not recognize basic research criteria such as authorship or sponsorship (if they differ), time period produced, and the ability to revisit a source as key signs of a source's validity.

If one is less interested in teaching primary research skills, there is a timely and useful political science book series on the environment edited by Thomas A. Eaton (2008), now in its thirteenth edition, that illustrates the wide range of topics an environmentally literate student should know, including: environmental philosophy debates over the precautionary principle; policy debates about endangered species and banning DDT globally; and consumer energy debates about car efficiency and the genetic engineering of food. Without requiring research, one still could emphasize the skills of identifying the assumptions and values being negotiated.

OVERALL COHERENCE

The point is not to debate pro- and anti-environmental stances and, thus, overall coherence can be a challenge to students. Although debate is understood in its most basic form as a resolution that can be affirmed or rebutted, it is more complicated than that when it occurs in public controversies. For example, the desire for an alternative fuel to oil could mean promoting solar, wind, or nuclear power, gas, ethanol, or coal; this is not a straightforward debate with merely two opinions. Further, one's identity does not predetermine one's position. Almost every year for the past decade, my undergraduate students have been asked to debate whether or not the Arctic National Wildlife Refuge should be opened for drilling and, undoubtedly, some students are surprised to discover that there are Native Americans who disagree with each other.

Endorsing Environmental Communication

Of course, some might say that those promoting environmental literacy across the curriculum have no obligation to consider rhetorical controversies because that ambiguity or inclusion of an opposing agenda is precisely what students learn in dominant society and the rest of their curriculum by default. There is merit to this point. In considering what environmental literacy will mean throughout the university, are we only accounting for the courses with "environment" in their title? Should we not recognize that most courses contain an implicit environmental message, whether it is focusing on the genetic causes of cancer over the environmental toxins that are known carcinogens or reading Nathaniel Hawthorne's descriptions of fields in which his protagonist is walking?

Indeed, the campus itself embodies environmental lessons about what is "cost efficient," "beautiful," and "worthwhile" versus what is not. Although environmentalism continues to transform our culture every year, it remains far from the dominant paradigm.

I'd like to suggest that there are at least two reasons why rhetorical controversy and, thus, engaging environmental communication remains vital for environmental literacy. First, as noted previously, one's ability to communicate about the environment in meaningful ways is predicated on the ability to be audience-centered and, therefore, able to anticipate differing opinions. To express a sense of exigency or urgency is not enough. We must find ways to teach students how to grapple with the exigencies of our times and find collective ways to respond to them. Second, students must learn how to analyze and to assess environmental controversies because we cannot predict all the dilemmas the next generation will face. The world is changing, and our knowledge also continues to shift with new information and technologies; that is why educators must teach critical research, thinking, and communication skills. In the end, teaching environmental literacy through advocacy and debates resonates with classic appeals that a university education should not only train students professionally, but also prepare them to act as more responsible citizens.

Research shows that how we communicate about the environment matters to a more sustainable and just world. We need to teach our students how to interpret environmental communication, as well as how to become agents of change themselves through more reflexive communication practices. Teaching environmental communication through rhetorical controversy better prepares students to be active and informed citizens in these uncertain yet urgent times. The environmental dilemmas we face are far too important for us to shy away from incorporating controversy into our curricula; we have an ethical duty to our future to foster a sense of concern about what is at stake in environmental debates and how our students may better communicate their own hopes for the future.

References

Cantrill, J. G., and C. L. Oravec. 1996. *The Symbolic Earth: Discourse and Our Creation of the Environment*, 95–122. Lexington: University Press of Kentucky.

Conquergood, D. 1995. "Storied Worlds and the Work of Teaching." *Communication Education* 42:337–348.

Cox, R. 2006. *Environmental Communication and the Public Sphere*. Thousand Oaks, Calif.: Sage.

DiChiro, G. 1992. "Defining Environmental Justice: Women's Voices and Grassroots Politics." *Socialist Review* 22:92–130.

Greene, R., and D. Hicks. 2005. "Lost Convictions: Debating Both Sides and the Ethical Self–Fashioning of Liberal Citizens." *Cultural Studies* 19:100–126.

Gore, A. 2007. *The Assault on Reason*. New York: Penguin.

Herndl, C. G., and S. C. Brown. 1996. *Green Culture: Environmental Rhetoric in Contemporary America*, 82–110. Madison: University of Wisconsin Press.

Higgins, R. R. 1994. "Race, Pollution, and the Mastery of Nature." *Environmental Ethics* 16:251–264.

Killingsworth, J. M., and J. S. Palmer. 1992. *Ecospeak: Rhetoric and Environmental Politics in America*. Carbondale: Southern Illinois University Press.

Little, A. G. 2007. "And Now, a Word from Our Detractor: GOP Strategist Frank Luntz Argues Enviros Are Failing—and They're Mean to Boot." *Grist Magazine: Environmental News and Commentary*. (January 31). At http://www.grist.org/article/luntz1/.

Luntz, F. 2006. *Words That Work: It's Not What You Say, It's What People Hear*. New York: Hyperion.

Madison, D. S. 1995. "Crossing Comfort Zones." *Communication Education* 42:313–316.

McKibben, B. 2006. *The End of Nature*. New York: Random House.

Meister, M., and P. M. Japp. 2002. *Enviropop: Studies in Environmental Rhetoric and Popular Culture*. New York: Praeger.

Muir, S. A., and T. L. Veenendall. 1996. *Earthtalk: Communication and Empowerment for Environmental Action*. New York: Praeger.

Nash, R. 1967/1982. *Wilderness and the American Mind*. 3rd ed. New Haven: Yale University Press.

Novotny, P. 2000. *Where We Live, Work, and Play: The Environmental Justice Movement and the Struggle for a New Environmentalism*. Westport, Conn.: Praeger.

Peterson. T. R. 1998. "Environmental Communication: Tales of Life on Earth." *Quarterly Journal of Speech* 84:371–393.

Pezzullo, P. C. 2001. "Performing Critical Interruptions: Rhetorical Invention and Narratives of the Environmental Justice Movement." *Western Journal of Communication* 64:1–25.

Pezzullo, P. C. 2007. *Toxic Tourism: Rhetorics of Travel, Pollution, and Environmental Justice*. Tuscaloosa: University of Alabama.

Proceedings: The First National People of Color Environmental Leadership Summit, Washington, DC, October 24–27, 1991 (Distributed by the United Church of Christ Commission for Racial Justice).

Smith, C. 1996. *Resisting Reagan: The U.S. Central America Peace Movement*. Chicago: University Chicago Press.

Williams, R. 1973. *The Country and the City*. Cambridge: Oxford University Press.

Overview

Doug Karpa
Campus Instructional Consulting

As outlined so far, environmental literacy encompasses a body of interdisciplinary knowledge including the social, economic, and ecological dimensions of human–environment interactions. We have suggested that this knowledge can be effectively organized around three broad themes: ecosystem services (or human dependence on ecosystems), ecological footprint (or human domination of ecosystems), and sustainability (or human alliance with ecosystems). We have also emphasized that being environmentally literate involves much more than merely being well-informed about the intertwined social, economic, and environmental questions of our age; the environmentally literate citizen also has the skills and the sense of engagement to make reasoned evaluations and to take action based on them. Thus, as we consider how to teach environmental literacy, we look for approaches that foster acquisition of the contextual *information* needed to assess issues, the *conceptual, analytical, and action skills* needed to interpret and apply new information, and, perhaps most importantly, a strong *sense of place and connectedness* to the world, both natural and social, to motivate action. In the essays in this section, each author describes an approach he or she has used outside of the traditional classroom context for promoting environmental literacy in these interconnected dimensions.

Students who become environmentally literate citizens will have developed an understanding of disciplinary thinking from the sciences, humanities, and social sciences, and, importantly, the connections among them, much as is advocated in liberal learning initiatives. Moreover, cognitive skills that undergird environmental literacy are closely related to various definitions of "critical thinking." The action skills and connectedness that form such an important part of environmental literacy are not so different from the engagement and the social connectedness goals of teachers focused on civic engagement and cultural awareness. Thus, successful teaching of environmental literacy moves student proficiency along a wide range of learning priorities—liberal, critical, civic, and cultural—in a wide range of disciplines and in thoughtful engagement with the world beyond the university classroom.

The Learners: The Demography of Teaching Environmental Literacy

The vision of environmental literacy in this book stems in part from an imperative for a society facing great challenges. Given this origin, our vision must reach beyond the already engaged students across the student body, engaging not only the uninformed but also those who are indifferent, resistant, or hostile to "the environment" and/or sustainability. Introducing students to the values of environmental literacy invites conflict with other, competing notions and priorities that prevail in society. In fact, this reorientation may not be so exceptional, since such conflicts are already part of much of higher education. Still, the wide variety of postures students hold with respect to the various facets of environmental literacy makes inviting them into the discussion, potentially, a complex task. Students not only bring an entire range of attitudes toward environmental literacy and its components, but they also differ in the cognitive skills and affective connections they have developed before arriving in our classrooms. For example, they may understand facts without having strong analytical skills, they may have strong analytical skills without any sense of connection to their world, or they may feel a strong connection to place without much factual understanding or analytical ability.

Contemplating Many Paths Toward Environmental Literacy

Teaching environmental literacy is thus a task of broad scope undertaken in a highly diverse context of student experiences, one that requires a variety of pedagogical tools. The chapters in this section propose teaching beyond the traditional four corners of the classroom. As a supplement, alternative, or even substitute for the more conventional approaches to teaching, the venues described in this section open a welcome door out of the classroom, where we find an entire other set of pragmatically useful tools to communicate with and foster growth in our students. Beyond the walls of the classroom, the teacher of environmental literacy may find those new ideas for teaching to be a breath of fresh air. The chapters in this section address the challenge of student diversity by bringing students into the complex "real" world. There they can practice an environmental ethic in which the authors in this section find two common threads.

First, these authors tend to conceive of environmental literacy as an opportunity for solving real-world problems. The pedagogies they describe do not so much distill or conceptualize the world for performance on the next exam as incorporate direct encounters with the environment that can provide a basis for lifelong learning. The real-world issues they reference are as diverse as the financial, institutional, legal, economic, cultural, and biological problems posed by factory farming in North Carolina and the messy matrix of human history and ecology involved in reading working landscapes. They carefully model the complex and ill-defined problems that students will confront as citizens. These encounters with the world become an appealing teaching tool because, by their very complex and ill-defined nature, they demand a fuller range of cognition to cope constructively with new knowledge and uncertain circumstances. Furthermore, teaching with actual examples from a familiar and immediate world, rather than with abstractions of those worlds, allows students to link their own lives and their own learning more directly.

A second strand in the chapters in this section focuses on fostering students' sense of connection to the place in which they live. There are many dimensions—ecological, cultural, economic, historical, and spiritual—to this sense of place, and its development is a complex process made all the more challenging by the itinerant nature of our modern society (and the homogenizing forces of corporate consumerism that tend to transform unique places into Anytowns). The authors present approaches that encourage students to examine their own conceptualizations of their place in the world and their relations to it, and which foster the capacity to create one's own sense of connection in a new place. For example, the chapter on service-learning approaches social and environmental worlds as "texts" for analysis. Other chapters describe ways to have students examine how landscapes are modified and used by human activities. In others, students may be invited become more aware of how they experience the natural world.

Possibilities Beyond the Classroom

Teaching and learning in the complex world outside the classroom requires sensitivity to the learners' stage of intellectual development that informs careful scaffolding of learning experiences. Craig Nelson describes a keystone conceptual framework for understanding both the development of learners and the kinds of teaching approaches that can support that development. In many ways, environmental literacy is grounded in this framework of holistic development, including cognitive abilities, affective postures, and senses of agency and ethics. All of the following approaches derive their power from their effectiveness at providing the structure for this holistic development, in large measure by incorporating the characteristics of active learning Nelson describes.

Nicole Schonemann, Andrew Libby, and Claire King describe how service-learning, with its emphasis on active learning through community engagement, provides a natural structure for developing environmental literacy that is amenable to any discipline. By working in collaboration with community organizations and incorporating opportunities for guided reflection on the service-learning experience, the world in which students live becomes a critically important "text" that enriches their understanding of course content and its connections to daily life, promotes problem-solving skills, and helps to develop a sense of ethics and agency in society.

Jim Capshew applies the principles of engaged and active learning to a university campus landscape. Students explore their local world to learn about the global environmental impacts of everyday student life through a lifecycle analysis of familiar examples such as such as chicken, bicycles, or notebook paper. By tracing the ecological footprints both upstream and downstream from their consumption, students are provided with a conceptual structure to understand the consequences of their activities locally and globally and to explore new models for meeting human needs that promote sustainable human–environment relationships. Investigating the lifecycle of familiar items from everyday life drives home new information about ecological connections and gives students complex issues to pursue in developing their skills and informational knowledge while developing an ethical sense of the impact of their actions. At another level, they are also practicing the self-authoring and critical thinking skills involved in creating their own sense of agency. By the very act of uncovering their connections, students are also reworking their own conceptions and narratives of their place in the world. Although the course is ostensibly about the ecological impacts of objects in the world, because it is about the students' use of those items, this course not only makes the world-at-large a text in the class, but it also invites the student into self-reflection.

Matt Auer emphasizes learning through the most primal of modes: the senses. He describes an experiential place-based learning that combines ecological and scientific understanding with the simple physical experience of the natural world. In engaging the natural world with all five senses, he moves his students beyond the classroom toward a more visceral sense of attachment to nature. He structures their analysis of these experiences so that students make their own observations and bring their own thinking to bear on ecological questions. Auer's "five senses" approach pays off with students' gaining scientific knowledge and analytical skills as well as increased environmental sensitivity.

As Keith Clay points out in his description of the use of nature preserves in teaching about the natural world, direct experience of nature is lacking in many students' lives. Visiting a nature preserve can thus be a novel experience for many students, and Clay describes how immersion in the relatively undisturbed habitat of a nature preserve helps to cultivate students' sense of wonder in, understanding of connection to, and acknowledgement of human dependence on the natural world. "Even students who are outdoor-oriented and have a good handle on the local flora and fauna can come away with a new understanding and appreciation of the small, hidden organisms that play critical roles in our ecosystem," he observes. This approach helps create a sense of connection to the local surroundings and awareness of the multifaceted nature of place. As Clay points out, the woods near his home campus of Indiana University are quite different from the redwoods of the University of California at Santa Cruz or the fern-draped live oaks of Louisiana State University. Wherever students make their home during the college years will offer fascinating features of the natural world, and nature preserves are one resource for helping students learn about how ecosystems underpin human community and the role human values play in shaping their relationships with the natural world.

Vicky Meretsky also highlights the importance of visceral experience, but to a different purpose. She does not use bounded environments like preserves to emphasize our place in the world, but rather she teaches through human-altered landscapes, asking students to consider the profound impacts of human activity. "Most of the world is not a park," she comments. Learning about the human forces that have created working landscapes, students develop the skills to read the human world around them so as to understand better how their own actions very literally shape the world. Meretsky invites students to consider some of the most difficult aspects of environmental literacy through an honest vision of environmental challenges and shows students how they can reimagine themselves and their place in the world in a hopeful way. Meretsky's teaching through "working landscapes" focuses on different phases in the development of environmental literacy: not only developing students' analytical skills but also moving them from initial despair at the pervasiveness of the human footprint toward hopeful understanding of how we can meet our needs more sustainably. "Our task is not to create students who loathe themselves or their needs," she writes, but to "create students . . . who can make choices that will leave as much as possible of our world for our great-grandchildren to worry about and delight in and care for."

All of these approaches take students out of the classroom and bring them *into* the world, creating opportunities for students to enrich their understanding of the ecological, economic, and social dimensions of human–environment interactions and develop their analytical skills in an ill-defined, multidisciplinary context. Furthermore, beyond conceptual or analytical learning, these approaches invite students to shape their own understanding of themselves and their place in the world, in terms of their dependencies, their impact, and their capacity for creating change.

Craig E. Nelson
Biology

Because of the ever-increasing magnitude and importance of the consequences of human actions on global ecosystems, effective education for environmental literacy is intrinsically one of the most important areas of post-secondary education. It is also one of the more complex. Environmental literacy requires integrated understanding of the ecological, social, and economic dimensions of human–environment interactions. For example, Bennet Brabson, as he explains in chapter 2 of this book, wants students not simply to understand the physics of energy and the relationships of energy to ecological, social, and economic dimensions; he also asks for a focus on a sense of place and of personal impact and responsibility. In terms of themes of this book, environmental literacy couples such broadly interdisciplinary understanding with key synthetic concepts such as ecosystem services, ecological footprint, and sustainability. Environmental literacy acquires even greater significance when we realize that it is also one of the areas in which student interest can help overcome the hurdles in the development of more effective ways of dealing with complex issues generally as well as those pertinent specifically to environmental understanding and action. This chapter will examine these hurdles and explore key ways to make education for environmental literacy more effective and more broadly significant.

Cognitive Development

In environmental literacy, as in scientific literacy generally, key tasks include, first, coming to grips with the paradox that the sciences and social sciences are fundamentally uncertain and simultaneously incredibly useful in dealing with external reality and, second, understanding how to appropriately constrain and qualify one's understandings in the face of this paradox, a goal that was clearly stated for education generally by Rousseau and Dewey (e.g. Oliver et al. 2001). The magnitude of the difficulty of these tasks for many students—and the consequent challenges for teachers—were first made clear by William G. Perry, Jr. (1970, 1998). The major steps in student thinking and the transitions between them are summarized in figure 9.1 with a brief indication of how they apply to understanding nuclear power.

Perry found that many students arrive at college expecting faculty to provide them with "facts" or truths to memorize, especially in science (Sergeant Friday, figure 9.1). For nuclear power (Nelson 1986: 200), students expect the faculty member to state clearly either that nuclear power is safe and should be developed immediately or that it is dangerous and should be banned. The first fundamental learning/teaching problem is to help students to understand how knowledge can be legitimately uncertain. As they come to understand this, students initially have no good ways of dealing with disparate views in the face of legitimate uncertainty. They conclude that, absent clear truth, all views must be equally valid (Baskin Robbins, figure 9.1). They think that since nuclear power has clearly been controversial, one just goes with whatever feels good. And just as if we were choosing flavors for our ice cream cones, there seems to the students to be no way of fairly critiquing anyone else's "opinions." Indeed, many students initially think that all attempts to decide which opinions are better and which are weaker are inherently narrow-minded.

Nevertheless, the fundamental learning/teaching problem has become exactly the task of learning to do valid critiques so as to separate stronger and weaker positions and arguments. Within the game of science (or economics, etc.), how do experts decide which ideas are stronger and which weaker? As the students learn these expert ways of knowing, they often in their hearts continue to believe that the validity of an opinion depends only on the act of choice. They then treat the more sophisticated approaches as "teachers' games" (figure 9.1) that one must adopt to pass exams. The question becomes, how does the particular economist or other faculty member guiding the class want me to justify my apparent

SGT FRIDAY

One Authority Has The Truth

Nuclear Power Either... (a) Is Really Safe or (b) Should Be Totally Banned

◄——— *UNCERTAINTY*

BASKIN ROBBINS

Opinions

Each Person's Views are Right For Her

Nuclear Power: Why Argue? Just Respect Each Other!

◄——— *COMPARISONS & CRITERIA*

TEACHERS' GAMES

Let's Really Understand Everyone's Arguments & Frameworks

Nuclear Power: Environmentalists Argue That .... Whereas...

◄——— *CONSEQUENCES & VALUES*
       FRAME ARGUMENTS

OWNED GAMES

Some Frameworks / Combinations Are
More Appropriate For Particular Contexts

Nuclear Power: Safe enough for Some Uses (Submarines)
But Not for Others (Power-Plants in Urban Areas) Because ...

FIGURE 9.1. Cognitive Development. Four modes of thinking relevant to undergraduate learning.

stand on nuclear power? The fundamental learning/teaching problem now becomes learning how to use consequences and values to balance different expert
positions (Owned Games, figure 9.1). Only as they learn this will they be able to
deal constructively with major issues in environmental and other realms. Once
here, they will be able to integrate and, to some extent, critique a variety of expert
opinions on diverse facets of the nuclear power issues. They also will begin to
understand how nuclear power can fit within a larger context (as advocated by

Brabson in his chapter in this volume) and even take stands based both on these large contexts and on their own sense of how the tradeoffs and risks should be managed.

Environmental issues both require these successive transitions and provide content that is seen by the students as sufficiently interesting and important to make the necessary rethinking worthwhile. And just as environmental issues make developmental transformations easier, a good working understanding of the developmental process allows faculty to anticipate student lapses and resistances and to scaffold the learning tasks so as to facilitate development and the deeper learning it allows. Perhaps the single greatest mistake faculty make is to assume that what is obvious to them will be obvious to students if only it can be explained clearly. In contrast, it is necessary to help students move though each of the transitions, often topic by topic (Nelson 1999). For example, on energy policy: Why is there uncertainty on key aspects (total exploitable petroleum reserves, amounts of key pollutants released by extraction, effects of toxins at chronic low levels, amount of petroleum-based energy required to produce a unit of biodiesel or nuclear energy, etc.)? Unless the current or historical uncertainties can be made clear, students will tend to want faculty simply to provide the "real" answer. Once the uncertainties are understood, attention can turn to addressing each aspect in a way that still recognizes the uncertainty and complexity. This typically involves learning to understand key disciplines (or "games") such as environmental toxicology and ecological economics. Glaser's chapter in this volume, a delightful and concise summary of ecological economics, presents a superb example of this strategy. Similarly, the chapters by Sanders and Auer suggest simple questions that students can ask about the place(s) in which they reside, questions which are initially largely discipline-based and start at the level of "facts." These authors illustrate the power of starting at the level of the individual discipline and building outward toward the larger syntheses and critical thinking, writ broad, that we collectively are suggesting in this book as the core of environmental literacy and of a more rational society.

Jumping too rapidly to environmental ethics or public policy can suppress real understanding by shortcutting the apperception of the frameworks that must underlie any effective address to these higher-level considerations. In short, the key lesson from our grasp of student development is that deeper understanding happens in predictable stages with predictable hurdles, and that these typically need to be addressed sequentially to produce deep and lasting understanding and a broad ethical consciousness.

Holistic Development

Development during the college years is not simply cognitive. And our goals in environmental education are not simply cognitive either. Rather, development when successfully fostered changes one's sense of self, agency, and ethics. It is precisely such shifts that we aim for in environmental education. We want the student to change from being told by authority who she is and what she should believe to a person who can actively work to change who she is and who constructs and takes responsibility for what she believes (change in sense of self). We want her to change from thinking that governmental authority is responsible for deciding what environmental issues should be addressed, and how, to knowing that she, like other citizens, has the privilege and burdens of helping make these decisions (change in sense of agency). And we want a shift from a black-and-white sense of values (nuclear power is always evil) to a much more nuanced and contextual sense of values (change in ethics).

Perry's focus, as his title proclaimed, was on intellectual and ethical development in the college years. His work stimulated several hundred follow-up papers applying his ideas, as well as scores of new empirical studies. Recent partial reviews are by Baxter Magolda (2001), Hofer and Pintrich (1997), and Knefelkamp (in Perry 1998). Among the most important were *Women's Ways of Knowing* (Belenky et al. 1986), King and Kitchner's *Developing Reflexive Judgment* (1994), and several books by Baxter Magolda (1999, 2000, 2001, and, with King, 2004).

Especially relevant here, Baxter Magolda (2001), partially following Kegan (1994), has shown that development is broadly multifaceted, with development of one's sense of self and the development of one's interpersonal identity being part and parcel of one's cognitive and ethical development. She terms this larger progress "holistic development" and emphasizes that its core is the development of "self-authorship." These shifts in sense of self and interpersonal identity provide a clearer window into the deep transformations required by successfully fostering environmental literacy and by successful higher education generally.

Perry (1970) had earlier partially addressed the shift in sense of self in his focus on a transition from a world defined by the views of authority to a world defined by one's own conscious choices, sometimes including the choice of a partial deference to authority. Belenky et al. (1986) found that as students transition to the owned games level of figure 9.1 their deeper understanding leads automatically to a sense of "mission." This commitment to making important changes is an outcome that we especially want as a result of environmental literacy. Several of the authors in this volume emphasize that education for environmental literacy is especially appropriate for goals that are implicitly or explicitly developmental and holistic:

No matter the field or professional goal, students provided with the opportunity to become environmentally literate will face and address questions relevant to their lives, daily choices, and ethics, as well as those of the society as a whole. Environmental literacy is an exercise in overcoming simplification and generalizations, and in thinking outside the box. (Brondzio, conclusion, this volume)

Educators of all disciplines can encourage their students to search in themselves for what truly brings them happiness, satisfaction, and joy, and to discover their highest aspirations for themselves and the world. This . . . will help students develop the inner freedom and strength to define for themselves what it means to be successful and useful members of society. . . . Awakening to, acknowledging, and courageously following our highest aspirations and hopes is not a selfish pursuit. Our highest aspirations connect us with each other and the universe. (Glaser, this volume)

But the foreseen costs of such commitments, the emotional burdens of facing persistent uncertainty and unsatisfactory tradeoffs, and the attendant shifts in responsibility, hold students back or even cause them to retreat to simpler views (Perry 1970). Meretsky (this volume) captures well some of the important challenges here:

Environmental educators have the potential to lay enormously heavy burdens on their students. Educators in other fields only want their students to change the world, or perhaps to save lives. We want our students to save the world. . . . Burnout is a very real possibility.

Simultaneously, these shifts require a redefinition of how one relates to peers and authority figures such as parents and teachers. Reluctance on the students' part to make these changes coupled with resistance from parents and others can make the adoption of more sophisticated ways of thinking difficult. One student studying evolution told me that "this is the first time my mother and I have disagreed on anything important and it has been quite difficult for both of us." The parallels to the policy and ethical facets of environmental issues are obvious. Students are held back in changing their environmental stances and understanding by the views that their parents or important peers hold. It has been fascinating lately to watch the changes by some parts of the evangelical leadership in the United States toward a much greater emphasis on environmental stewardship and more responsibility for those who are negatively affected by our environmentally significant collective choices. This changes the social context for many of our students, making it easier for them to commit to making environmentally positive choices.

Active Learning

The deep transformations required for holistic development and, hence, for the development of mature environmental literacy are facilitated by the interactions in small group learning. These interactions allow students to practice the new "voice" that is at the core of holistic development (Belenky et al. 1986). But small group interactions are important at all levels of learning, from arithmetic up (Whimbey and Lochhead 1999). A meta-analysis of the effects of small group methods in undergraduate science and related disciplines showed very strong average gains in learning, attitudes, and persistence (Springer et al. 1997, 1999). Similar analyses are available for cooperative learning (Johnson et al. 1998a; Smith et al. 2005), problem-based learning (Dochy et al. 2003) and college teaching and learning generally (McKeachie et al. 1986). Effective methods vary from brief interventions in large lectures (Mazur 1997) to total replacement of lecture with more interactive modes (partial review in Hake 1998). Several good handbooks available to college faculty include, to name just a few, Barkley et al. 2004; Duch et al. 2001; Evansen and Hmelo 2000; Johnson et al. 1998b; MacGregor et al. 2000; Michael and Modell 2003; Millis and Cottel 1998; Wilkerson and Gijselaers 1996. Several authors have dealt specifically with using active learning and other pedagogies to foster holistic development (e.g., Baxter Magolda 1999, 2001; Baxter Magolda and King 2004; Belenky et al. 1986; Nelson 1994).

Comparisons of alternative pedagogies in introductory physics were greatly facilitated by the development of pre-test and post-test instruments that have been used in a wide variety of institutions from high school to Harvard. Hake's summaries (1998, 2002) support several important conclusions. Adopting minds-on, active learning approaches doubles to triples the pre-test corrected net learning gain. No traditional lecture course has yet been found to match the average pre-test to post-test gain from active learning. Differences in quality of lecture have almost no effect on student learning. Differences in student quality have much less effect than most of us would have expected (i.e., the net gain from lecture, expressed as a fractional gain from pre-test to post-test averages, is about the same for students in high schools and at Harvard).

Startling as these conclusions from physics may be, the literature suggests that similar effects are probable across all of undergraduate science, technology, math, and engineering (Dochy et al. 2003; Johnson et al. 1998a; Springer et al. 1997, 1999; Smith et al. 2005). It is also now clear that students regard traditional ways of teaching science as discouraging and disrespectful and that those who complete majors in science typically do so despite rather than because of the teaching (Seymour and Hewitt 1997). Such effects from traditional lecturing cannot help but undermine the goals of any environmental literacy program.

Many of the chapters in this book seek intense, active ways to make the importance of the environment even more compelling to students, thereby hcightening the power of environmental learning to foster intellectual and ethical transformation. Sanders's sense of place is paralleled by Auer's multisensory approach to learning from a site outdoors, by Capshew's development of a somewhat similar, object-centered sense of a web of environmental connections, and by Meretsky's much larger-scale sense of working and non-working (and pristine) landscapes. More generally, Gross (this volume) and Schönemann, Libby, and King (this volume) focus on the roles of, respectively, action-based teaching and service-learning in more deeply transformative learning.

Additional Frameworks for Fostering Deeper Learning

I have focused on cognitive development fostered through active learning as a key aspect of holistic development. The goal, well illustrated for environmental literacy by the quotes above from Glaser and other authors in this book, is what Baxter Magolda (2001; Baxter Magolda and King 2004) terms "self-actualization" and what the authors of *Women's Ways of Knowing* (Belenky et al. 1986) term "constructed knowing." We are likely to get undergraduates to this point only if we systematically scaffold the transitions the students need to make. Gains within single courses are almost always small and somewhat illusory, as the students are giving the faculty what they think the faculty wants without having really adopted the new ways of thinking and being. Hence, as shown by the work that Mentkowski and Associates (2000) summarize, really reaching our goals requires a curriculum that *intentionally* works developmentally across all four years.

But understanding of holistic development and active learning is not sufficient to allow faculty to fully apply what is known about improving student learning in colleges and universities. For example, at a finer scale, faculty should also become closely acquainted with Piaget's ideas on the limitations on students' understanding of quantitative and formal ideas in science and social science and about the pedagogical steps that have been shown to be effective in helping students to transcend these limitations (e.g., Arons 1996; Herron 1975). At a larger scale, especially for the comprehensive goals of environmental literacy and action as described in this volume, faculty should integrate an understanding of holistic development with ideas of transformative learning (Cranton 2006; Mezirow and Associates 2000).

Similarly, for the transformative changes required for deep environmental literacy to be achieved, faculty will have to become much more expert at real assessment of learning. The course-specific approaches to the assessment of cognitive development suggested by King and Kitchner (1994, see their appendices) are an important start. An important question will be whether the development of functional environmental literacy is stage by stage parallel to that of cognitive development. Bennett (1986) has suggested just such a correspondence for the development of intercultural sensitivity. As a start, Uhl (2004) suggested three stages of ecological consciousness. Is "wonder" toward earth and its ecological systems accessible at a lower developmental level, "despair" over the extent of damage that humans are causing to earth and its ecosystems first accessible at an intermediate level, and informed "hope" that humanity will be able to create socially just economies that work with earth's ecological systems to create sustainable societies only accessible at the level I have called "owned games" (figure 9.1)?

Implications

It is of utmost importance that future leaders and members of the general public become much more deeply environmentally literate in the ways described briefly above and much more fully in this volume as a whole. One key to the requisite transformations of teaching is the provision of extra structure. This includes careful attention to tasks for each of the cognitive transformations and to the structure and dynamics of small group and of other learning tasks (Nelson 1996; Walvoord and Anderson 1998).

Payoffs include deeper learning of content, movement toward deeper understanding of complexity and tradeoffs, the development of a stronger voice with a sense of mission and the capacity for complex ethical decisions, better attitudes toward the areas we teach, and improved retention in our programs and in college. The effects on the achievement of underpowered minorities can be as large as a shift from 40 percent making A, B, or C to 96 percent doing so with no lowering of standards (Fullilove and Treisman 1990).

As noted above, environmental issues can motivate the students to do the deeper learning required to move from superficial mastery of content to dealing with complex cognitive and ethical issues. This will be vastly more effective if instructional design takes account of where the students begin, in terms of holistic development, and carefully constructs the cognitive scaffolding and social support appropriate to these starting points and to the students' subsequent progression. Simply posing ethically and cognitively complex problems is likely to be much less effective, even with well-prepared and hard-working students. Another way to put this: faculty have a tendency to design the courses that would be optimal for the faculty members rather than the courses that would be optimal for first-year students or other undergraduate audiences.

Indiana University Bloomington has been fortunate to have recently developed one of the world's best programs for fostering the scholarship of teaching and learning. It helps faculty move from content- and faculty-centered teaching to a practice that fosters deeper and more transformative learning. In the process, faculty must move from a focus on traditional methods to evidence-based and theory-framed approaches. The central thrust of this chapter has been an introduction to such approaches. Each of the instructional approaches described in the other chapters will benefit, in further development over time, from making the evidential and theoretical bases of the pedagogical theories and the corresponding assessments more explicit.

In teaching for environmental literacy, we ask our students to understand the evidence and frameworks that will lead them to assume responsibility for helping with environmental problems and issues. Must we not model that by mastering the evidence and theoretical frameworks that will better allow us to assume responsibility for the education we provide them?

Acknowledgments

Ella Ingram helped in the development of figure 9.1 and presented the summary behind this chapter to seminar participants. Lin Ostrom is one of a large group of faculty who helped deepen my understanding of the complexity of environmental issues and of their solutions during a series of meetings and symposiums that led to the founding of the Environmental Studies major in the College of Arts and Sciences and the various environmental programs in the then-nascent School of Public and Environmental Affairs (Nelson 1974). Jennifer Robinson and Doug Karpa are two of the most recent in a long series of faculty developers at this institution that traces back to Gene Ferris and Tom Schwen at the beginning of my career at Indiana University. My understanding of teaching would still be quite rudimentary had it not been for their guidance. The late William G. Perry, Jr., L. Lee Knefelkamp (now of Columbia University) and Carol Schneider (now of the Association of American Colleges and Universities) are among the individuals elsewhere who made major differences in my thinking and development as a teacher-scholar.

References

Arons, A. B. 1996. *Teaching Introductory Physics.* John Wiley & Sons.

Barkley, E., K. P. Cross, and C. H. Major. 2004. *Collaborative Learning Techniques: A Practical Guide to Promoting Learning in Groups.* Jossey-Bass.

Baxter Magolda, M. B. 1999. *Creating Contexts for Learning and Self-Authorship: Constructive Developmental Pedagogy.* Vanderbilt Issues in Higher Education.

——. 2001. *Making Their Own Way: Narratives for Transforming Higher Education to Promote Self-Development.* Stylus.

Baxter Magolda, M. B., ed. 2000. *Teaching to Promote Intellectual and Personal Maturity: Incorporating Students' Worldviews and Identities into the Learning Process.* Jossey-Bass.

Baxter Magolda, M. B., and P. M. King, eds. 2004. *Learning Partnerships: Theory and Models of Practice to Educate for Self-Authorship.* Stylus.

Belenky, M., B. Clinchy, N. Goldberger, and J. Tarule. 1986. *Women's Ways of Knowing.* Basic Books.

Bennett, M. J. 1986. "Towards Ethnorelativism: A Developmental Model of Intercultural Sensitivity." In Michael Paige, ed., *Cross-Cultural Orientation,* 27–69. University Press of America.

Cranton, P. 2006. *Understanding and Promoting Transformative Learning: A Guide for Educators of Adults.* 2nd ed. Jossey-Bass.

Dochy, F., M. Segers, P. Van den Bossche, and D. Gigbels. 2003. "Effects of Problem-Based Learning: A Meta-Analysis. *Learning and Instruction* 13: 533–568.

Duch, B. J., S. E. Groh, and D. E. Allen. 2001. *The Power of Problem Based Learning: A Practical "How to" for Teaching Undergraduate Courses in Any Discipline.* Stylus.

Evansen, D. H., and C. E. Hmelo. 2000. *Problem-Based Learning: A Research Perspective on Learning Interactions.* Lawrence Erlbaum.

Fullilove, R. E., and P. U. Treisman. 1990. "Mathematics Achievement Among African American Undergraduates at the University of California, Berkeley: An Evaluation of the Mathematics Workshop Program." *Journal of Negro Education* 59(3): 463–478.

Hake, R. R. 1998. "Interactive-Engagement vs Traditional Methods: A Six-Thousand-Student Survey of Mechanics Test Data for Introductory Physics Courses." *American Journal of Physics* 66: 64–74. Available at http://www.physics.indiana.edu/sdi/ajpv3i .pdf (accessed 2 April 2009).

——. 2002. "Lessons From the Physics-Education-Reform Effort." *Conservation Ecology* 5(2):28. At http://www.ecologyandsociety.org/vo15/iss2/art28/ (accessed 2 April 2009).

Herron, J. D. 1975. "Piaget for Chemists: Explaining What 'Good' Students Cannot Understand." *Journal Chemical Education* 52:146–150.

Hofer, B., and P. Pintrich. 1997. "The Development of Epistemological Theories: Beliefs About Knowledge and Knowing and Their Relation to Learning." *Review of Educational Research* 67: 88–140.

Johnson, D. W., R. T. Johnson, and K. A. Smith. 1998a. "Cooperative Learning Returns to College: What Evidence Is There That It Works?" *Change* 30(4): 26–35.

——. 1998b. *Active Learning: Cooperation in the College Classroom.* 2nd ed. Interaction.

Kegan, R. 1994. *In Over Our Heads: The Mental Demands of Modern Life.* Harvard.

King, P. M., and K. S. Kitchner. 1994. *Developing Reflexive Judgment: Understanding and Promoting Intellectual Growth and Critical Thinking in Adolescents and Adults.* Jossey-Bass.

MacGregor, J., J. Cooper, K. Smith, and P. Robinson, eds. 2000. "Strategies for Energizing Large Classes: From Small Groups to Learning Communities." *New Directions for Teaching and Learning* 81.

McKeachie, W., P. Pintrich, Y.-G. Lin, and D. Smith. 1986. *Teaching and Learning in the*

College Classroom: A Review of the Research Literature. The Regents of the University of Michigan.

Mazur, E. 1997. *Peer Instruction: A User's Manual.* Prentice Hall.

Mentkowski, M. and Associates 2000. *Learning that Lasts: Integrating Learning, Development, and Performance in College and Beyond.* Jossey-Bass.

Mezirow, J. and Associates. 2000. *Learning as Transformation: Critical Perspectives on a Theory in Progress.* Jossey-Bass.

Michael, J. A., and H. I. Modell, 2003. *Active Learning in Secondary and College Science Classrooms: A Working Model for Helping the Learner to Learn.* Lawrence Erlbaum.

Millis, B. J., and P. G. Cottel, 1998. *Cooperative Learning for Higher Education Faculty.* American Council on Education and Oryx Press.

Nelson, C. E. 1974. "Environmental Studies Program (at Indiana University)." In A. L. Pratt, ed., *Selected Environmental Education Programs in North American Higher Education,* 79–88. National Association for Environmental Education.

——. 1986. "Creation, Evolution, or Both? A Multiple Model Approach." In R. W. Hanson, ed., *Science and Creation.* Macmillan.

——. 1994. "Collaborative Learning and Critical Thinking." In K. Bosworth and S. Hamilton, eds., *Collaborative Learning and College Teaching,* 45–58. Jossey-Bass.

——. 1996. "Student Diversity Requires Different Approaches to College Teaching, Even in Math and Science." *American Behavioral Scientist* 40(2):165–175.

——. 1999. "On The Persistence Of Unicorns: The Tradeoff Between Content and Critical Thinking Revisited." In B. A. Pescosolido and R. Aminzade, eds., *The Social Worlds of Higher Education: Handbook for Teaching in a New Century,* 168–184. Pine Forge Press.

——. 2000. "Effective Strategies for Teaching Evolution and Other Controversial Subjects." In J. W. Skehan and C. E. Nelson, eds., *The Creation Controversy and the Science Classroom,* 19–50. National Science Teachers Association.

Oliver, J. S., D. F. Jackson, S. Chun, A. Kemp, D. J. Tippins, R. Leonard, N. H. Kang, and B. Rascoe. 2001. "The Concept of Scientific Literacy: A View of the Current Debate as an Outgrowth of the Past Two Centuries." *Electronic Journal of Literacy through Science* 1(1): 1–33. http://ejlts.ucdavis.edu/article/2001/1/1/concept-scientific-literacy-view-current-debate-outgrowth-past-two-centuries (accessed 1 May 2009)

Perry, W. G., Jr. 1970. *Forms of Intellectual and Ethical Development in the College Years.* Holt, Rinehart and Winston.

——. 1998. *Forms of Intellectual and Ethical Development in the College Years: A Scheme.* New introduction by Lee Knefelkamp. Jossey-Bass.

Seymour, E., and N. M. Hewitt. 1997. *Talking About Leaving: Why Undergraduates Leave the Sciences.* Westview.

Springer, L., M. E. Stanne, and S. S. Donovan. 1997. *Measuring the Success of Small-Group Learning in College-Level SMET Teaching: A Meta-Analysis.* National Institute for Science Education, University of Wisconsin. http://www.wcer.wisc.edu/archive/CL1/CL/resource/scismet.htm (accessed 14 April 2009).

——. 1999. "Effects Of Small-Group Learning On Undergraduates In Science, Mathematics, Engineering And Technology: A Meta-Analysis." *Review of Educational Research* 69(1): 21–51.

Smith, K. A., S. D. Sheppard, D. W. Johnson, and R. T. Johnson. 2005. "Pedagogies of Engagement: Classroom-Based Practices." *Journal of Engineering Education.* January 2005: 87–101.

Uhl, C. 2004. *Developing Ecological Consciousness: Paths to a Sustainable World.* Rowman and Littlefield Publishers.

Walvoord, B. E. F., and V. J. Anderson. 1998. *Effective Grading: A Tool For Learning and Assessment.* Jossey-Bass.

Whimbey, A., and J. Lochhead. 1999. *Problem Solving and Comprehension.* Lawrence Erlbaum.

Wilkerson, L., and W. H. Gijselaers, 1996. "Bringing Problem-Based Learning to Higher Education: Theory and Practice. *New Directions for Teaching and Learning* 68. Jossey-Bass.

James H. Capshew
History and Philosophy of Science

How can we encourage people to think deeply about the environment we live in? To understand basic ecosystem services and energy flows through the world? To creatively face the problems that human civilization has placed on the biosphere? In the midst of global climate change and worldwide environmental degradation, it has become clear than humans must act. But how can we, as individuals, make a difference in the face of these overwhelming forces? I would suggest that teaching and learning about the local context—the human culture and the natural landscape that surrounds each one of us—can serve perfectly. Indeed, we all have a certain amount of expertise in dealing with our local place-ways: how to navigate through them; where to find food and shelter; how to get our needs meet. Connoisseurs of the local can explain historical roots, provide esthetic judgments, or create new possibilities in place. Turning our attention to the local increases our knowledge of the world and our place in it, and opens a pathway for appreciation of our rightful place in the web of life. No longer can we afford to act as if the world exists only to meet the needs of the human population. Now we must nurture a fulfilling appreciation that humans belong to the world.

The local context, for millions of college students, is the campus, where they spend a significant portion of their time studying, playing, eating, and sleeping. But the university or college campus is an underutilized foundation for teaching the basics of environmental literacy and the ethics and practices of sustainability. As a physical place and as an institutional nexus of human resources, the campus can function as a laboratory and field site to illustrate environmental history, to illuminate general ecological processes and systems, and to investigate diverse responses to the current state of the environment.

The general theme of "campus as ecosystem" provides a broad avenue to grow environmental appreciation and ecological understanding, and has sufficient scope to customize courses to institutional needs for environmental literacy at all undergraduate levels. Such courses would take the ecological interconnectedness of abiotic features (e.g., rocks, soils, climate, etc.) of the local environment with various forms of life (e.g., bacteria, plants, animals, humans, etc.) as fundamental, treating them as parts of a whole community. This type of study is inherently interdisciplinary, valuing the insights, attitudes, and methods of fields ranging from geology, chemistry, and biology to demography, anthropology, and history. Courses can be tailored according to specific needs for content areas, cognitive skill development, or philosophical and ethical approaches.

Biologist Barry Commoner, seeking to capitalize on the enthusiasm of the first Earth Day in 1970, formulated a set of informal "laws" of ecology:

- Everything is connected to everything else.
- Everything must go somewhere.
- There is no such thing as a free lunch.
- Nature knows best.

These rubrics are pedagogically useful, and provide ways to connect study in most any discipline to environmental concerns.

Connecting to Students' Lives

Using the framework of "campus as ecosystem," a course organized around the lifecycle of objects encountered in the college lifestyle is a compelling way to introduce students to their place in the web of life. Exploiting items that a typical student might consume or use throughout a normal day, in such areas as food and drink, clothing, transportation, housing, and equipment, lifecycle analysis traces an object's origins "upstream" to its origins as well as "downstream" to its ultimate fate. It traces the linkages among objects ("everything is connected to everything else") and the idea that items, once consumed, do not dematerialize or disappear but go into some kind of waste stream ("everything must go somewhere"). Reflection on the costs, both financial and moral, of the college lifestyle ("no such thing as a free lunch") leads to consideration of philosophical and ethical questions, including contemplation of how we can learn from nature ("nature knows best").

Lifecycle analysis confronts students with the larger context of their daily choices and gives them exposure to some important environmental consequences of individual choices and collective decisions. Such a course would focus on such items as:

- Food and drink: water, beer, coffee, potato, corn, chicken, salmon
- Clothing and fabric: cotton T-shirt, nylon backpack
- Transportation: automobile, bicycle, bus, pedestrian
- Housing: dormitory room, downtown apartment, room in shared house
- Equipment: pencil, paper, personal computer, cell phone

To connect directly with students' lives, each unit would begin on the level of the *mesocosm* (the human scale), with an item of daily use. Students would learn about where the item came from, how it is transformed for use by humans, and its downstream destiny. The item would be analyzed on various levels, from "the big picture" context (*macrocosm*) of ecosystems to the unseen world of microorganisms and biogeochemical processes (*microcosm*) that support the biosphere.

Take chicken, for example: How did it appear on campus, both as a physical object and a social negotiation? Where is it going after being eaten, materially and culturally? More specifically, let's look at a Burger King chicken sandwich, prepared on campus at a local franchise, from frozen chicken raised on a factory farm in North Carolina, with attendant sanitary inspections, pollution issues, and refrigerated truck transportation. The class could discuss the history of animal domestication and agriculture and the rise of industrialized meat production along with the decline of family farms (capital flows, government regulations, faster transportation, etc.). Downstream analysis could include possible human physiological effects from hormones and antibiotics given to the chicken, impact on the community sewage system, and the infrastructure that supports fast food. Health and social benefits and costs, and the ethics of meat eating, could be explored through alternatives, including free-range chickens and vegetarian diets.

The bicycle is another rich, everyday example of environmental choice and impacts that could be drawn from the campus setting. Oftentimes students rediscover the joys of bike riding when they come to college after living in suburban places where families are tied to automobiles for most of their transportation needs. The physical environment may be challenging—narrow roads, steep hills, changeable weather—but the bicyclist is rewarded with great scenery, physical fitness, and participation in a vibrant culture of bicycling. The invention of the bicycle in the nineteenth century was a revolutionary advance in human-powered transport. No longer were humans confined to walking or running, or dependent on auxiliary sources of motive power that relied on animals or, later, on internal combustion engines. For local transportation, around campus and town, the bicycle is fast, easy to park, and is nonpolluting, counterbalancing rides in less than optimal weather conditions. Moreover, students studying overseas are often surprised at the extensive presence of bicycling in daily commutes in both developed and emerging countries, like the Netherlands and China. As a transportation system, bicycling has a soft ecological footprint in terms of manufacturing resources consumed and no special fuel requirements. But it has limitations in weight capacity, either for passengers or cargo. Furthermore, it might not be suitable for transportation for those less physically able due to health considerations or age, and the traffic infrastructure of many U.S. cities and towns does not support safe bicycle transportation. Thus bicycling offers a multifaceted example of the relationships among transportation, economics, and social organization.

Finally, items like notebook paper can serve as in-class examples of how we make constant but largely unconscious decisions about the environment. Paper, as a semi-permanent medium for written communication, has a long and rich global history. The transformation of plant fibers into stable sheets first occurred as a craft technique. Over time it became an industrial process, with wood as the raw material. Upstream, the technology of paper production leads to forests, natural as well as human-managed, and a discussion of what ecosystem services forests provide, including a central role in the global oxygen/carbon dioxide cycle. Case studies might include the Amazon rain forest, sometimes referred to as the "lungs of the earth," and conflicts over its management. In addition, many campuses will have local examples in nearby national and state forests, which typically invoke recurring controversies about how to interpret "appropriate use." Students might read and discuss Jean Giono's parable titled *The Man Who Planted Trees,* an inspiring story about individual determination and ecological restoration, and relate it to the changing role of wooded areas on campus as an example of stewardship. At the level of the student mesocosm, paper is a ubiquitous presence and often taken for granted as a resource. However, individual student usage, including trying to agree as a class to a standard paper allotment for notes, Xeroxing and computer printing, might provide "teachable moments" to discuss campus policies on resource use. In a larger sense, the university runs on paper, with student assignments, memoranda and policy documents, archives and libraries all utilizing this renewable resource. Once notebook or printer paper is discarded, it enters either the waste stream (destined for the landfill) or the recycling service. How paper gets recycled, the challenges of the market for recycled paper, and emerging alternative fibers for paper production are all topics for investigation.

Many colleges and universities are now grappling with how to educate their students to be environmentally literate citizens while also refashioning their campus operations to be more sustainable. At the same time, many institutions have come to value common-experience courses, especially for first-year and senior students. A multidisciplinary, integrative course on environmental sustainability, such as that described here, could offer powerful, real-world course content directly from the campus outside the classroom door.

A course revolving around lifecycle analysis reinforces many themes crucial to environmental literacy, including the major ecosystems and their associated services, the fundamentals of ecological footprint analysis, and the ethics and practices of environmental sustainability. Because course materials would be grounded in students' own campus experiences, they would gain knowledge of effective means to increase environmental sustainability. This could be applied immediately, not at some unspecified point in the future, for the collective good of the campus.

As students are learning the content and exercising skills (e.g., concept mapping, critical thinking, moral reasoning) while doing it, they are simultaneously embodying civic ethics and making a real difference in campus operations. Thus they can move from the wonder and despair that comes from learning about the human impact on the environment toward the hope that can be derived from reflecting on and taking control of one's own influence. Learning in place teaches us to be mindful about our place on the earth.

Acknowledgments

This essay is dedicated to the memory of Leah Woods Garlotte. I am grateful to the participants in the faculty seminar series that led to the Environmental Literacy and Sustainability Initiative, especially Douglas Karpa, and to those who consulted on an earlier version of a "green" course, including David Goodrum, Julia L. Jackson, Eric J. Nichols, J. David Perry, Laura Plummer, Heather Reynolds, Jennifer Meta Robinson, and Jiangmei Wu. Finally, I thank the editors of this volume for their patience and persistence.

Nicole Schonemann, Andrew Libby, and Claire King
Office of Service-Learning

Service-learning and environmental education are natural allies. Service-learning relies on the community as a text through which the lecture, reading, discussion, and reflective experience of the learner is writ large. Similarly, environmental educators have long held the premise that there is a text among the assigned readings for a course, required alongside the books, essays, and electronic reserves itemized in the syllabus, yet never found in the library or bookstore. The text is the world, the earth, the planet, the biosphere, the environment.

That there is a profound bioecological connection between physical location and the act of cognition has been well established. Equally true is the fact that learning in natural places plants seeds of commitment to that environment and offers students a chance to put down roots in the places where that learning happens. Such a benefit should be of compelling interest to state economies and regional private sectors that lament the loss of graduates to competing job markets out-of-state. Perhaps of greater importance is that situating service-learning in environmental contexts, a possibility in any discipline, can simultaneously advance the key content, skills and values that help students make connections between environmental literacy and their everyday lives. As the 2000 study by Patricia Madigan, Corporation for National and Community Service Fellow, explains: "Environmental service-learning helps students connect what they learn with how they live. High quality environmental service-learning programs are able to promote student leadership and decision-making, integrate and value the community voice, foster civic stewardship, develop cross-cultural connections, and plan for the program's sustainability."

As a program type, service-learning includes myriad ways that students can perform meaningful service to their communities and to society while engaging in academic reflection of study that is related to the service. As a philosophy of education, service-learning reflects the belief that education must be linked to social responsibility and that the most effective learning is active and connected to experience in some meaningful way. (Honnet and Poulsen 1989). Because service-learning is a form of experiential education where students perform a service that is clearly connected to the academic content of a course and meets a genuine community need, it is a strong match for environmental literacy and sustainability education.

The Basics of Service-Learning

Service-learning is often presented as a balanced approach (Furco 1996). In contrast to a practicum or volunteering, in service-learning the recipient and provider of the service are both intended and equal beneficiaries of the experience. Ideally, service-learning is a reciprocal relationship, a three-way partnership involving the course instructor, students, and community. This takes quite a bit of work and commitment on all parts—as each is a potential beneficiary, each also must expend effort in establishing and nurturing this relationship and experience. Because of the additional effort involved, we find instructors who adopt a service-learning approach to be among the most dedicated and committed to teaching. Community partner agencies must also realize that taking on a service-learning class entails a good deal of work on their part. It is important that community partner agencies understand that service-learning when done well yields benefits to the agency, but as with any group, student work varies. And since the service-learning commitment extends to the limits of the academic calendar, there may be a good deal of effort expended on the part of the agency in preparing the students for work for which they will no longer be responsible once the academic session ends. Despite these cautions, partnerships as a result of service-learning can be a tremendous experience for students, faculty, and community alike.

To assist students in making academic connections between what they are learning in their course and the work they perform at their service site, reflection is built into classroom activities and assignments. Reflection is the bridge between the service and the academics, making the course an integrated service and learning experience and providing an opportunity for the practical and the theoretical to merge. Without reflection intentionally and regularly built into the course, the students might enjoy a parallel service experience but without the understanding of how this ties to the academic content of the course. Reflection can be built into class discussions, group work, journaling, online discussion boards, etc. There is extensive literature on the importance of building reflection into the service-learning course as well as how to do so (Bringle and Hatcher 1999, 2001).

In the service-learning partnership, the community benefits as well. Community partner agencies are frequently underfunded and understaffed, relying heavily on volunteers; hence, service-learners are quite often a welcome force in the agency's pursuit of its mission. Moreover, service-learning can provide the context for better relations between the university and the community, each coming to see the other as a mutually beneficial resource. At its best, service-learning is an effective way to bridge the town/gown divide and allow for each community to learn from the other and work together on common goals. In the case of environmental literacy and sustainability education, the fruits of service-learning often extend beyond the agency and beyond the community to benefit the environment and society.

Types of Service-Learning and Applications to Teaching Environmental Literacy

There are multiple ways to categorize service-learning. For the purpose of this text we divide service-learning into two categories: direct service-learning and project-based service-learning. In direct-service learning, students essentially act as volunteers by providing service at a site over the course of the semester. From the perspective of the agencies where students might be placed, these students may appear similar to volunteers by working hours that allow the agencies to provide their services. But for the students, this service is an academic experience, intentionally and directly tied to the academic content of their course. Students take their experience back to the classroom as a companion text for the course—the text of real life experience. As a result of this reflection, students make connections between what they are experiencing and observing on-site and what they are learning in class.

There are many disciplines for which this is an appropriate model, and many courses at Indiana University already make use of this approach. For instance, a geography course that tackles the topic of sustainability includes a service-learning component where students work with university operations on data collection that will support campus sustainability efforts. Or, in a cross-listed biology/folklore ethnomusicology course on culture and the environment, students look at Jamaica as a case study on sustainable farming practices. In this class, during the week of spring break these students travel to Jamaica to work on organic farms. While providing their service, students are connecting readings on culture and biodiversity to what they are experiencing and observing first-hand. A number of recreational courses offered through the School of Health, Physical Education, and Recreation have also built in a direct service component. For courses with topics such as rock climbing, backpacking, and coastal kayaking, students learn not only skills but also how environmental recreation needs to incorporate respect and care for the environment. Rejecting a model that represents the environment as open only for exploitation and pleasure, these courses teach students how to protect and maintain the environment by involving a direct service-learning component. Thus, students in a rock climbing course not only climb in the Red River Gorge in Kentucky but also actively work on trail maintenance to minimize the damage left by human traffic. In each case, whether sustainability or environmental issues are an explicit topic of the course, students are engaged and learning about these issues.

Project-based service-learning is similar in theory, but different in practice. In project-based service-learning, students might not even visit the service site, but rather perform a service by creating a product that meets a stated community need. For instance, students in an introductory computer science course design a webpage, databases, and spreadsheets for local environmental organizations with limited resources, time, and technological skills to do so on their own. Students in marketing courses have also worked with various local agencies on the question of how to raise their visibility, increase student volunteers, or boost their donor base. In one case, a class studied social marketing in part by working with the residence halls to increase the popularity and desirability of recycling. And in a related effort, students in an anthropology class focused on qualitative research methods collected and analyzed data that assisted the residence halls in understanding barriers and successes of student recycling. While students may never actually work at the community partner site, students are practicing and demonstrating acquisition of skills and knowledge by creating a needed product. As with direct service, reciprocity and reflection are thoroughly integrated. It is perhaps worthy of note that none of the courses described above has environmental literacy or sustainability education as expressly stated academic course goals; however, having students work with community partners that do have this as a focus can facilitate environmental and sustainability awareness in students.

It is important to note that direct and project-based service-learning are not mutually exclusive. In many project-based service-learning courses, instructors have found that in order to create a product that truly meets the needs of that agency, students benefit from spending time working at that agency as well. For example, an event planning course in the School of Health, Physical Education, and Recreation has students not only plan and execute an event, but also provide some direct service so that they more fully understand the agency and the context in which the event is to occur. In this case, a group of students who provided direct service to the Sycamore Land Trust early in the semester planned an educational field visit for fourth graders at a local elementary school later in the semester.

Service-Learning Challenges, Logistics, and Opportunities

Before jumping headlong into service-learning, it may be wise to sound a note of caution here. Without doubt, there are numerous practical considerations of which faculty and community agencies should be aware when creating either direct service or project-based service-learning opportunities for students. For faculty, it is useful for courses intending to incorporate service-learning to address issues with broad social implications, employ disciplinary theories and concepts that can be clarified or further understood by application to practical situations, and emphasize attitudes and skills relevant to civic engagement. Moreover, faculty should bear in mind that teaching a service-learning course requires additional time to plan, meet with community partner agencies, work out logistics, orient students toward service and the agency, and structure regular reflection and evaluation. It is useful too, for faculty to be aware that some community agencies can accommodate more students with service hours than others and that some agencies may be overwhelmed with placement requests from students. For community partner agencies, it is important to clarify with faculty the maximum number of students the agency can supervise, the number of hours students will be expected to serve, who will provide orientation and training to the students, and whether the community partner will be asked to record attendance and evaluate individual students' performance at the agency, among other things.

The mutual understanding and reciprocity that is a hallmark of successful service-learning can be accomplished most easily through open and regular communication between faculty and the community partner agency. One useful approach toward that end is for faculty and community partners to spell out deliverables, responsibilities, and communication in the form of a contract among stakeholders. At its best, such a document provides faculty the opportunity to clearly articulate the learning objectives for the course to ensure its academic focus and rigor, while likewise providing the community partner with an opportunity to articulate the assets and needs of the agency and how the course may best draw upon those assets to fulfill that need. It is essential that everyone involved in planning the course work closely together, because the service-learning is neither an avenue for students to perform unreflective service nor a project driven entirely by the faculty's view on how to better conditions in the community. One especially encouraging example of open communication, mutual benefit, and reciprocity at work through service-learning at Indiana University was through an environmental education course in the School of Health, Physical Education and Recreation. In this course, undergraduate students worked with children at several local social service agencies to create on-site wildlife habitats that provide native and migrating species with the habitat they need to survive. Service-learning in this course was especially viable as its objectives paralleled those of the Wild City Initiative, a project of a local environmental organization, to certify the city as a Wildlife Habitat through the National Wildlife Federation.

Like the Wild City Initiative, which is an ongoing project in the local community, the scope of some service-learning projects may exceed the confines of one academic semester and continue on for several semesters, even years. These projects require multiple stages to be truly beneficial for an agency, and while challenging, offer the possibility for genuine continuity. Naturally, as a project evolves over time, it presents an ongoing opportunity for faculty members to change and modify their syllabus accordingly. For instance, one semester a public policy course could investigate the scope of an environmental problem such as student overuse of individual cars. The following semester, students taking the same course could add to the data gathered by researching approaches other cities have used for similar problems. Another semester, students in the same course could take the research of previous students to lobby local elected officials. As the course continues to evolve each time it is offered, students in subsequent semesters could assist the city with implementation and evaluation of the new plan. Rather than a hurdle to be overcome, such a multi-tiered service-learning project offers students a means of building on the work of their peers to make a sustainable contribution to the community and gives the students the understanding that environmental literacy encompasses a broad range of choices for engagement.

Another opportunity ripe for service-learning that could take place over multiple semesters and potentially spread to multiple sites through the community arises through campus-wide initiatives geared toward environmental sustainability. Any greening that occurs at the university can have a tremendous impact on the community in which it resides, as well, delivering a powerful message to the surrounding community as to its choice, use, allocation, and disposal of resources, its modes of transportation, and its purchasing ethic. Similarly, some successful service-learning projects begun on campus can be replicated at a variety of community sites. For example, an Indiana University religious studies course has explored environmental ethics through organic gardening and composting at a specific dormitory. This project has sustainability through continued gardening and composting at the site, as well as the possibility of expanding to other dormitories, the student union, and off-campus housing. Conversely, one site can be the location for multiple service-learning projects. Transforming a college union into a green building could encompass a broad range of classes studying and assisting in this transformation from a variety of angles across disciplines. Business students could explore the costs and benefits of incorporating local, organic food into union food services, students in public affairs or engineering courses could analyze graywater disposal systems, and physics students could conduct an energy analysis for installation of a solar photovoltaic roofing system.

While service-learning as a methodological approach is a valuable and immediate means through which students gain proficiency in the practice of applied health science, anthropology, finance, graphic design, environmental studies, and a panoply of other fields of inquiry, it often leads students beyond service to a mode of advocacy. Students in service-learning classes are frequently surprised by their sense of agency, that their youth and their incipient knowledge base have a value beyond the lecture hall and the exam grade. When they perceive themselves as efficacious, as resourcefully meeting a real community need or addressing a problem that lies beyond the pale of their meal cards and weekend plans, they gain a perspective and a *raison d'être* that bestows a new legitimacy on the knowledge they are busy acquiring. The field of environmental service-learning, with its place-based, problem-solving opportunity for multi-textual literacy, offers both the university and the community a powerful invitation to meaningful, satisfying, and ultimately long-term learning.

References

Bringle, R. G., and Julie A. Hatcher. (1997). "Reflection." *College Teaching* 45(4): 153.

Furco, A. 1996. "Service-learning: A Balanced Approach to Experiential Learning." In Corporation for National Service, ed., *Expanding Boundaries: Serving and Learning* 2–6. Columbia, Md.: Cooperative Education Association.

Honnet, E. P., and S. J. Poulsen. 1989. "Principles of Good Practice for Combining Service and Learning." In the Johnson Foundation Wingspread Conference. At http://service learning.org/filemanager/download/Principles_of_Good_Practice_for_Combin ing_Service_and_Learning.pdf. (accessed 27 April 2009).

Matthew R. Auer
*Public and Environmental Affairs
and Hutton Honors College*

The expressions "five senses" and "sense of place" share a common noun and a comparable purpose in environmental studies. Both have to do with orientation, and both are about connecting people to proximate spaces and places. But sense of place, unlike physical, organ-mediated sensory perception, has normative dimensions (Feld and Basso 1997). Conscience, no less than cognition, is inherent in the sensing of place; we can literally feel things in physical spaces, but particular physical spaces also evince particular feelings. The two together—the physical senses and subjective sensibilities—can provide students with a more indelible learning experience than either type of "sense" can afford on its own. In this chapter, we consider a field exercise that animates and integrates both the physical senses and the sense of place.

Lessons from a Woodlot

At many colleges and universities, campus environs offer suitable laboratories to test the five senses approach to environmental awareness and to inculcate students' sense of place. By the five senses approach, we mean the strategy of using all five traditional, physical senses to help discover and understand the world around us.

Consider wooded areas, including "pocket" woodlots that are too small to constitute forests but large enough to support different layers of vegetation (herbs, shrubs, understory, and canopy trees), animals, and other living and nonliving matter. These sites are ideal for promoting environmental literacy through the physical senses and through contemplation. It helps for the instructor to provide a bit of local history so as to portray a dynamic landscape, over time. Sense of place at this site is mutable, depending on who lived there, when, doing what. Instructors should not give away the whole story, however. A key learning objective is to encourage students to discover, on their own, how the site may have been used in the recent and much more distant past. Below, we also consider how students might go about conceptualizing the site's future.

A variety of natural resource markers, as well as remnants of human activities, provide students with ample hints about site history. These (primarily) biotic hints about the past can be detected through all of the physical senses. For the purpose of doing plant identification or vegetation measurement, it would be enough to measure the trees' diameters at breast height and toggle between different field guides to inventory the shrub and herb layers. Among the five traditional, physical senses, this approach leans most heavily on sight, and to some extent, touch, as the students steady their calipers or rulers against the tree stems.

But we can draw in the other senses, too. Manicured lawns that border many wooded areas are cornucopias of edible herbs. When properly washed, ground ivy (*Glechoma hederacea*) and wood sorrel (*Oxalis corniculata*) are nutritious and good tasting accompaniments to any salad, for example. The peppery tasting red clover (*Trifolium pratense*) is a key nitrogen-fixer in our fields and farms. It provides a good illustration of synergies between the natural economy and the market economy. Clover seed is deliberately mixed in with grass seed when pastureland is sown.

English ivy (*Hedera helix*) and euonymus (*Euonymus fortunei*) are typical groundcovers on many college campuses. They frequently invade campus woodlots, too. These two non-native species can become invasive pests. Their presence in the woods, and the nuisance they cause for other organisms, animate abstract concepts like ecological footprint. English ivy illustrates the ecological tradeoffs that flow from seemingly benign landscaping decisions.

Sights, textures, and tastes are part of the experience. But so is sound. The nasal "yank yank" call of the white-breasted nuthatch (*Sitta carolinensis*) is unmistakable and allows for positive identification even if visual confirmation is not possible. It is a means to tackle the topic of mutualism among birds, since nuthatches often flock with black-capped chickadees (*Parus atricapillus*) and tufted titmice (*Parus bicolor*). One theory has it that, by traveling as a flock, each bird is at less risk of predation. But the different species do not compete intensely for the same food sources. Sometimes these birds zone in on nearby seed feeders, which summons a comment about mutualism between birds and people. It is also a reminder that not all people–bird relationships are mutualistic. Some non-native birds, like the European starling (*Sturnus vulgaris*) and house sparrow (*Passer domesticus*), were introduced to North America, but are frequently considered pests in urban and suburban settings.

There are likely to be other pests in or near the woodlot, particularly if the site is bordered by pavement or other "human-introduced" features. Students should be on the lookout for ailanthus (Tree of Heaven, *Ailanthus altissima*). Olfactory senses are conduits for learning when students crumble the ailanthus leaf and take quick whiffs of this peanutty-smelling plant from Asia. On the back of each leaf are glands with translucent sap—the source of the peanutty odor. This sensory moment is a perfect entrée for the story of how ailanthus came to America. Ailanthus was a would-be food source for silkworms, but ultimately a failed experiment (the worms did not chew so much as eschew the plant). It is a fitting vignette for a field trip dealing with interactions between people and the environment. It is also a memorable experience, thanks in no small part to the memory-fixing properties of smell. Students are unlikely to misidentify the "peanutty-smelling" tree species in an essay or quiz.

Ailanthus is charismatic, but like many other species mentioned in this chapter, it is a headache for natural resource managers. Not only is it ubiquitous in and around urban playgrounds and parking lots, it also aggressively competes with native woodland trees for space, sunlight, nutrients, and water (Cronk and Fuller 1995). Ailanthus, an interesting tree that is easy to sense by our noses, nevertheless does not make sense for American forests. This is a normative statement, loaded with values and preferences that must be unpacked. In the unpacking are lessons about large ecological footprints (e.g., measured by sheer surface area covered by ailanthus) and sustainability (e.g., ecological costs, including impacts on biodiversity and forest stand dynamics; economic costs for controlling the problem; and social costs as valuable forest functions are degraded).

The ailanthus example reminds us that field sites for testing the five senses need not possess great physical beauty. Indeed, ecosystems exhibiting a strong human imprint are perfect settings for the five senses approach and for inculcating a sense of place. The visual cortex is especially important in the following example: Consider a faded candy wrapper near a weathered limestone bench in the woods. Coatings and ink in the wrapper have decomposed, but to what effect for the soil and vegetation nearby? This single candy wrapper is part of the ecological footprint of some "end user"—perhaps a student, staff, or instructor passing time at the bench weeks or months earlier. Students might consider the impact of that user's behavior in a variety of ways, with attention to scale and biophysical consequences, and effects on the values and sensibilities of other users of the woodlot. The biophysical impacts are limited in scope and scale. The immediate, physical effects may be confined to a few cubic inches of soil, and nonbiodegradable materials in the wrapper may have little or no long-term negative impacts on biota or on nonliving substances in the soil.

However, the normative impacts may be more pronounced. The candy-eater has enjoyed a private benefit (by eating the candy) and imposed a social cost (by tossing the wrapper in the woods) without incurring a private cost. Here is an opportunity to relate ecological footprint to the concept of economic externality. Future users of the woodlot, particularly those seeking to get away from the built-up and human-dominated areas nearby, have an impaired experience, thanks to the candy wrapper (and whoever littered). Even a vague (but unpleasant) memory of seeing that wrapper might inspire a visitor to stop visiting. Future picnickers, on noticing the wrapper, might leave their own litter there, deeming the woodlot's aesthetics already impaired.

Eventually, if the litter trend continues, the woodlot could suffer from a de facto tragedy of the commons. In classic illustrations of this concept, ownership rights are unclear or nonexistent and the resource (e.g., common pasture, fishery, or clean air) is easily accessed and exploited, leading to resource overconsumption and decline (Hardin 1968). In the woodlot context, the university is the owner. But because this space is spoiled by litter and is poorly maintained, future visitors begin to identify it as a waste place and someone else's management problem.

The candy wrapper illustration also brings into focus a larger, societal ecological footprint. Suppose the user is terribly fond of that particular brand of candy. Would it be possible to buy an unwrapped version in bulk, thereby reducing packaging waste? What are the main ingredients in the candy? High fructose corn syrup might top the list. Students might contemplate human–environment interactions, dietary and environmental feedback loops, and even politics. The U.S. fondness for sweets and the political power of manufacturers of sweeteners shape agricultural policies that favor (by subsidization) the industrial-scale production of corn over other foods (Pollan 2007). In fact, most corn grown in the United States is not so much a food itself as an input for other things people consume, such as sweeteners, beef, or decidedly non-food products like ethanol. Each of these commodities has an ecological footprint with measurable dimensions. For example, according to the U.S. Department of Agriculture, seven pounds of corn converts to about one pound of retail beef (Leibtag 2008: 14). Scientists have estimated that around 1,100 gallons of water are consumed in the production of every pound of corn (Pimental et al. 2004). Students might be encouraged to estimate how much water goes into the production of a pound of corn-fed beef. Outputs from conventional corn production include wastewater and residues from inorganic fertilizers and pesticides. Production of corn for ethanol, meanwhile, offers lessons on the second law of thermodynamics. Studies find that more fossil fuel energy goes into the production of corn-based ethanol than is available from ethanol's caloric value (Patzek 2004). All of these potential lessons —and more—can be catalyzed from a single, forlorn candy wrapper found in the woods.

Carrying out and Learning from the Exercise

It is important to plan ahead before any of the specimens from the woodlot can be studied, whether they are the ones that can be heard, touched, smelled and tasted, or, like the candy wrapper, observed and reflected upon. In a large lecture-type course, it may be necessary to divide students into smaller, more manageable groups. A maximum of thirty-five or forty students in the field works for instructors lacking a stentorian voice. Besides, any more field trippers will tend to trample the very sights intended for viewing, tasting, etc. The need to subdivide a large class requires either that the instructor conduct multiple trips with subsets of the class, or that teaching assistants and the instructor lead students during the same class session, but along different routes.

Learning opportunities should extend beyond the confines of this sixty- or ninety-minute field trip. Sensory perception can be fleeting, and in any case, the point here is to use the senses to stimulate other kinds of learning pathways. Otherwise, some students will learn disparate facts from the visit to the woodlot without making connections to larger patterns and processes. Names of plants and the phonics of particular bird calls may come easily to some students, but a genuine appreciation of ecological disturbance may not. Some students are "surface learners" who have trouble mastering "deep learning" (Marton and Säljö 1997).

Surface learners absorb and store bits of information, like names, places, and dates, and often rely on strict memorization and verbal constructions (such as mnemonics) to bank that knowledge. Sometimes surface learning occurs with the learner failing to make connections to broader concepts. Moreover, the classic scientific method—an abstract concept—may not take root unless the field trip becomes something more than a collection of sensory encounters. Inculcating the scientific method (and remedies for surface learning) includes having students follow up each observation in the field with reflection. Specifically, students are asked to summon and weigh alternative explanations for observed phenomena.

Testing facts against theories is a decidedly rational undertaking. It makes a suitable complement to the five senses approach, which, by itself, does not necessarily involve higher reasoning. In the field, deep learning occurs when students are inclined to ask, after each encounter with nature, "How did this state of nature come to be?" and "On what basis can I rule out other explanations for what I am observing?" An otherwise surface-prone learner will begin to systematically read the landscape as intended—identifying, for example, not just the distinguishing features and age of a row of sugar maple trees, but also the deliberate design of a farmer who planted or pruned those trees to mark a boundary between two properties. The latter illustrates affective learning. Students search for clues of past habitation (sense of history and place) and discover the intentions (values) of people who transformed the landscape.

Deep learning can be reinforced explicitly by having students jot their alternative explanations and tests of reasoning in a field notebook. Back in the classroom, field observations can be examined against theories of ecological disturbance and vegetative succession. It is also an opportunity to relate field data to the core course concern of drawing feedback loops between people and the environment. Scientific principles can be introduced or reinforced even if the first field observations did not rely on classic scientific methods. So while students remember ailanthus for its distinctive odor, their second encounter can inquire of that plant's preferred habitat or its impacts in wooded and urban settings.

Ailanthus's impacts are both ecological and socioeconomic, and when students consider the latter, they are recognizing, comparing, and contrasting normative (affective) aspects of nature and of nature's transformation. Ailanthus was a would-be feedstock for the silk industry, and hence the plant is associated with the value of wealth. It is also an ecological pest that crowds out native vegetation, has little food value, and is costly to eradicate. Identifying values in nature and from nature can be easily accomplished before the field trip, by encouraging students to contemplate values, explicitly. Instructors might consider Harold D. Lasswell's list of eight value terms, namely power, enlightenment, wealth, well-being, skill, affection, respect, and rectitude, which can be used to "classify the nearly infinite number of preferred outcomes" (1971: 18). Depending on the context, one can employ some or all of these terms to characterize peoples' interactions with and transformations of nature.

Sensory perception and the sensing of place, in the company of core content-based goals (concepts such as ecological footprint), skills (the scientific method), and values (enduring preferences for environmental quality), are the main substrates for learning in the field trip exercise described above. The content-based and science-oriented parts are conventional, whereas the five senses approach is somewhat unorthodox. However, we use the latter not strictly for the sake of being inventive. It is included based on students' apparent zeal for the approach and on their high post hoc performance on essays and exams, and because it reinforces knowledge gained using the conventional approaches. At a broader level, the five senses schema helps students read the landscape and unravel the mysteries of people/environment relationships in particular places. May Theilgaard Watts writes (1999: ix), "As we read what is written on the land, finding accounts of the past, predictions of the future, and comments on the present, we discover that there are many interwoven strands to each story, offering several possible interpretations." The five senses/sense of place exercise hones these interpretative skills, relying on a combination of science and perception, sleuthing and sensing.

The exercise also makes students cognizant of the environment's mutability and how alteration of the physical environment transforms how people perceive it. Even seemingly minor ecological disturbances can change the sense of place, quickly. The candy wrapper altered what had been a quiet, wooded get-away into an extension of a busy, human-dominated campus. If the wrapper induces a snowball effect of additional litter, a visitor to the woodlot may surmise, "People have been here" instead of "I can get away from people here." Yet the solitude and soothing qualities of the woodlot can be restored—and virtually any conscientious visitor can make that happen—by picking up the litter and carting it away.

Such revival would be unattainable were the woodlot razed to erect a new building. Sense of place would be irrevocably changed—or would it? Today, many campuses have adopted master plans calling for, among other features, "green buildings" that incorporate biological principles within built-up spaces. Suppose, for example, that the woodlot were transformed into a richly vegetated arboretum inside an environmentally friendly building. No doubt, the sense of place would change; the five senses would not mistake the place for an outdoor woodlot. But perhaps the quality of "getting away" would remain intact, as would the sense that this place, whether woodlot or indoor garden, is "naturalistic" if not genuinely natural.

To take advantage of these learning opportunities, students must use their imaginations, and it helps when the instructor is explicit about this obligation. Good, learning-inducing questions are helpful, too. Consider asking these: 1) Of the species encountered in the woodlot, which are memorable and by way of which senses? 2) Specifically, which features of this place remind us that it is not "pristine"—untouched by people? 3) Consider articles of litter in the woodlot and the products they represented before they became litter. Map the ecological footprints of the manufacturers of the pre-litter products and of their end users (the "final consumers"). 4) Imagine this particular place a hundred years from now. What will it look, sound, feel, smell, and taste like? 5) In this space, how will the sense of place change, and how might one go about preserving features of the current space that appeal to the senses?

References

Cronk, Q. B., and Fuller, J. L. 1995. *Plant Invaders: The Threat to Natural Ecosystems.* London: Chapman and Hall.

Feld, S. F, and Basso, K., eds. 1997. *Senses of Place.* Santa Fe: School of American Research Press.

Hardin, G. 1968. "The Tragedy of the Commons." *Science* 162: 1243–1248.

Lasswell, H. D. 1971. *A Pre-View of Policy Sciences.* New York: American Elsevier.

Leibtag, E. 2008. "Corn Prices Near Record High, but What about Food Costs?" *Amber Waves: The Economics of Food, Farming, Natural Resources, and Rural America,* 6(1): 10–15

Marton, F., and R. Säljö. 1997. "Approaches to Learning." In *The Experience of Learning.* Ed. F. Marton, D. Hounsell, and N. Entwistle. Edinburgh: Scottish Academic Press.

Patzek, T. W. 2004. "Thermodynamics of the Corn-Ethanol Biofuel Cycle." *Critical Reviews in Plant Sciences* 23(6): 519–567.

Pimentel, D., B. Berger, D. Filiberto, M. Newton, B. Wolfe, E. Karabinakis, S. Clark, E. Poon, E. Abbett, and S. Nandagopal. 2004. *Water Resources, Agriculture and the Environment.* Report 04-1 (July). eCommons Library of Cornell University. At http://ccommons.library.cornell.edu/bitstream/1813/352/1/pimentel_report_04-1.pdf (accessed 3 April 2009).

Pollan, M. 2007. "Weed It and Reap," *New York Times,* November 4.

Watts, M. T. 1999. *Reading the Landscape of America.* Rochester, N.Y.: Nature Study Guild Publishers.

Keith Clay
Biology

> I went to the woods because I wanted to live deliberately, to front only the essential facts of life, and see if I could not learn what it has to teach. . .
>
> —HENRY DAVID THOREAU, *Walden: or Life in the Woods, 1854*

In this chapter, I emphasize the importance of natural areas as a powerful context for teaching and learning environmental literacy. Natural environments can provide memorable, visceral learning experiences that enhance understanding and retention of content and foster affective learning goals such as the development of a sense of place. While there are many challenges to integrating natural areas into a curriculum for environmental literacy, such as proximity and accessibility, the benefits of learning in a natural environment are worth the effort.

Teaching Efficacy

Natural areas provide an effective format for teaching key environmental concepts and principles. Scientific concepts can be very abstract to students who have no personal experience or connection to the subject matter. Classes in ecology, organismal diversity, and taxonomy, for example, stress the incredible biodiversity of tropical rain forests and coral reefs. But traditional classroom lecture techniques such as PowerPoint presentations of organisms and habitats pale in comparison to the experience of being there in person. As a university faculty member I have taught field courses in several regions of the United States as well as in Central America and the Caribbean. These experiences emphasize that seeing for the first time a monkey foraging in the tropical forest canopy or a shark swimming above them during a reef dive has more of an impact on students than the most carefully crafted lecture or energetic teaching performance. Indeed, I am still blown away by the incredible diversity of sponges on my first and only wall dive in the Cayman Islands, but am hard-pressed to remember a single lecture from my undergraduate and graduate school experiences.

Our biology department conducts an exit survey of all graduating majors, and one of the most common comments is that they wished they had the opportunity to take more of the "ology" courses: ornithology, herpetology, entomology, ichthyology, ecology, etc. For most people, their interest in biology comes from seeing organisms in their natural environment. Seeing a flock of sandhill cranes fly over, or a carpet of wildflowers in the spring, is more real than any lecture in a cavernous classroom. I know that I am a better teacher, and my students are better students, outdoors in the real world rather than in a classroom.

Many institutions of higher education have dedicated natural areas, or are close enough to other natural areas to make them accessible for teaching. Urban universities and colleges can access city parks or less developed parts of campus. Even abandoned lots and brownfields exhibit biodiversity and ecological interactions of educational value, while they simultaneously illustrate human impact on ecosystems. At Indiana University a system of preserves was recently established to provide an outdoor classroom and living laboratory for the environmental sciences. While a forest preserve in the Midwest is hardly a tropical rainforest, it offers its own distinctive beauty, such as the profusion of wildflowers in the spring and the dazzling colors of deciduous trees in autumn. And much of the pre-European fauna still exists or is making a comeback. The woods are full of wild turkeys, bald eagles are not difficult to spot, and timber rattlesnakes are starting to reappear. These observations provide entry to basic concepts of environmental literacy such as ecosystem services and sustainability.

Ecosystem Services

What are the important concepts and perspectives that students can learn from a simple walk in the woods? There are many. Perhaps first and foremost is the critical notion that we are part of nature and our existence is completely dependent on natural processes. For people whose lives exist largely inside buildings and automobiles, it is easy to become complacent and presume that clean water comes from a faucet, food comes from boxes on the supermarket shelf, and that local climate is determined by setting the thermostat. The notion that we are dependent on a myriad of ecosystem services is easier to appreciate in the woods, away from the trappings of our modern society. A babbling brook originating in a forested watershed provides a powerful contrast to the ditch draining the local mall's parking lot, and the biodiversity of the forest is far greater than that of human-dominated landscapes.

An important related concept is the interconnectedness of life. Trees release oxygen to the atmosphere, their leaves are fed upon by insects, and their seeds are dispersed by birds or mammals, which in turn feed on the insects. And everything eventually dies and decomposes, sustaining the soil that supports the forest. Birth, death, cooperation, and conflict are all readily evident in nature. A dead tree standing in the forest represents a beginning as well as an end.

An additional environmental concept is that there are many ways to make a living in this world, i.e., there are many ecological niches for organisms. There are autotrophs (green plants) that just need sunlight, soil nutrients, and water, heterotrophic predators that hunt and kill to survive, parasites and pathogens that exploit a living host for their nutrition, and decomposers that feed on anything dead that drops into their laps. These life form types are superimposed upon a matrix of physical habitat types: aquatic vs. terrestrial, forest vs. field, above-ground vs. below-ground. All of this generates and sustains diversity, and that may be the most important lesson that comes from our walk in the woods. Even students who are outdoor-oriented and have a good handle on the local flora and fauna can come away with a new understanding and appreciation of the small, hidden organisms that play critical roles in our ecosystem. The whole ecosystem is greater than the sum of its parts.

Affective Learning Goals

The direct contact with natural environments and reflection about their functioning lead directly and inevitably to a critical examination of human values and principles related to environmental literacy. Even though our nature preserve is by definition relatively undisturbed, the evidence of human influence is everywhere. Very few trees there are older than eighty years, emphasizing that basically all of the Midwest was once deforested. In areas where the trees have grown back, is the forest the same as it once was? For example, no large predators such as wolves or cougars remain—they were all hunted out. As a result, deer populations are uncontrolled and are having a detrimental effect on native plant biodiversity. Should humans step in (again) and attempt to address this ecological imbalance by reducing deer populations through hunting, contraception, or reintroduction of large predators? These types of considerations raise the Orwellian question of whether all animals are created equal or whether some are more equal than others. Many humans choose not to eat meat, but many animal species persist only by killing other animals and eating them. Are predators of lesser value? Or could they be playing a key role in ecosystems by preventing plant-eating animals from becoming too abundant and threatening ecosystem sustainability?

Past and present disturbances, and our fondness for the showy and exotic, have resulted in the invasion of many natural areas by an ever-growing list of aggressive exotic species, such as garlic mustard, autumn olive, purple loosestrife, gypsy moth, zebra mussel, and West Nile virus. What are the consequences of these species, and should we care? After all, humans are the ultimate invasive species, and other invaders are just following in our footsteps. As with predators, are native species inherently more valuable than invaders? And if so, where do we fit in along with our domestic livestock, garden plants, and pets?

Natural areas have been and still are used for waste disposal. Likewise our rivers, lakes, and oceans are major waste repositories. In southern Indiana the many deep ravines and sinkholes have long provided easy and free dumping grounds. Our preserve has several such ravines full of broken glass, rusty appliances, junked cars, and old tires. While the flotsam and jetsam of human existence is more easily seen in the abandoned lots of the inner city, it is all too common in natural areas as well. The capacity of natural systems to absorb our waste is limited and possibly already exceeded. All of these examples go to the larger issue of environmental stewardship. What kind of world, and woods, are we going to leave for future generations? The poet W. H. Auden suggested that "A culture is no better than its woods."

Another important contribution of natural areas and dedicated preserves is to instill a sense of place in students. Charles Darwin wrote, "A traveler should be a botanist, for in all views plants form the chief embellishment." The heavily wooded hills and valleys of southern Indiana create a tangible sense of place for Indiana University that is every bit as important as the built campus or the local college strip. When alumni and visitors come to campus, many think of the local woods and natural areas. Likewise, students at University of California–Santa Cruz are nestled in a redwood forest, the Louisiana State University campus is populated with live oak trees draped with *Polypodium* ferns and almost all Flor-

ida State University students at one time or another have gone swimming in
Wakulla Springs, the largest freshwater spring in the United States. My local
environment is characterized by the painted sedge (*Carex picta*), a woodland
plant that blankets the forest understory. It is an extraordinarily abundant species, but surprisingly its range is largely limited to the hills of southern Indiana.
Returning from a trip, I know I am getting close to home when I begin to see the
painted sedge growing on the hillsides. It defines my environment more than any
highway, building, or shopping center, which reflect business calculations replicated in thousands of locations. Understanding where a particular species grows,
why it grows there, and why it does not grow elsewhere can teach us a lot
about our own environment. Nature is continually telling us that there are some
environments—the southeastern coastal areas or the California chaparral, for
example—where maybe we should not live or at least not build permanent
structures, despite our formidable technology and engineering capabilities.

Dedicated University Preserves

All educational institutions have libraries that represent repositories of human
knowledge and accomplishment. Likewise, music departments have pianos and
astronomy departments have telescopes requisite to their educational mission.
Should not natural environments also be an essential part of environmental
literacy? I would argue that dedicated natural environments are as essential to
environmental literacy as books, and that environmental education is incomplete without meaningful exposure to natural systems subject to minimal human
influence.

In the particular case of Indiana University, the largest forested region in the
lower Midwest is literally at our doorstep. Within a twenty-minute drive are a
national forest, two state forests, the largest park in the state, as well as an
extensive municipal nature preserve. These and other lands have been central to
Indiana University's history of research and teaching in the natural sciences. For
example, zoologist Carl Eigenmann conducted pioneering studies of blind cave
fish in a nearby state park, and Alfred Kinsey, before his transformation into a
researcher in human sexuality, studied hybrid toad populations in a natural area
just north of campus. Despite this history and wealth of publicly owned natural
areas, the university established its own dedicated natural areas for teaching and
research.

University-owned natural areas are not unusual and in fact may be the normal
state of affairs. However, I am hard pressed to point to any database or statistical
summary on what proportion of institutions of higher education own and man-
age natural areas. I suspect it is the majority, but it would be a useful research
endeavor to gather these numbers. Many cities evaluate adequacy of parkland

and other greenspace on a per capita basis. A goal might be for every institution of higher education to have natural areas equivalent to one acre per ten students. Alternatively, each institution should strive to establish dedicated natural areas of at least the same size as the extant campus. Separate from their educational value, these natural areas would help to offset the environmental impacts of the main campus.

A tenth of an acre per student might be a pie-in-the sky goal given the financial pressures most institutions face. Purchase of natural areas is likely to be low on the hierarchy compared to a new research building or a bigger football stadium. Likewise, geographical considerations suggest this goal might be more difficult to reach in some areas than others. Urban campuses in high-priced cities are in a very different position than land-grant universities in rural locations. The best situation entails institutions having the foresight to obtain and dedicate their own natural areas for posterity. For institutions not so fortunate, partnerships with local parks, state and national forests, land trusts, and the like may suffice.

The overriding goal for these natural areas is to serve the teaching and research missions of the university. Natural areas not under the control of the university may serve different goals and uses at odds with an educational mission. The university does not depend on the city or county to provide its library and should not depend on the city or county to provide its outdoor laboratories either.

Logistical Challenges

There are certain logistical and management issues unique to dedicated preserves and natural areas that are not generally problems for more traditional learning environments. First and foremost is getting the word out to faculty and students about the preserve and encouraging their use of it for teaching and research. In the case of a well-known and centrally located facility, such as Curtis Prairie within the University of Wisconsin–Madison Arboretum, awareness is very high and little advertising is required. However, the Indiana University Research and Teaching Preserve is much younger, and probably most people on campus are only vaguely aware of it. In addition to an informative and attractive website, such events as open houses, guided hikes, natural history programs, availability of scientific experts, media coverage, and direct solicitations all represent mechanisms for informing faculty and inspiring their enthusiasm. For students, participation in field classes, service projects and other volunteer activities, recreational activities, employment opportunities, and word-of-mouth all help to raise awareness and interest. This all takes time, but eventually a university preserve becomes as essential a part of campus as the library or performing arts center. Many preserves also have a lab or multiuse classroom facility where people can gather, out of the rain or cold, for lectures, labs, seminars, or natural history presentations. This type of built facility combined with the surrounding natural environment opens up the possibility for use well beyond the natural sciences. Classes in the arts, journalism, law, psychology, economics, history, and literature, to name a few, can all benefit from using a preserve's facilities and natural history expertise to provide learning experiences that deepen understanding of disciplinary content while enhancing environmental literacy of students in the broadest sense. The preserve could also serve as a forum for partnering diverse courses, one from history and one from ecology, for example. By explicitly engaging students in the social, economic, and ecological dimensions of a preserve—for example, its cultural, political, and land-use history as well as its geological, ecological, and evolutionary history—such interdisciplinary collaborations have great potential for promoting student environmental literacy, including an enriched sense of place and a multifaceted understanding of ecosystem services and ecological footprint.

One more pragmatic issue concerns transportation to and from campus. This is costly both in terms of money and class time. Many campuses have preserves that are within easy biking or walking distance. However, more remote sites also have their benefits by being far from the hustle and bustle of campus life and by providing long-term housing and dining opportunities, which create a sense of camaraderie and common purpose among students. The ratio of travel time to on-site time is minimized with multi-day trips, but overnight trips also provide challenges for students with families, jobs, or other responsibilities. Another important issue is accessibility to disabled students. By definition, natural areas are undeveloped, or lightly developed. Creative strategies are required to make natural areas a resource for all. A third issue is the potential conflict between the intended purpose of the preserve and casual recreational use by students and non-students. Should a preserve be fenced in with a locked gate or open to local hikers and nature lovers? A proliferation of unleashed dogs, vandalism, or environmental degradation suggests that access by the general public might need to be limited. Finally, university preserves and natural areas often fall under the auspices of different administrative units with different missions than traditional classroom education. For example, the actual land of a natural area might fall under the physical plant department, while its educational uses may fall under an academic dean. At best, networking across a range of offices and divisions may be necessary. At worst, a preserve becomes a political football in larger conflicts and bureaucratic infighting.

Separate from its other educational values, a nature preserve is a gift for the future. It sets aside a bit of our primeval landscape when most of the rest is being gobbled up by human progress. In a hundred years, natural preserves will be far more valuable, and valued, than they are today. This contrasts with the built environment of the campus that requires constant upkeep and renovation. A preserve will increase in quality without upkeep as the forest grows older and is protected from disturbance. We can only hope that it will remain a living laboratory and not become a museum. Lyndon Johnson captured this idea well. "If future generations are to remember us with gratitude rather than contempt, we must leave them more than the miracles of technology. We must leave them with a glimpse of the world as it was in the beginning, not just after we got through with it." The bottom line is that fostering environmental literacy will be more effective when students can study natural processes and human–environment interactions in real environments. Dedicated natural areas associated with educational institutions help to ensure those opportunities.

Vicky J. Meretsky
Public and Environmental Affairs

Most of the environment is outdoors. It isn't surprising, then, that many of our best opportunities for teaching about environmental issues are out there, too. Outdoor learning is more than just an excuse to escape the tyranny of four walls and little desks. The outdoors is both an obvious classroom for environmentally related topics and a uniquely rewarding one. As earlier chapters in this volume by Sanders, Auer, Clay, and Vogelsang and Baack all attest, lessons learned outdoors can be powerful, vivid, and long-lasting. Landscapes show us our species' own impacts on lands and waters and allow us to compare the outcomes of different actions and practices. While teaching us about the land, outdoor learning also teaches us about ourselves, and about the impacts of the ethical choices we make in our lives.

Virtues of the Outdoor Classroom

The outdoors is an obvious classroom, but I will not immediately dismiss the obvious. Outside, everyone becomes an explorer: everyone has a chance to see a new bird, hear a chorus of would-be-mating frogs, feel the soft spongy moistness of a well-rotted log. As a teacher of ecology and conservation biology, I work hard to help students understand how interconnected the different parts and processes of the world are. In the classroom, students can find this confusing, as they wrench their minds away from the current brainful of information to reach back to what they learned last week, or to reach forward to what we'll discuss next week. In the field, or the forest, or the swamp, the connections are immediate, even intrusive. You cannot look at a tree without seeing the birds that feed and nest in it, without seeing the other trees crowding in around it, without seeing the grapevines that use the tree for support even as they conspire to steal its sunlight. What was difficult to visualize in the classroom is constantly on display outdoors, and students are often able to find the connections for themselves.

In my experience, many of us who teach outdoors seek out the serene and seemingly unspoiled places to be our "classrooms." For many of us, these are the sources of our own renewal, and our desire to share them is a generous, if not entirely selfless, gesture. How better to defend what we love than to ensure it is loved by many, many people, until it is too important to too many to despoil? And what better way to convert the unconvinced than to show them that forests and meadows and mountains are beautiful and moving and mysterious? By sharing such sights with our students in their own towns and counties and states, we give them an opportunity to be proud not only of our national treasures, but also of their own, nearby treasures. As Scott Sanders explains movingly in his chapter, we get a wonderful return on our investment of time and passion by showing students these special places.

Working Landscapes

Indeed, these days, parks are the only part of the outdoors that many people deliberately experience. But most of the world is not a park. Increasingly, we humans are urban creatures. Fewer and fewer of us grow up exploring out of doors, much less working there. The resulting disconnect from the "natural world" can be an important component of environmental problems, and taking people outdoors is an obvious part of the solution, once the electronic distractions have been left behind. But if our goal in promoting environmental literacy is to nurture environmentally informed citizens, then we must take students beyond the delight and discovery and awe of our parks and preserves to the more complex learning opportunities of working landscapes.

Working landscapes—farms, mines, urban and suburban and industrial areas, landfills, commercial ports, dams—are the places to go to see human impacts in action. Too often, the necessary processes of human existence—raising food, constructing roads and buildings, mining metals, producing goods, processing wastes—are unexamined in the context of environmental education. Or if examined, they may be condemned as entirely negative activities that a more enlightened species would avoid entirely. But we must eat. We must have shelter. And no species is without impacts on others. Our task is not to create students who loathe themselves and their needs. Rather, we seek to create students who can distinguish between needs and wants, and who can make choices that will leave as much as possible of our world for our great-grandchildren to worry about and delight in and care for.

Walking in parks and preserves teaches us about the diversity of plant and animal species and about the fascinating interwoven processes that support natural systems. But walking in working landscapes teaches us how we humans affect the land and its ecological webs. We become students of a surprising variety of practices we never considered before. Learning to read landscapes forces us to be inquiring, engaged.

I challenge my students to extend their studies to the trips they take during semester breaks, and to the landscapes they travel going to and from school. No more driving down the highway, zoned out. Now we have to learn to pay attention to the land around us. Why is this field that was in corn last year in soybeans this year (rotation planting to "outwit" corn borer)? Where are they getting all the water to irrigate that alfalfa field outside Tucson (from oversubscribed water sources, of course, but maybe also graywater recycling)?

No more flying from coast to coast glued to the movie. Now we get to find out why, as you go west, you find those odd, perfect circles on the landscape (center-pivot irrigation), or why some lakes have those odd snaky shapes (dammed rivers backing up into canyons and valleys) instead of big wide shapes (glacial scrapes, melted glacial remnants). What are the impacts related to these patterns? Which land-use practices are gentler? Which practices exist because of "perverse incentives," suggesting we need to change some aspect of our economy, of our values?

Walking on a plowed field, seeing the differences (are they good, bad, neutral?) between plowed soil and forest soil, looking at buffer strips that protect the low areas from erosion and improve the water quality of nearby streams—these are ways to make a working landscape real, to see the choices made, the impacts reduced, and the impacts aggravated. Talking to a farmer teaches even more—what does the buffer strip cost in lost potential income? What farm policies encourage soil and water conservation or even wildlife conservation, and what policies make it necessary to plow every available inch in order to remain in business? How do international policies affect our local landscapes?

Even on a field trip to a park or preserve, I use the variety of landscapes along the way to raise these points (walkie-talkies can spread the discussion among vehicles). Once at our destination, we can discuss in more depth the needs and practices that produced both our protected landscape and the working landscapes we traversed. Often we can see memories of working landscapes in the protected landscape, which raise questions about why people were moved to protect the area. Keith Clay, Matt Auer, and Keith Vogelsang and Eric Baack, in their chapters, describe the importance of landscape history in teaching from the landscape.

Working landscapes usually come with working humans, with their own understanding of the landscape and its role. Environmental educators regularly acknowledge and calculate the human costs of obvious mismanagement of the environment—a toxic spill, or a mud slide on a deforested mountainside. But human costs may also result from trying to improve our management of the environment—farmers and ranchers who can no longer profitably farm or graze, miners without new mines to work, lumber mills facing retooling costs for working smaller logs. As we try to embrace a holistic approach to solving environmental problems, we must also be willing to include the human problems, an impressive balancing act. Farmers and miners and loggers meet demands for goods and services—provide food, building materials, energy. Consumers create demands for these goods and services. If we cut off supply in one place, without diminishing demand, other people in other places will profit from the demand, producing impacts on those places and on yet other people. Inserting these ideas into our lessons links our students to global social and environmental issues and expands the interconnectedness we teach in a local landscape to include the interconnectedness of global climate and markets.

Of course, all landscapes are working in some way. Our parks and preserves not only provide serenity and beauty and recreation—they also provide ecological services in abundance. With their memories of past land uses, they provide lessons in passive as well as active ecosystem restoration. What land uses leave the longest signs on the landscape? What practices restore ecosystem services most rapidly? Even roadsides and railway rights-of-way have their positives and negatives. Some of these areas have saved prairie plants from extinction; others are highways for invasive species

From Local Landscape to Global Citizenship

Understanding working landscapes as well as parks and preserves is the business of informed citizens. We need to comprehend both kinds of places. We need to understand why we use the land as we do, and what changes we might make to permit our actions to be sustainable. And as we begin to contemplate sustainability seriously, we begin to come to grips with difficult ethical questions for which society has not yet provided answers.

Few environmental educators have the financial support needed to take students to developing countries to allow them to see and contemplate the environmental choices being made under entirely different economic, social, and environmental regimes. But we can invite students who are standing or walking in our own working landscapes to contemplate working landscapes under these other regimes. What factors will be foremost in the minds of people in these places when they think about their land? What will they value? What will their experience have taught them? We can ask, "You, our students in the United States, take national parks for granted. How would it change your views to have grown up in a country that had none?"

Just as we can make a transition for our students from local working landscapes to working landscapes elsewhere, we can move our discussion from how our choices shape our local landscapes to a discussion of how our choices affect landscapes elsewhere. By linking familiar landscapes to more distant landscapes in our own country and elsewhere in the world, we begin to develop global citizens prepared to tackle the hardest questions—questions of what it means to be responsible, of what fairness means at the global level. By posing these questions while we, ourselves, are standing on the land, we help our students remember that these are not only academic questions. They are questions whose answers will be written on the land and on its citizens.

Balancing Despair and Hope

Environmental educators have the potential to lay enormously heavy burdens on their students. Educators in other fields only want their students to change the world, or perhaps to save lives. We want our students to save the world. We may even see our students as a substantial part of what we are doing to save the world. Burnout is a very real possibility, given the seriousness of the environmental issues facing that world.

One of the greatest benefits of teaching outdoors, in using both working and preserved landscapes, is the opportunity to model and teach humility and hope. Because working landscapes so clearly demonstrate the impacts of our local, regional, and national choices with respect to the environment, they provide an excellent opportunity to discuss our personal environmental footprints. When you are standing in one hundred acres of protected forest, the news that local development in the past year has created one thousand new acres of built landscape has meaning with new depth. Knowing that the wetland in which you stand is expected to be a grassland in fifty years, due to climate change, may put a new face on the old admonishments about energy conservation. Conversations about small changes or life changes both have more immediacy.

Instructors who invoke the power and urgency of real landscapes also have responsibilities. Young, idealistic students are entirely able to develop a sense of responsibility too crushing to bear. They neither created the world they inherit, and to which we as environmental educators introduce them, nor can they, individually, render it pristine and perfect. We owe them the honesty of our own thoughts on responsibility to the environment, and our own hard-won lessons on surviving the burden Aldo Leopold described with such devastating clarity:

> One of the penalties of an ecological education is that one lives alone in a world of wounds. Much of the damage inflicted on land is quite invisible to laymen. An ecologist must either harden his shell and make believe that the consequences of science are none of his business, or he must be the doctor who sees the marks of death in a community that believes itself well and does not want to be told otherwise. (Leopold 1953: 165)

I always regret the recognition I see in my students' eyes when I read them this passage. But Leopold provides a balance of equal strength: "We shall never achieve harmony with land, any more than we shall achieve absolute justice or liberty for people. In these higher aspirations the important thing is not to achieve, but to strive" (Leopold 1953: 155).

When we teach outdoors, particularly in working landscapes, the wounds are often plain to see. If we make reference only to the wounds, students have the chance to feel shame and despair. If we can point out the striving—the buffer strips that would have been planted in crops in the past, the protected areas that were once over-harvested forests or eroded farmland, the hybrid cars, the solar panels—they have an opportunity for hope and so do we. If we share with them the changes we have seen in our lifetimes, we give them a longer frame of reference and a sense that they are not alone in the longer and larger struggle for sustainability and fairness. The only points I make in any class for which I am thanked every year, without fail, are these last, about recognizing the risk of despair and coping with the knowledge that brings it.

It has been several years since I had a class that met outdoors several times in a semester. Now I think of my field trips and outdoor classes as events I will mine repeatedly in the classroom. By taking advantage of all the landscapes and features I can, and all the history of the land we visit, I build a pool of common experience and knowledge that is real and vivid to my students, even from a campus walk. By taking photographs during a field trip and using them later in the classroom, I take my students fleetingly back outside to the richness of the experience rather than to the memory of the last lecture. Because I can use these "flashbacks" to cover some topics in the classroom, I can take time with my students in the field to discuss regional, global, and philosophical issues evoked by the landscapes around us.

The final reminder I give students about the outdoors is to go back. Often. It is my final advice regarding teaching outdoors. We owe ourselves the chance to refresh our energy and enthusiasm, too. When you're tired of being good and high-flown, take a walk outside. Watch something else fly. Remember why you got yourself into this in the first place. Read some landscape stories. Get wet and muddy. Take other people with you. If you can get back to discovery and wonder (and a sense of humor: remember, woodpeckers survive a whole lifetime of banging *their* heads all day) then there's reason to hope.

References

Leopold, L. B., ed. 1953. *Round River: From the Journals of Aldo Leopold.* London: Oxford University Press.

Overview

Jennifer Meta Robinson
Communication and Culture

The complex environmental, social, and economic challenges faced by society require our "thinking collectively at disciplinary crossroads," as Whitney Schlegel, Heather Reynolds, Victoria Getty, Diane Henshel, and James Reidhaar note (this volume). In the case of teaching environmental literacy across the curriculum, such thinking will mean fostering not only students' proficiency in diverse knowledge and skill domains but also their facility in assessing and supplementing those areas that they do not know sufficiently. To successfully negotiate these challenges, we will need to draw on broad resources and constituencies, sharing models, success stories, and cautionary tales of individual insights, group collaborations, and institutional initiatives. While parts 2 and 3 of this book outline some of the core knowledge and teaching methods appropriate to teaching environmental literacy and sustainability through the lens of various disciplines, both inside and outside the traditional classroom, part 4 speaks to the potential that the authors have found in building broad-based collaborations among faculty, campus administration and services, and students.

As we have indicated, environmental literacy—with its evocation of complex problems requiring sophisticated, multifaceted responses—lends itself to the exercise of new, collective means of teaching and learning. Major funding agencies such as the National Science Foundation and the National Institutes of Health recognize the potential of "multidisciplinary," "interdisciplinary," and "transdisciplinary" research to address complex issues. Thus, various ways of constructing useful disciplinary crossroads can be employed, sometimes bringing multiple perspectives to bear on a single problem (multidisciplinarity), sometimes seeking to truly integrate diverse disciplines into a new paradigm (interdisciplinarity), and sometimes collaborating across the usual disciplinary limits to allow people to operate as experts in new domains (transdisciplinarity). Even individual scholars now identify themselves as knowledge domain boundary-crossers, borrowing methods traditional to one field in order to apply them to another or applying the theories and findings of one field to subjects typically considered by another. Students and faculty alike are energized by the possibilities of moving beyond conventional departmental lines.

The urgency of our planetary dilemma challenges us to think in terms not only of how to make the most of traditional course structures in advancing environmental literacy and sustainability, but also of how to create and support other approaches and to make use of the implicit educational messages communicated through practice. Universities teach about sustainable human–environment relationships through the examples they set, either positively or negatively, in decisions relating to infrastructure, architecture, and community relations. For example, a campus-wide focus on civic engagement and liberal education prioritizes the roles that students can play in shaping our collective future. Similarly, visible university support for campus greening projects that facilitate students' collaboration with faculty, administrators, and staff to make the campus a more sustainable environment can teach powerful lessons about self-authorship and civic responsibility. Such projects can extend the teaching space beyond classrooms and courses to all of the spaces that students spend time in, creating an action-based teaching ethic.

The role of cross-disciplinary initiatives in support of environmental literacy and sustainability includes supporting faculty members as they move from roles as interested citizens into experts who can contribute to general understanding and education through one or many disciplinary lenses. While some faculty may have long been interested in sustainability and green issues and may have already seen their disciplinary research and teaching in that light, others may be just exploring what they can contribute to the conversations around a green campus. In her chapter titled "Environmental Literacy and the Curriculum—An Administrative Perspective," Catherine Larson moves from a personal to a campus-wide perspective on what it means to support this activity from an administrative position. As an expert in Hispanic literature and an Associate Dean for Undergraduate Education in the College of Arts and Sciences at Indiana University, Larson recalls how, from an initial sense of being an "outsider," she came to embrace the concept of environmental literacy as a basic competency for all citizens, a unifying theme for all disciplines, and a possible organizing theme for an entire campus, from academics to physical operations, purchasing, and administration. Larson provides an overview of key curricular initiatives that emerged from the environmental literacy movement at Indiana. These initiatives, which include service-learning and campus greening activities, green certificates, leadership minors, web-based, traditional, and topics courses, freshman learning groups, and special seminars and conferences, begin to address the challenge of weaving environmental literacy into the existing fabric of curricular initiatives, administrative structures, fiscal constraints, and student groups already existing at a large research university. She places particular emphasis on campus-wide targets of environmental literacy and sustainability, including greening projects that are instructive not only for direct participants but also for all members of university community who come into contact with them. She also endorses service-learning as a logical pedagogy for greening because it connects meaningful community service with academic learning, personal growth, and development of civic responsibility (see also Schonemann, Libby, and King in this volume). Larson further advocates that the institution convey the value that it places on these activities through such recognition as a "Green Diploma" or other certification. In these ways, the teaching of environmental literacy and sustainability moves beyond classrooms to more obviously interdisciplinary settings integral to everyday life.

During the Indiana University experience, it became increasingly clear that we needed to engage the full range of stakeholders involved in making the transformation to sustainability. While the project began as a multidisciplinary *faculty-*centered seminar, we quickly broadened our notion of a crossroads to include graduate students, physical facilities staff, administrators, undergraduate students, and community members. In her chapter "Faculty, Staff, and Student Partnerships for Environmental Literacy and Sustainability," Briana Gross explores the potential of including representatives from a wide range of stakeholders. Moreover, she explores the possibilities of extracurricular learning opportunities for students. While she was an Indiana University doctoral student in biology and chair of the Council for Environmental Stewardship, Gross observed firsthand the catch-22 common to campus greening or sustainability initiatives. To be successful, she says, greening initiatives require both grassroots support from the student body and top down support from high-level campus administrators. Yet each type of support can be difficult to attain without the other. Gross argues that promoting environmental literacy in the student body through a pedagogical approach to campus greening can help to bring top down and bottom up forces together. As an example of such an approach, Gross describes how students, staff and faculty, with resources and support from campus operations and administrators, naturalized several campus planters with native prairie plants and created accompanying signage and literature. Among the elements contributing to the success of this initiative, Gross identifies a clearly defined and modest scope, a prominent profile (in this case due to location in a high-traffic area of campus), and an obvious common ground of intersecting interests and benefits.

In "Food for Thought: A Multidisciplinary Faculty Grassroots Initiative for Sustainability and Service-Learning," Whitney Schlegel (human biology), Heather Reynolds (biology), Victoria Getty (dietetics), Diane Henshel (public and environmental affairs), and James Reidhaar (fine arts) take on the challenge of leveraging for-credit courses that create greening experiences beyond the classroom. They describe a project that brings four different courses from four different fields—biology, nutrition, environmental science, and fine arts—together with three local not-for-profit agencies to "nurture students in their cognitive, social, ethical, cultural, and global identities." Organized around the common learning theme of food literacy, the courses used collaborative service-learning projects developed to foster students' interdisciplinary understanding and sense of civic engagement, both on campus and in the wider community.

All of these approaches support faculty and students as they use the strengths of various crossroads in a collective effort to move toward a more sustainable future. Such models for networking across campus and community, supporting growth and discovery by individuals, and realizing the potential of institutions will help to develop environmentally sound, socially equitable, and economically vital campuses and to produce graduates who can contribute to a sustainable world.

15

Environmental Literacy and the Curriculum: An Administrative Perspective

Catherine Larson
Spanish and Portuguese

When I was first invited to join an environmental literacy working group at my university, I feared that as soon as the experts began talking, I would be found out as the ringer in the group—I was not a true, deep, forest green, though perhaps a light shade of chartreuse. My area of research is not a scientific discipline but Hispanic literature. Furthermore, my life outside this institution has precious little to do with sustainability or the interconnectedness of the environment, society, and the economy, although I possess a fair amount of intellectual curiosity and my family does recycle pretty enthusiastically. Still, I wasn't really sure why I had been asked to participate, other than the fact that I was the associate dean for undergraduate education in the College of Arts and Sciences, and the faculty leaders of the group were most likely making strategic invitations. Because I work with the curriculum on both macro and micro levels on a daily basis, I decided to become involved, and I became a believer in the power of this grassroots effort to change policy and to affect the way we all "do" the business we do. In fact, what I came to understand and embrace was that this concept—

helping to create more environmentally literate citizens (students, faculty, staff, and administrators), greening the campus by involving academic programs, the physical operations of the university, and purchasing decisions—really is for everybody. We all coexist on this planet, and we all share the responsibility for determining its future.

Pedagogical initiatives involving environmental literacy are intended to educate people, to make them more aware of their individual and collective choices, and literally to change behavior. In what follows, I will explore from an institutional perspective some of the ways in which such an initiative might work at a large, public university. As an associate dean from the liberal arts and sciences, it is fair to say that my perspective emanates from there. I will also consider how such an initiative might be woven into the fabric of academic life of an entire university.

Inclusiveness

The question of ownership is central to discussions linking the environment to pedagogy in a university setting—and, I would submit, it should be as all-encompassing as possible. The environmental literacy initiative that was developed in our university was, from the beginning, conceived of as belonging to everyone, from newly arrived freshmen to members of the Board of Trustees, from the person responsible for purchasing zucchini for the residence halls to the faculty member teaching a course on the relationship between the environment and public policy. The governing philosophy, then, was that the initiative should require each of us to take ownership, although in a number of different ways. Clearly, because the constituent groups are so varied, the overall initiative also requires a menu of options and opportunities that will enable everyone to buy in. In the early days of the project, as I went through my own process of coming to terms with the issues at stake, I had three key questions regarding the relationship between this initiative and the curriculum: 1) What teaching and learning strategies might enable us to foster environmental literacy, and how should they be prioritized? 2) How could we make at least some of the working group's suggestions happen operationally? 3) What policy issues would specifically relate to undergraduate education at the level of the College of Arts and Sciences? For example, would we need to consider changing degree requirements for all students—and how might that affect everything from programming the degree audit system to time-to-degree issues? What might be the intended and unintended consequences if we added a required environmental literacy course? Could we achieve many of our goals by heading in other directions—and, if so, what might they be?

Strategy

The first concept with which I came to terms was one I have already noted: the issues involved in environmental literacy are not just a "science thing"—they affect all three of the distribution areas that comprise the arts and sciences: the arts and humanities, natural and mathematical sciences, and social and historical studies. Because these issues are central to what the arts and sciences are all about (not to mention other obvious connections with the schools of education, journalism, public and environmental affairs, and law, among others), it made sense to me that we needed to explore ways of intercalating a variety of educational activities into our curriculum and into the fabric of campus life—one single initiative would not be enough. Like many universities, ours has been engaged in ongoing debates about campus-wide general education (or core) requirements for all undergraduate majors, so the possibility of adding a course in environmental literacy to the requirements already in place in each school slid seamlessly into discussions of a general education curriculum. The questions we raised are representative of issues discussed at large and small schools across the country. Would a required environmental literacy class for every single undergraduate student at this institution make good sense? Should there be a requirement solely for majors in the College of Arts and Sciences, or should the professional schools be encouraged to participate in the changes we were starting to envision? Rather than consider one course, should we propose a number of "green" curricular offerings that could count for general elective credit toward graduation? Some people proposed creating a minor. Others suggested the possibility of a green certificate (somewhere between a minor and a major), which could be earned if students took a certain number of courses from all disciplines labeled "green" in the course catalogue. All of these ideas have real-world implications and raise legitimate questions: a campus-wide or college-wide graduation requirement would necessarily slow time to degree for every student involved. What departments or schools would "own" such a course in a responsibility-centered budget management environment, one in which each individual unit (or responsibility center—for example, each school) would have real-world incentives to generate credit hours, as they would supply revenue to the unit? Where is the line in the sand between recommending such a core course and actually requiring everyone to take it?

A Diverse Approach, Building on Existing Strengths

Ultimately, we began to focus on a few key curricular initiatives, some new and some bringing together elements from the curriculum that already exist, ones that speak to the specific needs of our institution, its administrative structures, and its financial management realities, as well as our varied student groups. The first element actively includes our campus-level Office of Service-Learning in helping to incorporate green service-learning projects into courses in a number of disciplines. The Office of Service-Learning works with instructors, departments, and the community to forge viable connections for the creation of meaningful student projects, allowing them to move from conceptualizing environmental literacy issues to dealing with them in a hands-on manner. It has become clear that this type of experiential learning experience for our students is a key initiative, and since service-learning support already exists on campus, we will be able to build from a solid base. Moreover, because experiential learning is growing in popularity across the country, its potential for application at virtually any college or university seems a very safe bet.

Another existing initiative that dovetailed beautifully with our environmental literacy initiatives is a relatively new minor on campus. The LESA (Leadership, Ethics, and Social Action) minor, under the umbrella of the Department of Political Science in the College of Arts and Sciences, by definition encourages students to get involved with important social issues and to take leadership and ethically responsible roles in grappling with them. It is clear that many of the students pursuing the LESA minor are—and will continue to be—attracted to the environmental literacy initiatives discussed in this book and will form a symbiotic relationship with them. The LESA minor is unique to Indiana University, but many other schools have similar curricular options that could be adapted to meet their own students' needs and interests from an environmental literacy perspective.

Another green curricular possibility arises from our experience in designing and running large-scale web-based courses. The College of Arts and Sciences already has an extremely popular web-based offering, "Traditions and Cultures of Indiana University," as part of a group of centrally run experimental courses. In this online course, students explore a variety of topics, from the Lilly Library's rare Gutenberg bible to Alfred Kinsey or the impact of research on Crest toothpaste on the university. We are exploring the possibility of utilizing the expertise and environmental interests of faculty who originally designed "Traditions and Cultures" to create a similar web-based course that would focus on environmental issues. If the first course is a good indicator of potential success, the second course should do extremely well, with hundreds of students enrolled per year.

In addition to this web-based course, we anticipate that existing courses in a number of disciplines will be modified, with or without an additional service-learning component, and that others will be developed. As green courses become a part of each student's thinking about his or her course of study, the university will need to have sufficient classes available to meet student demand. In our case, the College's joint undergraduate degree program (with the School of Public and Environmental Affairs), the B.S. in Environmental Science, will surely be affected, and courses in biology, chemistry, geography, geology, physics, human biology, and sociology—and, conceivably, in English, political science, fine arts, economics, philosophy, and comparative literature—will also be impacted. Course and project development will take place in myriad places and with a wide variety of permutations. All of this will require coordination and will no doubt need the collaboration of the campus's internal grant systems and other financial support resources.

Many colleges and universities across the country have a course or an entire curriculum aimed at giving freshmen a solid foundation for future studies. At Indiana University, the College of Arts and Sciences requires a course in its Topics/Freshman Seminar curriculum of every student receiving an undergraduate degree in the College. These courses can range from freshman seminars with as few as 20 students to large lecture/discussion courses with 60 or even 120 students, and they are targeted at first-year students, providing opportunities to be taught by professors rather than graduate students, to learn how one of the three distribution areas (arts and humanities, natural and mathematical sciences, and social and historical studies) approaches the central questions of its discipline, and to focus on critical thinking and writing. The ability to think critically will help prepare our students to integrate what they have learned into their own value systems as they make decisions about the environment, both now and in the future. The Topics curriculum—or its version in other institutions—is a natural home for courses dealing with these issues, and I feel certain that in the future, we will make a conscious decision to include some of them in our curricular offerings.

The university also combines residential living with academics in the Freshman Interest Group experience, in which in their fall semester, small groups of first-year students living in the same residence hall select a topic of interest, take three of their classes together, and are provided with peer and faculty mentors to help guide them as they transition in. The FIGs could also be ideal for promoting sustainability in that a green FIG could combine environmentally focused courses in the hard sciences, social sciences, and humanities for students interested in the topic. Those students would then have a specific site from which to try out some of their ideas, perhaps working in collaboration with their residence halls to promote awareness among their peers of the decisions made in bringing the food to their dining hall tables each day or the greening of their living space. Indeed, the residence halls in general offer an ideal site for exploring the concept of the ecological footprint and developing sustainable practices.

Extracurricular Elements

Seminar series, working groups, and conferences are examples of other elements that can help make environmental literacy a part of the campus culture. On our campus, the environmental literacy working group engaged in an intensive two-year project, in which the first year was principally devoted to a well-attended seminar speaker series and the second focused on working group meetings throughout the academic year, as faculty and graduate students from a wide range of disciplines explored ideas for giving the project form and coherence. In fact, I have never seen, let alone participated in, a more effective interdisciplinary, grassroots project; the fact that so many people continued to participate so actively over the course of two years is nothing short of a miracle in academe these days. A solid organizational structure and in-house funding from several programs aimed at fostering multidisciplinary problem-solving were key to the success of the seminar and working group. Working group members also helped to organize an annual Bioneers conference, a meeting that focuses on solving current problems facing the planet and its inhabitants and featuring plenary presentations by prominent, visionary thinkers. Indiana University, in partnership with the city of Bloomington, was one of a select group of satellite partners for the Bioneers conference from 2004–2007, purchasing live feed of the plenary talks and projecting them here on our campus; we also organized our own local workshops on various sustainability topics such as local food, recycling, etc. (see http://www.bioneers.org for more information). These efforts brought together students, faculty, and the community in a unique way, and although Indiana University is no longer a satellite partner, there are plans to continue the local Bioneers conference using plenary recordings from previous years. One goal is to involve students even more actively in both planning activities and participating in those we already have in the pipeline. These activities and approaches have worked well for us; they could certainly be adapted for other institutions.

By far, the majority of the ideas and initiatives outlined above utilize elements from the curriculum that already exist and bring together current faculty even more than they involve inviting outside specialists to inspire the masses. In the difficult financial times that characterize the realities of campuses across the country, it makes even more sense to build on what has been proven effective and is already working well, rather than beginning a dozen projects from scratch. An approach that builds on existing foundations will, I believe, help us create something that will really work at our institution, because it will be woven into the fabric we have created together up to this time. A number of these initiatives are aimed at freshmen—again, a logical step in that we hope to begin with our newest students the process of teaching and learning about the environment that will, over the course of time, truly promote literacy. The number and nature of our environmental literacy initiatives will no doubt evolve over time, but we are beginning with a broad menu of possible choices and a great deal of enthusiasm —key ingredients for future success.

Faculty, Staff, and Student Partnerships for Environmental Literacy and Sustainability

Briana L. Gross
Biology

Many colleges and universities have some type of organization dedicated to environmental issues such as stewardship, sustainability, or the catchall focus of "greening." Such campus greening or sustainability initiatives can face a catch-22. To be successful, greening initiatives require both grassroots support from the student body and top down support from high-level campus administrators. Yet each type of support can be difficult to attain without the other. On one hand, high-level administrators might stipulate that broad support for environmental stewardship must be shown before any changes are implemented. Similarly, campus departments that are designed to serve student needs will not provide environmentally friendly alternatives until there is sufficient student demand. However, even if moderate support for environmental stewardship is shown, it may be difficult to elicit further interest without the assistance of administration and support staff. Many institutions thus struggle with the question of whether changes in environmental policy should come from the top down or the bottom up. There is no easy answer to this question, of course—

forcing change from the top down can result in resistance, but waiting for an environmental movement to occur in the absence of any information or encouragement is a difficult prospect. Even when individuals in every sector of the university would like to see a green campus, as is frequently the case, the prospect of any one department striking out on the road toward this goal can be daunting. In this essay, I detail how collaborative projects can successfully bridge the top/bottom divide faced on many campuses and also promote environmental literacy in the undergraduate student body.

One specific example of how environmental literacy and sustainability can be initiated in a way that combines elements of top down and bottom up efforts comes from Indiana University Bloomington. The organizations responsible for campus sustainability at IUB have gone through several incarnations, something that is probably not uncommon for an institution of higher education. Efforts mainly began with the formation of the Council for Environmental Stewardship (CFES), which was made up of representatives from staff, student, and faculty groups from across the IUB campus, and was created with the goal of moving the university toward sustainability through academic, operational, and administrative efforts. The CFES took the approach of creating working groups centered on topics of interest or importance to the IUB campus. Among the many projects completed between the CFES's inception in 1998 and its disbandment (due to budget cuts) in 2006, one of the most successful and well liked was the Prairie in the Planters project. Initiated by the CFES's Green Landscaping working group, this project effectively brought together a number of campus and community groups.

The Prairie in the Planters project was organized by a Biology Department faculty member who was leading the Green Landscaping working group and a graduate student from the School of Public and Environmental Affairs, whose work on the project contributed to her master's degree in environmental policy and natural resources management. The project involved using native plants to beautify several large planters in a high-traffic region of the campus, creating examples of the native prairie that once dominated parts of Indiana. Implementing this project depended on input from the architect's office, help with tools, mulch, and other supplies from the landscaping division, greenhouse space and supplies from the Biology Department, and volunteer efforts by students, staff, faculty, and Bloomington community members associated with an initiative to register the city as a National Wildlife Federation Community Wildlife Habitat (http://www.nwf.org/community/). Funding for plants was provided by the CFES and a National Wildlife Federation Campus Ecology fellowship awarded to the graduate student. The project was complemented with permanent signage at the planter site and pamphlets describing the benefits of environmentally friendly landscaping practices and tips for implementing native landscaping on campus. The integration of efforts by faculty, graduate and undergraduate students, support staff, and Bloomington citizens extended the breadth of the project across the campus and to the community. The use of signs and pamphlets, as well as the striking visual presence of the native plants, made the planters a prominent feature on the campus, helping to raise ecological consciousness and promote a sense of place in students. In general, the project is an excellent example of using the physical campus as a pedagogical tool.

Elements of Success

There are many features of the Prairie in the Planters project that contributed to its success. From a purely practical perspective, the explicit goals and relatively modest size of the project allowed it to be completed in only about a year. The clearly circumscribed nature of the plan made seeking assistance from other departments on campus less daunting for both the organizers and the potential donors. While it might at first be considered restrictive to limit the scope of environmental projects, it is likely that many small successes will have a more positive impact on a given campus than any project left half-completed. Note also that the size of the project is appropriate for undergraduate participation; i.e., it could have been integrated into a course and completed by a group of students over the span of a semester or a year. Although this project was undertaken outside of a formal course structure, it represents an excellent example of how one might integrate pedagogy and greening to promote both environmental stewardship and environmental literacy.

Another important element contributing to the success of the project was the fact that it provided a mechanism to institute campus greening and promote environmental literacy that was appealing to *all* the members of the campus community. Although the project involved students, faculty, administration, and staff, no single group was required to take on the entire burden of the project. Thus, the campus administration and staff supported a greening effort (top down) organized by students and faculty (bottom up). This project sidestepped the major roadblocks usually involved in greening efforts by virtue of its cooperative nature; change was not forced on the campus by the administration or operations, and the individuals organizing the project were not required to complete it in the absence of a support network. Perhaps most importantly, the project revealed the common ground that is shared by many members of the campus community, but is rarely explored. The project allowed the CFES to meet goals of promoting environmental awareness and stewardship on campus, contributed to the degree work for a master's student, and assisted a community group in their work to promote natural landscaping citywide. Furthermore, the campus architect's office and landscaping division were happy to promote a grounds project that fostered student ownership and pride in the campus landscape. When students' attitudes toward the campus grounds change in this way, the goals of maintaining and improving the grounds become easier. The enthusiastic public response to the planters by passers-by (staff, student, faculty, and community) bodes well for the future of campus greening projects.

Transfer of Ideas

The Prairie in the Planters project cannot be considered extraordinary in comparison to green landscaping or habitat restoration projects that are being implemented on campuses across the United States (e.g., the National Wildlife Federation Campus Ecology program, described at www.nwf.org/campusecology). Nonetheless, it serves as a useful illustration of two major issues surrounding environmental literacy and sustainability.

The first issue returns to my focus at the beginning of this essay. Although an increasing number of institutions are making sustainability a priority and even hiring people in the position of sustainability/environmental coordinator, there are still many places where this is not high on the list of priorities. What if you are an individual who is not lucky enough to be at an institution with a commitment to sustainability? In that case, you might be facing the catch-22 of trying to show, simultaneously, that there is sufficient enthusiasm for environmental stewardship from the administration, the staff, and the students before any real institutional support has materialized. In this situation, even a modest project that integrates contributions from multiple groups can make a convincing case that such an attitude actually exists. Indeed, projects like the Prairie in the Planters doubtless helped to generate momentum for a well-supported Task Force on Campus Sustainability, with areas of focus that include environmental restoration and environmental literacy.

The second deals with the use of "place as pedagogy" for promoting environmental literacy in both an unstructured and a structured manner. The way a campus is maintained and presented to students will influence their understanding of the importance of sustainability, even when it is not presented in a formal manner. What is communicated to a population of thousands of undergraduates when environmentally harmful practices, such as the use of chemical fertilizers and pesticides, are used to create a "beautiful" campus? How can they develop an appropriate sense of place at a university when most of the plants are exotics that would never survive in that location without human assistance?

More formally, campus greening projects present rich active learning opportunities that can be integrated into course syllabi as service-learning. Basic service to plant or maintain restored, natural landscapes could be appropriate for almost any course (although, ironically, these areas will actually need less care than traditional landscaping areas). At a more complex level, a comparison between traditional landscaping practices and green landscaping practices might serve as an explicit focus for discussions dealing with such aspects of the human ecological footprint as chemical and land use policies. The positive side of this discussion, of course, would deal with the role of the natural landscape in terms of ecosystem services and our ability to restore them as a part of a commitment to sustainability.

The power of place as a pedagogical instrument cannot be underestimated; that is, once the campus *is* green, it can serve as a constant reinforcement of the importance of environmental stewardship. Thus, the pedagogical approach to greening a campus proposed in this book is a logical plan of action, and many campus environmental groups might benefit from approaching education and greening simultaneously. Producing environmentally literate graduates clearly has important implications for the future of the environment and society at large. Happily, introducing a program of environmental literacy will likely also have an impact on the campus where students are trained. An environmentally literate student body would be more likely to support campus greening, providing steady reinforcement for cooperative efforts once the initiative is underway.

17

Food for Thought

A Multidisciplinary Faculty Grassroots Initiative for Sustainability and Service-Learning

Whitney Schlegel, *Human Biology*

Heather L. Reynolds, *Biology*

Victoria M. Getty, *Health, Physical Education, and Recreation*

Diane Henshel, *Public and Environmental Affairs*

James W. Reidhaar, *Fine Arts*

Thinking collectively at the crossroads of disciplines is difficult intellectual work that is essential if higher education is going to be able to turn out students who can address the interrelated environmental, social, and economic challenges of twenty-first-century society. Our ability to bring to the forefront new knowledge exceeds the capability of the human mind to retain this factual information. This mandates that meaningful connections be made visible and that education be not merely about the transmission of factual knowledge, but rather about fostering ways of knowing and habits of mind that will continually renew our intellectual resources and provide innovative ways for approaching the complex problems facing humanity.

A challenge for faculty thus lies in developing new models of teaching and learning that prepare students to work within uncertain intellectual boundaries

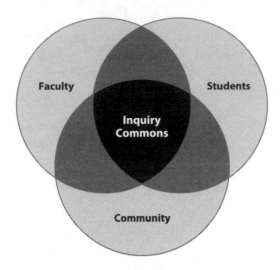

FIGURE 17.1. Our inquiry commons: multidisciplinary service-learning with a common theme.

and to connect existing knowledge to complex problems; to recognize the multitude of disciplines necessary to work toward solutions to these problems; and to understand diversity and advocate for social justice and change. Learning communities have been shown to support student and faculty work at disciplinary crossroads. Service-learning has been demonstrated to engage students and faculty in ways that allow them to think more critically and deeply within their disciplines and foster understanding of the connections between disciplines that can then facilitate the application of knowledge to solve real world problems. The Food for Thought (FFT) Project developed and tested a novel model of multi-course and multi-partner service-learning as a means of increasing student interdisciplinary understanding and civic engagement. Our model operates very much within the framework of the *Teaching Commons*, where faculty, students, and community come together to engage in experiential learning, dialogue, and reflection (Huber and Hutchings 2005). Organized around a central theme and a common set of community partners, with built-in support mechanisms for cross-disciplinary sharing and collaboration, we define this special type of learning community as an "inquiry commons" (figure 17.1).

Opportunity for Change

Change occurs through opportunity, and in early 2006 two interdisciplinary initiatives on the Indiana University Bloomington campus, Human Biology (HUBI) and the Environmental Literacy and Sustainability Initiative (ELSI), merged their collective expertise to put forth a successful project proposal for the Dean of the Faculties Scholarship of Teaching and Learning Leadership Award. The project sought to provide a transformative and transdisciplinary learning experience for students, one that would foster their cognitive, social, ethical, cultural, and global identities. The experience of the ELSI team with environmental literacy and service-learning, coupled with the experience of the HUBI team with the development of learning communities, interdisciplinary curricula, and tools for documenting and supporting integrative teaching and student learning, provided for a strong collaboration. The three broad goals for the FFT project included: (1) to develop and test *a novel model of cross-disciplinary service learning* as one approach to fostering student interdisciplinary understanding, intellectual and personal development, and civic engagement, (2) to develop and implement *new and integrative models for assessing student learning* and for finding ways to make visible the *connections between teaching and learning,* and (3) to provide a model for *learning communities* consistent with that of a *teaching commons* as described by Huber and Hutchings (2005).

Both HUBI and ELSI had experience pioneering distinctive learning experiences that were grounded in the theoretical frameworks and assessment of student learning set forth by Perry (1970), Kegan (1994), Belenky et al. (1986), King and Kitchener (1994), Chickering and Reisser (1993), Piaget (1970), Magolda (1999), and Magolda and King (2004). Both HUBI and ELSI embraced and employed holistic and integrative approaches to teaching and learning. These approaches aim to foster cognitive maturity, integrated and ethical identity, and mature relationships that enable effective citizenship and are consistent with those championed in *Greater Expectations: A New Vision for Learning as a Nation Goes to College* and most recently in the LEAP Report (National Leadership Council for Liberal Education and America's Promise report; Association of American Colleges and Universities 2002 and 2007, respectively).

Learning Communities

The collaboration of learning communities with a shared purpose has been shown to facilitate institutional change (Cox and Richlin 2004). Furthermore, faculty learning communities create connections for isolated teachers, establish networks for those pursuing pedagogical issues, meet early-career faculty expectations for community, foster multidisciplinary curricula, and encourage community in higher education.

Early leaders of learning communities in higher education include Alexander Meiklejohn (1932), John Dewey (1938), and Joseph Tussman (1969). Meiklejohn, who instituted the Experimental College at the University of Wisconsin in 1927, wrote of the importance of curricular structures, coherence, and community with a sense of shared values in addressing the fragmentation of the learning experience and environment in higher education. Meiklejohn and Dewey shared a vision for teaching, learning, and community that is perhaps captured best by Mervyn Cadwallader, an early dean at Evergreen State College, an institutional model for integrated studies and learning communities. He writes, "Meiklejohn and Dewey arrived at the same terminus: the need to provide education for citizenship, a curriculum of political morality, and a call to teachers to be endlessly experimental rather than doctrinaire (Cadwallader 1984: 286)."

The organic process that our FFT learning community employed is rooted in Tussman's learning community experience at Berkeley, "A dominating idea must come first. The curriculum must grow out of a simple idea and be developed by a group committed to the idea" (1969: 52–53). Interdisciplinary learning communities support faculty and students in ways that allow for forward thinking about the design of assessment tools and research studies (Lynd-Balta et al. 2006). Central to the FFT learning community was inquiry, asking questions about student learning, collecting evidence of student learning, sharing this evidence and building upon the work of others with the purpose of transforming the practice of teaching in higher education. For there to be an understanding of what an environmentally literate person looks like, and how teaching and learning align with this curricular goal, there needs to be a teaching commons that has at its core the scholarship of teaching and learning: a community that is asking questions about student learning and teaching practice and examining the evidence, making this work public, and building upon the work of others in ways that allow for teaching as a scholarly endeavor.

The questions that provided the foundation for the FFT learning community innovation and inquiry were: How do interdisciplinary teams of students and faculty work together with multiple community partners to enhance student learning and civic engagement? How can such a complex teaching process be documented? How do you capture evidence of student learning in this community-focused learning environment?

The Model

An emergent vision and creative process is at the core of transformative and sustainable innovation and change. Our vision was that of an inquiry commons, a novel curricular model comprising multiple service-learning courses across a range of disciplines, organized around a central theme and a common set of community partners. With help from Campus Instructional Consulting and the Office of Service-Learning, blending two independent faculty learning communities, ELSI and HUBI, offered the necessary coherence, support, and sense of common purpose to undertake the implementation of this inquiry com-

Table 17.1. Faculty, Courses, and Community Partners

Faculty/Discipline	Course	Community Partners
Victoria Getty Applied Health Science	Issues in Dietetics HPER-N401	· Indiana University SPROUTS (Students Growing Organics Under the Sun)
Diane Henshel Environmental Science and Policy	Risk Communication SPEA-E412/512	· Indiana University Hilltop Garden and Nature Center
James Reidhaar Studio Art	Graphic Design Studio COLL-S452	· Mother Hubbard's Cupboard
Heather Reynolds Biology	The City as Ecosystem COLL-E105	

mons. An Office of Service-Learning Advocate for Community Engagement (ACE) and a graduate student assistant provided additional logistical support to the FFT project. ACEs are undergraduate students who act as a liaison between community-based organizations, instructors, and service-learners.

The courses taught involved a range of disciplines (environmental science and policy; nutrition; biology; and graphic design) and students (freshmen to graduates, non-majors and majors), and the community partners included a food pantry, a student organic garden group, and a garden and nature center (table 17.1). Two key elements of our model were a central organizing theme and the collaboration of multi-class teams of students on service-learning projects related to this theme.

We chose food literacy as a model interdisciplinary theme. As an important element of environmental literacy, food literacy cuts across critical social, economic, and environmental issues at local to global scales, providing ready access points for a wide variety of disciplines and student backgrounds. Early in the planning process, faculty and community partners came together to develop a common understanding of food literacy. Using affinity mapping of concepts, the group defined food literacy as the understanding and motivation to act on the interrelated social, economic, and ecological dimensions of food production, distribution, preparation, consumption, and waste management, recognizing the roles of individuals, communities, and societies at local to global scales. Developing this common understanding of food literacy was an essential first step in identifying common interdisciplinary ground among faculty and insuring consistency in learning goals across courses.

Service-learning is a form of experiential learning that when coupled with reflection allows for students to connect the classroom with life experience in ways that develop higher-order thinking and empowers them with a sense of identity, place, and connectedness in the world (Kolb 1983). To accommodate the hundred or so students involved, faculty and community partners developed twenty-five service-learning projects that drew on the common and unique expertise and skills available in each class. Examples of service-learning projects include development and marketing of food- and agriculture-related lesson plans, development of plans for food waste composting and community outreach, and development and administration of patron surveys.

Other teaching and learning tools included two hours of direct service to a community partner, group and electronic reflection sessions, and student electronic portfolios (e-portfolios). The e-portfolio, derived individually and linked to others, is one tool that allows for the complex nature of the learning outcomes such as those sought in HUBI and ELSI to be revealed by students and linked with faculty pedagogical intention and reflection (Yancey 2001). Electronic portfolios are a central form of assessment for HUBI, and it has integrated a longitudinal e-portfolio into its undergraduate degree program using the Carnegie Foundation for the Advancement of Teaching and Learning (CASTL), Knowledge Media Lab (KML), KEEP (Knowledge, Exchange, Exhibition, and Presentation) Toolkit (http://www.cfkeep.org). The very process of generating a portfolio allows for students and faculty to "go meta" and in doing so facilitates deeper understanding of learning. The Peer Review of Teaching Project, building upon earlier work (Hutchings 1998), led the way for the scholarly faculty course e-portfolio. We employed individual faculty e-portfolios as well as an overall project e-portfolio in the FFT project.

Emerging Outcomes

Student, faculty, and project e-portfolios offered a framework for collecting and evaluating evidence of student learning and other data sources that were central to our inquiry. The faculty course portfolios were a place for reflection on individual courses and analysis of student e-portfolio work, while the project portfolio provided for documentation and analysis of the multidisciplinary service-learning project model (table 17.2). Results indicate that the model was supportive of student learning across a range of class levels and disciplines. The model facilitated student understanding of the community and connected their learning to genuine concerns within the community in a manner that promoted civic engagement. This model also helped students recognize and value the multiple perspectives and expertise necessary to solve authentic problems and complete multifaceted projects.

Student work captured in the student e-portfolios demonstrated student grasp of the environmental, economic, and social dimensions of food and food production and a dramatic change during the semester in their thinking about food. At the start of the semester students in all four courses thought of food as a

Table 17.2. Summary of Data Collected and Assessment Tools

Student	Faculty	Community Partners	Project
Demographics Coursework Service-learning course projects Reflections E-portfolios Service-learning surveys	Course e-portfolios provide a formal, consistent framework for each faculty member to evaluate student learning outcomes, develop plans for course improvement, and make visible their scholarship.	Functionality of product Level of satisfaction	Project e-portfolio brings faculty together in assessing overall project success, developing plans for project improvement, and disseminating program outcomes.

personal source of physical well-being, essential for health and energy. They viewed food within the community as driven by culture and tradition, and issues of world hunger dominated their global perception of food. Student thinking about food changed to reflect an understanding of how food choices impact the environment, the economy, and social well-being at individual, local, and global scales and that these choices often pose ethical dilemmas. A student in the biology course writes, "I now see that food is not just for nourishment and pleasure. Its production and consumption have infinite effects in the world. When one thinks about food, one must keep in mind that it does not just affect those who eat it, but also those who produce it, the community in which it is produced and sold, and its source, the environment." A graphic design student writes, "Should I design for unhealthy food? For cigarettes? For alcoholic beverages? Am I selling the truth or a lie?"

Student work with their multidisciplinary service learning teams and community partners allowed them to apply their course knowledge and moved them from positions of basic awareness to informed action. A student taking the biology course writes, "I mentioned previously that feeding the world was most important, so now that I'm aware that we actually could be doing that if it weren't for the high demand for meat production, I've tried to eat meat only once or twice a week." A graphic design student writes, "I think I've learned how to appropriate the techniques of corporate advertising, so that I can subvert them and apply them to 'the other side.'" A student in risk management writes, "This course, along with the community aspect of it, has taught me to bridge the gap between research and application; in other words, I should use what I have learned by applying what I know to my life and live it out in actions."

Furthermore, the multidisciplinary composition of the student service-learning teams appeared to enhance the quality of the products they produced for the community partners. A poster designed to promote awareness of and encourage food waste composting provides an especially nice illustration of the synergy possible with multidisciplinary expertise. Here, students from three courses came together, combining graphic design expertise; leadership, organizational and communication skills; and knowledge of ecosystem ecology and principles of sustainability; and they produced an end product that was visually appealing and provided a strong organizational identity for the community partner while expressing the economic, environmental, and social benefits of composting. In conclusion, this multidisciplinary service-learning model triangulates faculty, students, and community partners and fosters learning communities that facilitate communication, collaboration, knowledge sharing, and innovative solutions to complex problems. We anticipate broad utility of this approach in advancing teaching and learning about other inherently multidisciplinary issues.

References

Association of American Colleges and Universities. 2002. *Greater Expectations: A New Vision for Learning as a Nation Goes to College*. Washington, D.C.: Association of American Colleges and Universities.

Association of American Colleges and Universities. 2007. *College Learning for the New Global Century: A Report from the National Leadership Council for Liberal Education and America's Promise*. Washington, D.C.: Association of American Colleges and Universities.

Belenky, M., B. Clinchy, N. Goldberger, and J. Tarule. 1986, 1997. *Women's Ways of Knowing*. New York: Basic Books.

Bransford, J. D., A. L. Brown, and R. R. Cocking, eds. 2000, *How People Learn: Brain, Mind, Experience and School*. Washington, D.C.: National Academy Press.

Cadwallader, M. 1984. "The Uses of Philosophy in an Academic Counterrevolution: Alexander Meiklejohn and John Dewey in the 1980s." *Liberal Education* 70: 275–292.

Chickering, A. W., and Reisser, L. 1993. *Education and Identity*, 1–542. San Francisco: Jossey-Bass.

Cox, M. D., and Richlin, L. 2004. *Building Learning Communities: New Directions for Teaching and Learning*, 1–163. San Francisco: Jossey-Bass.

Dewey, J. 1938. *Experience and Education*. New York: MacMillan.

Huber, M. Y., and Hutchings, P. 2005. *The Advancement of Learning: Building the Teaching Commons*. A Carnegie Foundation Report on the Scholarship of Teaching and Learning in Higher Education, 1–187. San Francisco: Jossey-Bass.

Hutchings, P., ed. 1998. *The Course Portfolio: How Faculty Can Examine Their Teaching to Advance Practice and Improve Student Learning*. Washington, D.C.: American Association for Higher Education.

Kegan, R. 1994. *In Over Our Heads: The Mental Demands of Modern Life.* Cambridge: Harvard University Press.

King, P. M., and Kitchener, K. S. 1994. *Developing Reflective Judgment: Understanding and Promoting Intellectual Growth and Critical Thinking in Adolescents and Adults.* San Francisco: Jossey-Bass.

Kolb, D. 1983. *Experiential Learning.* New York: Simon and Shuster.

Lynd-Balta, E., Erklena-Watts, M., Freeman C., and Westbay, T. D. 2006. "Professional Development Using an Interdisciplinary Learning Circle: Linking Pedagogical Theory to Practice." *Journal of College Science Teaching* 35(4): 18–24.

Magolda, M. B. 1999. *Creating Contexts for Learning and Self-Authorship: Constructive-Developmental Pedagogy*, 1–345. Nashville, Tenn.: Vanderbilt University Press.

Magolda, M. B., and King, P. M. 2004. *Learning Partnerships: Theory and Models of Practice to Educate for Self-Authorship*, 1–342. Stylus.

Mansilla, V. B. 2005. Assessing Student Work at Disciplinary Crossroads. *Change* 37: 14–21.

Meiklejohn, A. 1932. *The Experimental College.* New York: Harper and Row.

National Research Council. 2003. *Transforming Undergraduate Education for Future Research Biologists: BIO 2010.* Washington, D.C.: The National Academic Press.

Perry, W. G. 1970. *Forms of Ethical and Intellectual Development in the College Years: A Scheme*, 1–285. San Francisco: Jossey-Bass.

Piaget, J. 1970. *Science of Education and the Psychology of the Child.* D. Coltman, trans. New York: Orion Press.

Tussman, J. 1969. *Experiment at Berkeley.* London: Oxford University Press.

Eduardo S. Brondizio
Anthropology

When compared to the array of civic and educational challenges in front of U.S. students today—immigration and economic crisis, evolutionism vs. creationism, marriage and family, religion and government—one may rightfully question whether an emphasis on environmental literacy is indeed appropriate for centers of higher education. What makes teaching environmental literacy relevant in the midst of economic and ideological divides that are currently shaping the world in general and the United States in particular? The answer, one may argue, is that environmental literacy serves as a means to engage students and the community in general in discussing and learning about the economic, ecological, geopolitical, ideological, civic, cultural, and historical interconnections of our changing world. As we learn to accept the facts and implications of global climate change, for example, we understand that new forms of thinking about energy, food, transportation, and our sense of place, as well as about global commodity markets and resource ownership are required.

Environmental literacy is an exercise in balancing cultural, economic, and environmental values. Several of the concepts presented in this volume fall exactly in between these notions. For instance, one can hardly separate concepts like sustainability and equity from cultural notions of well-being and development, not to say modernity and progress. In this sense, few topics serve the exercise of teaching critical thinking and civic engagement—prime tasks of institutions of higher education—so well as environmental issues. No matter the field or professional goal, students provided with the opportunity to become environmentally literate will face and address questions relevant to their lives, daily choices, and ethics, as well as those of the society as a whole. Environmental literacy is an exercise in overcoming simplification and generalizations, and in thinking outside the box. We hope that our three themes (ecosystem services, ecological footprint, and sustainability) allow students to reflect and think critically about the interface between environment and different aspects of society, regardless of their background. Likewise, these concepts provide heuristic tools for students to understand the aggregated impact of their individual choices and political positions.

One of the key challenges of environmental literacy is to overcome ideological stereotyping. Environmental issues in general and environmentalism in particular invite popular, as well as political and academic, profiling. While much improvement has happened since the 1980s Brundtland commission articulation of a "business friendly" concept for sustainable development, myth and misinformation still tend to surface during times of high economic and political stakes. How many times have you heard the expressions "environmental whacko" or "greedy businessman" during the past few years? Stereotyping has been a dominant tool of discourse, ideology, and confrontation about environmental issues, and most often a successful way of diverging productive discussion into political propaganda. Most people lack the basic information and historical understanding of society's environmental problems to identify and properly react to stereotyping. As a result, labels tend to be reinforced, differences highlighted, and solutions weakened. University campuses are no exception, and students tend to reproduce these views and label "others" as unethical, dreamers, unrealistic, or selfish. One of the goals of environmental literacy is to recast these debates through a process of fostering critical thinking while respecting differences in values and political positions. Essays in this volume as well as our classroom experiences show that in most cases debates based on simplistic, dichotomist positions are empty of meaning, content, and solutions.

A prime challenge to be overcome through environmental literacy is the tendency to teach complex problems through single explanatory variables and simple causality. It is commonplace to put emphasis on variables such as population growth, poverty, or economic maximization to explain a variety of environmental problems (e.g., deforestation, pollution, resource depletion), at a variety of scales (e.g., county, country, biome, global). From debates between developing and developed countries during the 1972 Stockholm conference on human environment (e.g., poverty vs. pollution) to today's debates about protected areas (e.g., use vs. conservation), there is a tendency to favor simple explanations to environmental problems over explanations that include historical, political, economic, and geopolitical aspects of society and environment. As some essays in this volume illustrate, environmental problems have historical dimensions and vary according to level of analysis and time-scale. Simple explanations, especially when applied to other parts of the world (e.g., population growth, poverty, and lack of education in developing countries) help to distance our individual and social contribution to environmental problems. As a result, many students on university campuses find no connection between their consumptive behavior, their political positions or lack thereof, and larger environmental problems.

This issue falls within the classic debate between "structure and agency," a prime topic to consider in fostering classroom discussions. While we understand that large-scale variables are important (e.g., demographics, market economy), environmental problems result in no small measure from aggregated patterns emerging from individual actions, flowing from a process where both dimensions of society—structure and individual agency—influence each other. Fostering a better understanding of these connections may improve our chances of changing our own behavior as well as the structural conditions underlying environmental and social problems.

An important paradox underlying the debate on global environmental change and sustainability today is the mismatch between political, social, and environmental boundaries. A similar tension exists between our conceptions of the human species vis-à-vis our conceptions of ethnicity and nationhood. Perhaps appropriately, global environmental problems are often cast as a problem at the level of the human species. However, we tend not to see ourselves as a species, but rather as cultural groups and nation-states. Similarly, we tend to see the global environment not as one, but as a mosaic of nation-states. These are important issues in today's context, particularly because they underlie concerns about national sovereignty, global commodity markets and resource ownership, and economic development. Current debates, for instance, about the Kyoto Protocol, or tropical deforestation for that matter, are cast exactly within these terms: primarily as issues of geopolitical concern. In order to understand the subtleties of these issues an environmentally literate student should use the "glasses" of the social and physical sciences, and the humanities. Global environmental problems are as much an issue of the physical environment as of geopolitics and trade; environmental issues cannot be separated from the aspirations of national and local forms of resource ownership and use and cultural views of development.

Every social challenge offers an opportunity for education. By considering the environment's intrinsic relationship with society and our daily lives, this volume contributes strategies and offers an optimistic approach to engage students in addressing the paradoxes society faces today, such as achieving its aspirations for economic development while considering its ability to do so in an equitable and environmentally sound manner. This volume has avoided the debate on "skills" vs. "content" vs. "affective goals" so common to initiatives aiming at fostering critical thinking among university students. All are interconnected and interdependent, at least when it comes to environmental literacy. Similarly, the examples and cases discussed here highlight the importance of integrating top down and bottom up approaches to implement environment literacy programs on the university campus and in the community. We hope these examples will contribute to new programs and exciting teaching scholarship resulting from the combined efforts of university administration, faculty and students across disciplines, and the communities where they belong.

APPENDIX

ELSI Core Strategy: "A Pedagogical Approach to Greening IU"
(http://www.indiana.edu/~elsi/strategy.html)

Rationale: Global environmental crises and the growing interdependency of environmental, social, and economic issues motivate environmental literacy as a basic competency for twenty-first-century education. By environmental literacy we mean an understanding of the ecological, social, and economic dimensions of human–environment interactions, including how to live day to day in a sustainable fashion. We submit that higher education has the responsibility and resources to lead the way in meeting this new educational challenge and see environmental literacy as a fundamental civic necessity and a core learning goal for all students.

Learning Goals: Environmentally literate graduates will possess the information, skills, and values to help our complex, global society move toward sustainability— meeting present needs without compromising the ability of future generations to meet their needs. The basis of sustainable societies are socially just economies that run on renewable, nontoxic sources of energy and resources with ecologically appropriate levels of population and consumption. Broadly, environmentally literate graduates will have gained information, skills, and values in the following areas:

The fundamental life-support processes that ecosystems provide ("ecosystem services")

The status of the global environment (humanity's "ecological footprint")

The theory and practice of sustainability

A sense of place: personal, cultural, historical

An understanding of the social and environmental outcomes of individual behavior (e.g., consumption)

The interrelationship of economy, environment and social equity

The role of policy and market forces (e.g. ecological economics)

Ecological design principles and their application to the built environment and to agriculture

Strategy: ELSI recognizes that the university learning environment itself is a powerful form of pedagogy, ideally as a deliberate positive model of sustainability (Orr 1994). Our core strategy is therefore to create an experiential learning initiative to green the IUB campus. This strategy will integrate activities across departments and schools, offering learning experiences beyond any one academic specialty.

"Greening" refers to changes in academic programs, physical operations, and purchasing that move a campus towards sustainability. As students move about campus buildings and grounds every day, they receive important messages about human–environment interactions. Typically, these messages reinforce the paradigm that the earth's resources and capacity to assimilate wastes are infinite and that each individual's energy and resource use is disconnected from the welfare of other humans, other organisms, and the local to global ecosystems in which they are embedded. Alternatively, the campus environment, including buildings, grounds, energy and resource use, waste production, and academic focus can foster an understanding that humans are embedded in and dependent upon the web of life, that our personal and collective lifestyle choices have both local and far-reaching impacts on other humans, other organisms, and ecosystems, and that sustainable societies must live within the regenerative and assimilative capacity of earth's biosphere. The campus greening movement gained strength in the 1990s and now involves hundreds of campuses nationwide (examples include Penn State, Oberlin College, and University of Georgia). In addition to educational benefits, the greater resource use efficiency of green campuses can lead to considerable economic savings and help to stimulate the local economy. Furthermore, green campuses have also become an important recruiting draw.

Because it connects meaningful community service with academic learning, personal growth, and development of civic responsibility, service-learning is a natural educational framework for greening activities. While "community" has traditionally referred to the local municipality, it can also apply to the campus community. Indiana University already has a strong service-learning presence on campus through the Office of Service-Learning (OSL, http://www.indiana.edu/~copsl/). The OSL has been an active participant in ELSI and is enthusiastic about expanding service-learning opportunities to green IU Bloomington.

Sustainability is inherently interdisciplinary, and we plan to promote campus greening service-learning projects throughout and between a wide range of disciplines and courses at IUB. We will adopt Penn State's categorization of the campus environment into ten sectors: energy, water, material resources and waste disposal, food, land, transportation, built environment, community, research, and decision-making. Green service-learning projects with strong environmental, economic, and/or social emphases will be promoted within each of these ten sectors.

Key Components:

Environmental Literacy and Sustainability Coordinator—A position dedicated to developing, coordinating, promoting, and acquiring funds for this initiative will be key. We recommend that this be a top-level administrative position.

Website Interface—An engaging website will provide a high-profile presence for this initiative and serve as an important means to communicate information and opportunities, to present the results of greening projects, and perhaps ultimately to provide virtual tours of "Green IUB." We would like this website to have a link from IUB's homepage. We are hoping to partner this website with a web-based course on the "Green Campus of IUB." The course would examine our local environment using ecological concepts and findings from a variety of disciplines and perspectives. The course design, inspired by the successful "Traditions and Cultures of IU" web course co-developed by Jim Capshew and Tom Gieryn (with logistical and technical support from Instructional Support Services), is in the planning stages.

Service-Learning Grant Program—Small grants for development of green service-learning projects will be an important incentive for faculty. The Office of Service Learning has successfully used grants to promote service-learning throughout the campus curriculum.

"Green Diploma" Certification—Students who complete a given amount of green service-learning could be eligible for a green diploma certification (perhaps also accompanied with a green banner to wear over the graduation gown, similar to those given out for honor students). Such a program would help promote awareness of our program. Various kinds of green certification for graduates already exist at other universities, and are an appealing form of recognition for many students.

Signage—Attractive and eloquent indoor and outdoor signage will be an important means of making the pedagogical nature of greening projects explicit. We envision that each greening project will culminate with such signage. A few examples already exist on campus, such as the signs posted at the Prairie in the Planters green landscaping project behind Jordan Hall.

Local Bioneers Conference—Bioneers is an educational nonprofit that promotes solution-oriented ecological and social strategies for sustainability. David Haberman, then Chair of Religious Studies, spearheaded an effort to bring, via teleconferencing, the annual Bioneers Conference Plenary Speakers to the IUB campus. The Union Board agreed to sponsor the 2004 event, and we hope to make this an integral part of the IUB greening strategy. City of Bloomington community groups sponsored the Bioneers telecast at IUB in 2003, and the faculty and students who attended were inspired and impressed.

Community Outreach—collaboration with like-minded City of Bloomington groups can allow sharing of resources and knowledge, enhance a sense of place and civic ethic in students, and support IUB's role as a productive member of the larger community. One particularly exciting prospect is partnerships with the City of Bloomington Sustainability Commission.

Assessment—Evaluating progress through time is essential. Initially, we envision developing a survey to gauge the baseline level of environmental literacy at IUB (e.g., via random samples of graduating seniors), with annual follow-ups to assess progress. Longitudinal audits of IUB's course offerings, operations, and purchasing practices would be a complementary form of assessment, some of which would naturally take place as a part of service-learning projects.

CONTRIBUTORS

John S. Applegate
Walter W. Foskett Professor of Law
Maurer School of Law
Vice President for Planning and Policy
Indiana University

Matthew R. Auer
Dean, Hutton Honors College, and Professor
School of Public and Environmental Affairs, Indiana University

Eric J. Baack
Assistant Professor
Department of Biology, Luther College, Iowa

Bennet B. Brabson
Professor Emeritus
Department of Physics, Indiana University

Eduardo S. Brondizio
Professor and Chair
Department of Anthropology
Associate Director
Anthropological Center for Training and Research on Global Environmental Change (ACT)
Adjunct Professor of Environmental Sciences
Indiana University

James H. Capshew
Associate Professor
Department of History and Philosophy of Science, Indiana University

Keith Clay
Professor
Department of Biology
Director
Indiana University Research and Teaching Preserve, Center for Research in Environmental Science
Adjunct
School of Public and Environmental Affairs, Indiana University

Victoria M. Getty
Director
Didactic Program in Dietetics, Indiana University

Christine Glaser
GreenFire Consulting Group, LLC, and Earth Literacy Program, Saint Mary-of-the-Woods College, Indiana

Briana L. Gross
Postdoctoral Research Associate
Department of Biology, Washington University, St. Louis

Diane Henshel
Associate Professor
School of Public and Environmental Affairs, Indiana University

Doug Karpa
J.D. candidate
University of California Berkeley School of Law

Claire King
Associate Director
Indiana University Center for P-16 Research and Collaboration

Catherine Larson
Professor
Department of Spanish and Portuguese, Indiana University

Andrew Libby
Assistant Director
Office of Service-Learning, Indiana University

Vicky J. Meretsky
Associate Professor
School of Public and Environmental Affairs, Indiana University

Emllio F. Moran
Distinguished Professor and Rudy Professor
Anthropology
Professor
Environmental Sciences
Adjunct Professor
Geography, Indiana University

Craig E. Nelson
Professor Emeritus
Department of Biology, Indiana University

Phaedra C. Pezzullo
Associate Professor
Department of Communication and Culture, Indiana University

James W. Reidhaar
Associate Professor
Department of Graphic Design, Indiana University

Heather L. Reynolds
Associate Professor
Department of Biology, Indiana University

Jennifer Meta Robinson
Senior Lecturer
Department of Communication and Culture, Indiana University

Scott Russell Sanders
Distinguished Professor
Department of English, Indiana University

Whitney Schlegel
Director
Human Biology
Associate Professor
Department of Biology, Indiana University

Nicole Schonemann
Director
Office of Service-Learning, Indiana University

Lisa H. Sideris
Assistant Professor
Department of Religious Studies, Indiana University

Keith M. Vogelsang
Research Associate
Department of Biology, Indiana University

INDEX

DATE DUE

NOV ~~27 2010~~

APR 0 2 2012

Demco, Inc. 38-293